DEMOCRACY AS FETISH

RSA·STR

THE RSA SERIES IN TRANSDISCIPLINARY RHETORIC

The RSA Series in Transdisciplinary Rhetoric is a collaboration with the Rhetoric Society of America to publish innovative and rigorously argued scholarship on the tremendous disciplinary breadth of rhetoric. Books in the series take a variety of approaches, including theoretical, historical, interpretive, critical, or ethnographic, and examine rhetorical action in a way that appeals, first, to scholars in communication studies and English or writing, and, second, to at least one other discipline or subject area.

Other titles in this series:

Nathan Stormer, *Sign of Pathology: U.S. Medical Rhetoric on Abortion, 1800s–1960s*

Mark Longaker, *Rhetorical Style and Bourgeois Virtue: Capitalism and Civil Society in the British Enlightenment*

Robin E. Jensen, *Infertility: A Rhetorical History*

Steven Mailloux, *Rhetoric's Pragmatism: Essays in Rhetorical Hermeneutics*

M. Elizabeth Weiser, *Museum Rhetoric: Building Civic Identity in National Spaces*

Chris Mays, Nathaniel A. Rivers, and Kellie Sharp-Hoskins, eds., *Kenneth Burke + the Posthuman*

Amy Koerber, *From Hysteria to Hormones: A Rhetorical History*

Elizabeth C. Britt, *Reimagining Advocacy: Rhetorical Education in the Legal Clinic*

Ian E. J. Hill, *Advocating Weapons, War, and Terrorism: Technological and Rhetorical Paradox*

Kelly Pender, *Being at Genetic Risk: Toward a Rhetoric of Care*

James L. Cherney, *Ableist Rhetoric*

Susan Wells, *Robert Burton's Rhetoric: An Anatomy of Early Modern Knowledge*

Ralph Cintron

DEMOCRACY AS FETISH

THE PENNSYLVANIA STATE UNIVERSITY PRESS
UNIVERSITY PARK, PENNSYLVANIA

Library of Congress Cataloging-in-Publication Data

Names: Cintron, Ralph, author.
Title: Democracy as fetish / Ralph Cintron.
Other titles: RSA series in transdisciplinary rhetoric.
Description: University Park, Pennsylvania : The Pennsylvania State University Press, [2019] | Series: RSA series in transdisciplinary rhetoric | Includes bibliographical references and index.
Summary: "A multidisciplinary study of democratic politics that draws on ethnography, political theory, and rhetorical analysis to demonstrate how the rhetorics of democracy have become fetishized"—Provided by publisher.
Identifiers: LCCN 2019034476 | ISBN 9780271084855 (hardback) | ISBN 9780271084862 (paperback)
Subjects: LCSH: Democracy. | Rhetoric.
Classification: LCC JC423 .C56777 2019 | DDC 321.8—dc23
LC record available at https://lccn.loc.gov/2019034476

Printed in the United States of America
Published by The Pennsylvania State University Press, University Park, PA 16802–1003

The Pennsylvania State University Press is a member of the Association of University Presses.

It is the policy of The Pennsylvania State University Press to use acid-free paper. Publications on uncoated stock satisfy the minimum requirements of American National Standard for Information Sciences—Permanence of Paper for Printed Library Material, ANSI Z39.48–1992.

Contents

1

Putting a Text into Motion

Arrival Scene

I live in downtown Chicago, and I walk a lot. Rather often, I cross one of the bridges spanning the Chicago River. Sailboats and powerful motorboats often plow in both directions of the river during late spring, summer, and early fall. They are either going to or coming from Lake Michigan. We are in the midst of the sensorium of the city. My understanding of *sensorium* differs a bit from the standard dictionaries since I do not use the word just to refer to the mind, brain, or body "as the seat of sensation." Rather, I use the word to talk also about the external world—a place—as a sensorium. In other words, one can talk about an entire city or a forest as a sensorium and in the process link objects to perceiving subjects. Indeed, the goal would be to reimagine the distinction between the two through the sort of phenomenological work that interested Maurice Merleau-Ponty.[1] And if one wanted to, one could take another step and show how rhetorical theory is but a species of the sensorium—but that, dear reader, is a future project, or at least another stroll on another day around the city.

I am standing on one of the bridges overlooking the Chicago River. As I look into the boats, I notice the faces passing under me. Such lovely faces. They are filled with pleasure, or so it seems to me, as they take in the vast sensorium. They seem to bask in it, to glide through it—to be, in a sense, a bit above it. It is as if these people had set aside, for a while at least, their worries, obligations, and pressures. Perhaps they have stepped outside their routines, and so they relax into the sensorium itself—hence the pleasure, the enjoyment, the sitting back on a cushion and looking up at the fantastic buildings rising up from the banks of the river. They have sufficient wherewithal, I suppose, to make this moment possible. They smile, and one of them even waves at me. I wave back. We are mysteries to one another, but we wave. Perhaps somewhere above us in an office or an apartment someone takes a short break, and they find us. They spy the boat, they spy me, but we down here will never know of it. Their gaze is already moving beyond us to the larger scene. Our small moment is not sufficient to keep their attention.

Wherewithal can always afford indifference, and sometimes those who exercise indifference seem to think that they have the moral privilege to do so. What ideological program enabled this? Who has wherewithal and who doesn't, and what is its rationality? *Wherewithal* is an interesting word. It suggests the accumulation of money, but at the same time it suggests more than money. It also suggests power, influence, and even ease of being. Those with wherewithal, more than likely, have more freedom (a fraught concept to be sure) at their disposal than those without. One of the understandings of the word *freedom,* according to the *Oxford English Dictionary,* is "liberation from the bondage of . . . worldly ties." I would like to understand wherewithal, then, as a kind of ability or potential to move beyond "worldly ties"—that is, to move beyond material limitation. Wherewithal, then, has the ability to untie. Such a person floats upward, untethered. Is there much doubt that the accumulation of money goes particularly far in the gathering up of other qualities, such as power, influence, ease of being, and freedom, too?

It should be obvious: the accumulation of money is, indeed, a kind of freedom from the bondage of worldly ties. Hence today economic terms are enmeshed inside democratic terms, and both sets of terms sometimes function as spiritual ideologies. Karl Marx and Kenneth Burke are just two of the theorists who have noticed that money can function as secular transcendence (wherewithal).[2] But more vivid—because it is all too real—is the example of President Donald Trump, who during his presidential campaign in 2016 signed dollar bills thrust at him by his followers. Reporters speculated on the meaning of these events. For instance, Mark Leibovich, writing for the *New York Times,* suggested that candidate Trump seemed to be at these moments a kind of "high priest" of the "nation's secular religion: aspirational consumerism."[3] Did his followers receive these signed dollar bills as actants, as totems? Ministers and politicians such as candidate Trump, who tap deeply into the vulnerabilities and desires of their followers, seem to be working, in Leibovich's words, a kind of "prosperity-theology . . . , the idea that you follow a minister because he is rich and has his own plan and implicitly and sometimes explicitly promises that you, too, will be rich."[4] Something of his wherewithal just might rub onto lives less successful—one more version of the reproductive power of money begetting money. Friedrich Nietzsche might say that we continually sing to the god of happiness: "Our happiness. . . . We have discovered that happiness; we know the way. . . . [But] *this* is the sort of modernity that [makes] us ill."[5]

This notion of wherewithal can be translated into a conceptualization called "two cities." My Puerto Rican activist friends on Chicago's north side and my Mexican activist friends on the south side use the idea of "two cities" to signal the growing wealth of downtown versus the less wealthy neighborhoods that spread out toward the northwest, west, and south. The city is in the hands of developers and real estate interests, my friends complain, and it all starts in the mayor's office and with his need to raise property values in order to increase taxes and bail the city out of debt.[6] The encroachment of "gentrification," the closing of neighborhood public schools, the increasing number of charter schools, the aesthetics of sandblasted brick, master chefs transforming eating into art, the proliferation of festivals across the city, the pleasantries of a summer evening in this very liberal city that has pushed gunshots to just a few neighborhoods—the trope of two cities becomes a complaint or a celebration depending on where you spend most of your time. My activist friends are pretty much fed up with "liberals," and so they turn to a wherewithal of their own making that they sometimes call a "critical space." They have created some remarkable successes through this counter-trope. Still, this Other wherewithal, this critical space, is haunted by not having the same clout, ultimately, to restrain the uprooting, material forces of money and investment spreading from the first city toward the second. So wherewithal: who has it, who has less of it, and how does it instantiate a whole host of fantasies and phantoms that constitute modernist politics and economics?

←↨→

How Did This Book Start?

In ethnographic fieldwork.[7] I have done fieldwork across multiple sites: in Kosova[8] as well as in Mexican, Mexican American, and Puerto Rican neighborhoods in Chicagoland. My Chicago fieldwork began within a year after taking up a teaching position at the University of Illinois at Chicago in 2000. In Chicago, my fieldwork comes from aldermanic offices, from being a member of a Puerto Rican activist group that I call the PRA, and from being on the board of directors of LUCHA, a nonprofit that provides affordable housing. I have also done fieldwork among groups that oppose immigration rights.[9] As for Kosova, I began sporadic fieldwork there in 2001 as part of a mental health project led by Professor Stevan Weine and the International Center for the Study of Human Responses to Social Catastrophe at the University of Illinois at Chicago. The real work, however, occurred in 2007–8, when I was a Fulbright Scholar housed in the Department of Political Science at the University of Prishtinë, Kosova's major public university.

Let me introduce the fieldnote from 2008 that was written in Kosova and that crystallized what later became this project. I was reflecting, at the time, on how the whole of Eastern Europe seemed to be urgently cultivating liberal democracy and free-market practices, but there seemed to be, underneath it all, something chaotic that was not going to be repaired anytime soon. In the Kosovar case, the unease was exacerbated by the constant tensions between Serbia and Kosova, and the stubborn rates of unemployment that hovered, by all accounts, at around 40 percent year after year[10] despite the efforts of the international democratic, free market regime that was engineering the new liberal order.[11] "Democracy here functions more like a fetish, or a kind of empty container that gets filled with everyone's private miseries, and there is the hope that somehow democracy will solve these personal and collective lacks. Many put before the fetish of democracy their memories of incompleteness: perhaps their desires for a national identity after decades of Serbian control, for a voice in the public sphere, for property and even wealth, in short, for opportunity—or they bring before it their ongoing poverty, their unemployment, their frustrations with corruption and political immobility."

My Kosovar fieldwork suggested that democracy was releasing a plethora of desires and a sense of potential that could not be satisfied merely through the establishment of democratic institutions. The leaders of the newly emerging political parties responded to these desires much like "village head-men" passing out favors, promises of employment, and money. That is, democracy functioned through patronage organized around loyalties to family, friends, and regional networks.[12] "Big-man" or "head-man" politics—this was the conclusion that my graduate students in political science at the University of Prishtinë and I kept testing out over a year's time. We kept pointing to an earlier era, at least as early as the Ottoman, in which families of influence kept local order and councils of head-men made decisions. "Big-man politics" grafted itself onto national formation politics of the nineteenth and early twentieth centuries, then regrafted itself onto the communist era, and regrafted itself again onto the globalization era of democracy and markets.[13]

Head-man politics, then, looked like the historically enduring structure encountered by international management teams created by the United Nations, such as the United Nations Mission in Kosovo (UNMIK) and later by the European Union (EU), for example, the EU Rule of Law Mission in Kosovo (EULEX). These international institutions attempted to establish laws and codes, many of which went unobserved because they came from the EU and not the Kosovars[14] or because the laws tried to rupture the growing solidification of the informal economy and its new networks of corruption. The general population became increasingly disaffected and labeled their political situation as a kind of "fake democracy" or "democracy without democrats." They wanted genuine democracy, but it is not clear, in Kosova or elsewhere, exactly what democracy does to cure rampant corruption when the economy cannot get off the ground.

I remember watching the celebrations in 2008 when Kosova, for the first time in its history, became an independent nation. A large, bright-yellow sculpture spelling "NEWBORN" was unveiled. Over the next few weeks, more and more graffiti began to appear across the surface of the sculpture. The extent to which many of the graffitists intended to disfigure the sculpture is not absolutely clear, but this national symbol seemed to symbolize simultaneously the aspiration to a national identity and the complex dissatisfactions with the realizations of this aspiration—in other words, the precariousness of a newborn state. I do not wish to overinterpret, but later, "NEWBORN" was repainted, not just once but many times, with wildly different designs. The sculpture seemed to function as an objective correlative of a newborn country saturated in nationalist sentiments but perpetually unsure of how to materialize an adequately working system.

What does my Chicago fieldwork tell us? Are Chicago and Kosova comparable? In one sense, we might expect them to be opposites. On the one hand, the United States represents the epitome of a mature democracy; on the other hand, Kosova represents the epitome of an emerging democracy. But this distinction between the former and the latter became one of the central questions driving the weekly meetings between my Kosovar graduate students in political science and me. My students incessantly wanted to know how democracy worked in the United States. There was a moment in which I reached back into my Chicago fieldnotes in order to pull out what had become, for me, an unforgettable scene in 2004 inside an aldermanic office. The scene spoke not to any idealization of democracy as deliberative and all-inclusive but, rather, to the necessity of corralling power and then fighting to maintain it if things were going to get done. The context of the scene concerned a Puerto Rican alderman famous for his strong commitment to affordable housing, but in his private moments he suspected that he was losing the fight, for in his view speculative investment in property (the capitalization of poor communities—that is, gentrification) can only be slowed but not prevented. Still, he remained a formidable obstacle to developers and realtors who wanted to rush into his ward and gentrify. They had harassed him with lawsuits and run their own candidate against him in every election. At the end of one day after watching him arm wrestle developers who had been seeking his permission to build in his ward, I asked him about his understanding of the term *democracy*.

> Democracy, what democracy? I can't have democracy around here. I'll lose the place. Look, the city is complaining I won't sign off on some of the mayor's appointments. The city calls me. They tell me that this is unheard of, "why aren't you signing off?" I reply: "I want my legislation passed." I submitted eight pieces of legislation that basically hit the developers hard. I want all permits to conform to the redevelopment area and that no demolition can take place without the alderman signing off on it. If democracy says I gotta play fair with these guys, this community loses.

I asked my students if he was a kind of village head-man, minus the bribes and kickbacks (to the best of my knowledge), strong-arming the mayor's office until he got his goodies that, he thought, would favor the fraction of his "village" that supported him? Meanwhile, did he forcefully block the "voices" of those inside and outside his "village" by denying them a place at the table? If a raw fight for power is what underlies both mature democracies and emerging democracies, how do we establish the differences?[15] Both snippets of fieldwork seem removed from democracy as a set of virtuous institutions and practices, and certainly not the "end of history."[16] Democracy does not sit above the fray determining just laws through reasoned deliberation. Rather, democracy functions more like a figure of speech embedded in the fray, helping to organize powerful enthusiasms on behalf of one agenda or another. That is, particularly in the alderman's case, one group can name their cause as a furtherance of democracy, which then encourages a rival group to name their opposing cause as leading to even more democracy. As the anthropologist Julia Paley says, there is no "a priori definition of democracy"; rather, "the discourses labeling certain regimes as democracies are strategically deployed by groups with strong interests in particular definitions and contested by others differently situated in relations of power."[17] When dealing with his constituents in Chicago, the alderman could mobilize the discourse of "democracy" to fight for affordable housing, but when dealing with his rivals, he could not afford to act "democratic." What the alderman knew in his bones was the following: if acting democratically in some instances but refusing to do so in others helped him stay in power, so that he could continue to do what he thought was "right" and "good" for the benefit of a particular fraction, then so be it. There was no doubt that his rivals played the same game with that elusive term *democracy*. I happened to agree with the alderman, and so I thought that his maneuverings were the correct ones, that both his and his rivals' use of "democracy" were self-serving, and, finally, that pious definitions of democracy, such as democracy as deliberation, are foolish and, in some contexts, harmful.

In sum, the relationship between political majorities (the alderman in this case) and political minorities produces rhetorics that fetishize democracy. On the one hand, majorities, the winners, must fetishize democracy because that is the virtue term and system that enabled their self-interest to move into the foreground. On the other hand, political minorities, the losers, must also fetishize democracy because if they are to move their beliefs into the foreground, they must whitewash their cause as something other than narrow self-interest. That is, in order to contest in the democratic arena, it behooves all causes and beliefs to bathe their interests in democratic rhetorics. As I explain more fully later, these rhetorics lend virtue and justice, even inclusivity, to whatever they are attached.

Fieldwork, then, in an "emerging democracy" and a "mature democracy" narrowed my lenses until persistent underlying commonalities came into focus. What I saw was how desires were shaping democracy's meanings in ways that seemed to override its institutional form. Another recurring commonality was the necessity of power. Power must be in place if democracy is to succeed. For instance, the local example of the alderman suggests that in order to defend the "rightful" or winning cause, there are instances when one must make distinctly undemocratic power plays. These commonalities emerging from fieldwork and reinforced through reading particular scholars eroded my confidence in concepts such as "deliberative democracy" and "participatory democracy."

←↕→

If Democracy Is a Fetish, Does That Mean Democracy Is an Illusion?

I discuss the workings of the fetish most particularly in the next chapter. A central point I make is that the ideas of self-deception or, more strongly, false consciousness are certainly important to my analysis, but they do not summarize my entire position. Indeed, I am more disposed to thinking of fetishization as productive of the democratic system itself. That is, fetishization is consonant with the system and enables democracy to flourish. It is simplistic to say, for instance, that we ought to clean up our self-deceptions and thereby improve our political lives and philosophies. Rather, the fetish and fetishization are productive of who we are, and we cannot remove their threads, for they belong to the fabric of our most precious actions and truths. Without them, we do not know ourselves. They help to establish our meaningfulness and our purpose. They create the political world and us in it. To repeat: they are productive of who we are. In sum, no amount of "knowing," no matter how vast, can lift the shades of not knowing. Similarly, no amount of self-transparency, which is what "knowing thyself" amounts to—or, for that matter, political transparency—can achieve transparency itself. Both the self and politics are constituted through their shadiness.

Let me turn to the notion of inclusion in order to examine how democracy indeed creates a deception, a fetishization. Inclusion is something that has been extended historically to citizens. For instance, different marginalized groups have received batches of rights because as citizens they have a right to have rights.[18] But this expanding inclusivity withers when it arrives at the undocumented. What this fact reveals, I argue, is that democracy is always territorialized. Democracy, or any political order for that matter, must be territorialized—that is, grounded by the self-serving interests of nation-states. One of the primary interests or obligations of nation-states is to determine its rules of belonging. International law is somewhat split on the matter, as we will see later, but, basically, it grants the sovereign nation the right to distinguish those who juridically exist (citizens) from those who do not. It is not as if noncitizens (the undocumented) do not have any rights—indeed they do through such instruments as the Fourteenth Amendment of the United States Constitution or universal human rights proclamations. But the powerful fact of the undocumented is that oftentimes their material presence is deeply woven into the socioeconomic lifeways of the citizenry. That is, they are absolutely present with us, but are they protected and represented politically? Not necessarily.[19] The artifice of law reveals a curious split: material being is not necessarily consonant with legal being. This cleavage of material being from legal being is one that only the state can make. Further, the very beingness of the included is constituted through the excluded. That is, inclusion depends on exclusion: for instance, democracy establishes its legitimacy through "rightful" voters limited to the citizenry, which excludes those noncitizens who can only vote fraudulently even if they are deeply present in the body politic. It is in the nature of democracy to not see any of this as a problem because democracy relies on this cleavage to come into existence. Therefore, we fetishize democracy (we deceive ourselves) when we say that democracy is synonymous with inclusion.

The fact of the undocumented, then, reveals that democracy is always territorialized. People may want something more from democracy, but this "something more" is its deterritorialized version, which must wait in the wings, a potentiality waiting to be summoned into actuality. If it is true that democracy is a kind of container containing millions of desires, then democracy will remain forever a potentiality generating excessive hope and excessive frustration. Ultimately, my position is rather blunt: fetishization signals a longing to live inside what we do not have. That is, democracy seems to be split between its deterritorialized versions—which exist as abstract, fetishized ideologies—and its territorialized versions, which are the only ones that can be experienced. We invent or fetishize in order to erase the dissatisfactions of our experience. As I will explain, fetishization signals how prone we are to rhetorical leaps. People leap from those things that limit them toward those things that seem limitless. I call this leap the rhetorical architectonic of limitation → limitlessness.

To provide some detail for these claims about fetishization, let us go back to the revolutionary moments of the eighteenth century and consider them through the eyes of Thomas Paine. Paine was no lover of aristocracy: "The more aristocracy appeared, the more it was despised: there was a visible imbecility and want of intellects in the majority, a sort of *je ne sais quoi*, that while it affected to be more than citizen, was less than man. It lost ground from contempt more than from hatred; and was rather jeered at as an ass, than dreaded as a lion. This is the general character of aristocracy, or what are called Nobles or Nobility, or rather No-ability, in all countries."[20]

His solution, of course, was the establishment of a whole new order based on merit. He claimed along with his fellow revolutionaries that "men are all of *one degree*, and consequently that all men are born equal, and with equal natural right. . . . The equality of man, so far from being a modern doctrine, is the oldest upon record" (39). By establishing equality as foundation, nations could tap a much larger pool of talent for political leadership and thus not be limited to the "No-ability" pool of incestuous monarchs and aristocrats. Paine did not call this move the "release of potentiality," but that term, which is central to the analyses in this book, is applicable to all sorts of moves that I call "modernity" or, more specific to our era, "managerial modernity."

In sum, this release of potentiality, which in theory would lead to better governance because it was merit-based, led to a kind of fetishization or idealization of the representative system:

> The representative system diffuses such a body of knowledge throughout a nation, on the subject of government, as to explode ignorance and preclude imposition. . . . There is no place for mystery; nowhere for it to begin. Those who are not in the representation, know as much of the nature of business as those who are. . . . In the representative system, the reason for everything must publicly appear. Every man is a proprietor of government, and considers it a necessary part of his business to understand. It concerns his interest, because it affects his property. He examines the cost, and compares it with the advantages; and above all, he does not adopt the slavish custom of following what in other governments are called leaders. (169)

Paine knew well the limitations of aristocracy and monarchy, and from that position he could easily imagine an opposite system of governance stripped of faults—that is, a representative system founded on transparency between the leaders and the led. And further, because the leaders and the led were equals, talent and ability could rise legitimately on their own merits without being suppressed by an illegitimate overclass of aristocrats. In effect, meritocracy, as a politics of the horizontal, was the rightful replacement of the vertical politics of aristocracy and monarchy. Because we live in the wake of Paine and others of like mind, this particular release of potentiality continues to have moral urgency and thus to produce us and our institutions. The representative system and meritocracy as truths in comparison to the falsity of monarchy strikes most people as nearly self-evident. Where, then, is the self-deception or false consciousness? What Paine is missing is that meritocracy today functions as a kind of stealth aristocracy or, in my phrasing, the "oligarchic condition." It was not so much Paine's self-deception as it was his inability to peer deeply into the structures of representative democracy and to predict their unfolding. For instance, he claims that representation functions as a kind of transparency, but representation is the relationship between the one—the few—and the many. The representative (the one) cannot possibly represent the masses (the many) but can represent a faction (the few).

Let us go deeper into the relations of "the one," "the few," and "the many." If democracy is a political structure that sanctions the release of potentiality, which includes the release of desire, then political life can often resemble a monstrous swarm of desires, each one claiming that it ought to be heard because "democracy" says so. Democracy institutionalizes this right to be heard even as it encourages forbearance to enable opposing desires to listen to each other in order to be heard. But when do we forbear; when do we listen? We listen best when our investment in some final claim is modest. But if the investment really counts, if it springs forth from a deep desire, how do we make such a thing a clear object open to others' clear evaluations? For the most part, we can't—thus the hocus-pocus of forbearance and tolerance. The desires of "the one" will listen best to those of "the few" but not "the many." Further, "the many" resemble split factions seeking to capture "the one," and if the investments belonging to these factions are worth fighting for, then each faction will seek to undermine its counter-factions because democracy "rightfully" warrants agonism. The power of a lobby, campaign financing, gerrymandering, and battles over inheritance laws that pit the rich against the many are just a few examples in which "the few" capture "the one" temporarily and never permanently. Of course, each faction wants permanence, for that is the goal of final claims and ultimate investments.[21]

So Paine's fetishization of representation as transparency is not a consequence of self-deception. If anything, it is due to the inability to see the structural limitations of representation—that is, the actual mechanics of how representation might be territorialized. The many or totality simply cannot be transparently represented by the one. This means, in effect, that the oligarchic condition exists at the dead center of democracy. Democracy, then, is a mixed system composed of both democratic and oligarchic tendencies. In liberal democracy, the oligarchs consist mostly of wealthy individuals or powerful interests. In socialist democracies, the oligarchs could represent collective interests. At any rate, Paine fetishized democratic representation and its transparent possibilities. I do not see democratic representation the way Paine did but, for all that, I appreciate how such fetishizations produced a viable political world. Both the writer and reader of this book are consequences of that production. We cannot filter out from ourselves some sort of "beingness" that has not been produced from it. History was produced through a myriad of fetishizations. As stated earlier, without them we do not know ourselves. They help to establish our meaningfulness and our purpose. They create the political world and us in it. They are productive of who we are.

←↨→

What Is Meant by Rhetoric in This Book?

The term *rhetoric* has at least two inflections in this text. I label the first *democratic rhetorics*. Here are some specific terms within democratic theory that function as democratic rhetorics: *equality*, *freedom*, *liberty*, *the people*, *inclusivity*, *rights*, *justice*, *transparency*, and so on. The history of rhetorical theory might understand these terms as "special" or "specific" topics that belong especially to democracy because these are the common terms within the boundaries of democracy's meaning. That is, they seem to be content terms that belong to democracy talk. The second inflection of rhetoric that I mobilize might be described as "universal elements" because they concern elements of language use that are much more than content terms. These "universals" possess generative force that results in our capture. Rhetorical theorists will immediately notice that my use of terms like *specific topics* and *universal elements* both harkens back to and deviates from standard rhetorical theory—particularly theories of topoi as consisting of special or specific topics versus universal topics.

So the democratic rhetorics (equality, freedom, and so on) are the topoi or commonplaces through which we articulate our thoughts about democracy. I am not overly strict about what to include or not include as a key term or democratic rhetoric. There is a fundamental elasticity regarding which terms ought to be listed and even more elasticity within the terms themselves. The elasticity of each term, internally, is so profound that each one seems to be structured as a contradiction. Indeed, each term can be used to make elaborate propositions that seem reasonable, even indubitable, but frustratingly contradictory or paradoxical. In other words, the democratic rhetorics seem to lead to antinomic propositions.[22]

This antinomic quality that inheres inside each of the modern democratic rhetorics recalls our discussions of Thomas Paine. He warred against aristocracy on behalf of the equality of all. (Granted, he didn't mean "all" the way we try to understand it today.) Paine links equality to merit and both terms to competition. This linkage of equality-merit-competition is not accidental but structural—that is, as soon as we claim human equality as foundational, we have leveled the dominance, say, of aristocrats and unleashed a massive competition among "equals." Equality, then, is synonymous with the maximization of competition, and this explains Paine's premises to a tee—the fact, for instance, that he advocates simultaneously for human equality and the expansion of competitive commerce. These notions of equality as furthering competition may strike the contemporary progressive left as odd, for the left begins from another premise—namely, that equality's leveling power is meant to temper avarice and the seeking of advantage. Moreover, they say, equality does not demean, whereas competition always runs that risk. So from the perspective of the contemporary progressive left, equality is, at minimum, an ethos or ethic of self-restraint that we ought to observe and, at maximum, a set of laws with the capacity to forcefully restrain. Thus one can build opposing propositions and worldviews from the same topos, "equality." Those who advocate for equality as competition build a world around a term such as *equality of opportunity*, whereas those who advocate for an equality that never demeans build a world around a term such as *material equality*—that is, a distribution of resources and a set of restraints on vertical accumulation and hierarchy caused, in their view, by "free competition." So goes the antinomy.

A further point: when opposing positions such as the left and right root themselves in equality, they have rooted themselves in what rhetoricians have called a "god term" or "virtue term." Indeed, all the democratic rhetorics are essentially virtue terms because they are associated with the release of potential, perhaps the most significant justification of democracy itself. I talk about the release of potentiality throughout this book, and I provide a cursory discussion of it in this chapter, but for now my claim is that virtue exacerbates the antinomic problem. That is, when our propositions become foundationally right (virtuous), how do we acknowledge the virtue of opposite propositions? If my position regarding what an "equal world" ought to look like is virtuous, can my opponent's worldview also be virtuous? If my structural analysis of the antinomy is correct, the answer is yes: each proposition may be both virtuous and well reasoned. But this structural analysis is too abstract. From the perspective of human self-interestedness that jealously guards its personal investments, the answer is an unqualified no. That is, if our position is essentially virtuous, then we are justified to dig in our heels. *We* are on the side of virtue, truth, justice—and *you* aren't. Hence the opposing propositions and worldviews that we build through a term such as *equality* eventually rub against each other with little resolution. Or perhaps a resolution will be forced on us by a vote, or courts, or police—and that will satisfy only the winning party. The losing party will not be easily compelled by public institutions to set aside its deepest, virtue-laden investments.

So the topoi of equality and related notions such as "horizontal politics" can be aimed by the progressive left against, for instance, concentrations of elite power or aimed by conservatives against big government. Both attacks can occur in the name of "the people." "The people" is another virtue term that can point us to antinomic propositions. In other words, all the democratic rhetorics seem to have the ability to generate contrary premises and propositions that are virtue-filled. Moreover, what is occurring at the level of topoi suggests that this structural antinomy is also occurring at another scale—namely, the democratic body politic. In what sense is the body politic also antinomic, and what are the implications of such a claim? I am saying more than the standard notion that different people hold different opinions about, say, justice or equality. I am saying, rather, that the democratic body politic itself—its forms of life, its laws and policies for determining what counts as a "just" economy, its ideas about welfare, and on and on—is significantly ordered by the structural antinomies already buried inside its virtue terms. So the "beingness" of the body politic becomes the material expression of its core virtue terms, meaning that the structural antinomies buried in the terms themselves help to generate the body politic. In sum, when people offer what they think are their own individual opinions about, say, the "nature" of freedom or liberty, they are, more than likely, handing over received antinomies that also reappear in laws, policies, and the platforms of political parties. A consequence of this is that public discourse, to a significant degree, seems to be constituted by semantic repetitions.

And here I want to introduce the idea of the "escape route." Each pole of a structural antinomy acts as an "escape route" from the other pole. That is, the mind often encounters specific ideas that do not feel suitable, that seem limiting or confining. Thus it needs an escape route, another roadway pointing in another direction. Structural antinomies represent preexisting escape routes offering an opposite, or at least different, way to think about things. My analysis of structural antinomies, then, is more than an abstract analysis of virtue-filled topoi, propositions, and the democratic body politic. That is, escape routes should tell us that structural antinomies are linked to viscerally passionate matters and mechanical ones as well. For instance, humans always confront confinements and limitations. Hence they need other interpretations that appear to break free of limitation; they need conceptual escape routes, but these routes are, to a significant degree, preexisting and thus formulaic or mechanical. In sum, every belief in the body politic must have at least one escape route because every belief shrinks the totality of possibility. Each escape is fairly standardized—that is, believed by many. Its "common sense" is what makes it a commonplace. The democratic topoi and the antinomies therein register these routes of escape in the common mind. These routes, then, are more familiar than original, but people locked inside their logics do not necessarily know that.

I can already hear objections to what I have said. Many will ask: Can the body politic be only understood as a catalogue of its virtue terms? Isn't the body politic more than that? Doesn't democratic deliberation point to the possibility of new thinking? Isn't the idea of structural antinomies a kind of overly narrow *argument machine*? After all, today's left and right seem to be similar expressions of the same thing and not opposites of each other. Isn't there an unwarranted cynicism regarding your take on the democratic topoi as virtue terms, and doesn't this cynicism empty democratic political life of all substantive value, making hard-won commitments look like dry leaves blowing in the wind? I do not necessarily disagree with these objections. At my most cynical moments, I indeed say something like, "Freedom is a hackneyed virtue term that the state and vested interests promote in order to manage populations, and in turn populations suck at freedom's teat even as they justify nasty actions in the name of freedom, as when one party attempts to dismantle the prior party's laws and policies because its 'freedom' represents a more 'genuine' understanding of freedom itself." And making my position even more cynical, I can also believe that opposing groups do not necessarily fight over virtues and principles but simply defend their self-interested economic position by defeating the competition—whose suffering is thoroughly enjoyed—in spectacles of raw Machiavellianism.

Beneath my arguments and the objections to them, which I hear frequently, is a deep and ancient problem. The problem concerns the role of the sovereign in the making of political life and, finally, the role of violence in the making of sovereignty. Democracy, obviously, is a type of sovereignty, and, I argue, violence functions deeply inside democratic life. Some key texts for thinking about all this are Thomas Hobbes's *Leviathan*, Carl Schmitt's much later reflections on Hobbes, and Walter Benjamin's "Critique of Violence."[23] Broadly, the democratic rhetorics as god terms or virtue terms and the body politic as structurally antinomic participate in sovereign violence. I argue that the democratic rhetorics seem to hide violence, even as they embody it. To briefly explain, I start with Hobbes's notion that the human passions must be bracketed off in order for civil society to emerge. His "war of all against all" acknowledges that underneath social order is a dark, violent world waiting to erupt, a world of desperation, self-preservation, fear, ambition, the enjoyment of destruction, the sweetness of revenge, the pleasures of power, and so on. For Hobbes, the only way to overcome this seething world and achieve peace, which is our rational duty, is to voluntarily renounce our natural right to everything. This renunciation is called "contract," and it replaces self-interest with the possibility of social relations, but in so doing we become vulnerable to others who might break the contract. Our only protection, then, is the covenant to not break contract that we make with others and, most particularly, with the Leviathan whose coercive power will ensure peace.[24]

In sum, Hobbes's vision does not contain the open-ended optimism typically associated with democratic life. Hence Hobbes is not a run-of-the-mill liberal. Indeed, his sense of the unruly passions and the necessity for an authoritative, coercive state makes him a kind of anti-liberal or illiberal, and thus he is useful for my thinking. I argue that anti-liberalism does not, in fact, contradict liberalism but runs alongside it (or is in ratio with it) without ever being eradicated because our crudest passions are never tamed. When and how does anti-liberalism appear? It appears, I argue, when people make final claims or stake their lives on absolute truth statements about, say, religion.[25] But any claim that becomes absolutist ("my version of equality or freedom is more correct and virtuous than yours") runs the risk of becoming a final claim. Final claims are the bases for Hobbes's war of all against all. Wars do not begin without final claims. For Hobbes, civil society comes into being through the Leviathan's monopoly of violence (and what state can afford to not monopolize it) that tames our propensity to war and final claims.

In contrast to Hobbes's brutish view of life and politics is the view that encourages democracy toward an ever-deepening inclusivity, fairness, and so on. In the latter view, the democratic rhetorics display themselves in all their optimism, but they occult the fact that they, too, operate as final claims. The optimistic view is held by the progressive left, activist nongovernmental organizations (NGOs), and, generally speaking, an educated professional class that manages, for instance, the bureaucratic and educational sectors of democratic life. Its habits and practices suggest that this class in particular has absorbed the ideological subtleties of what it means to live in a democracy. This class most easily ascends a democratic society's rungs of power and becomes its best managers and advocates. This class works hard to uphold a genuine belief in diversity and equality, a conviction that all should be treated fairly, and that forbearance and self-restraint are important personal qualities because final claims are themselves a kind of breach of propriety. The irony, however, is that these convictions regarding democratic life become, themselves, final claims. Those, for instance, who feel disadvantaged by equality or feel that rhetorics of inclusivity jeopardize their economic standing find themselves marginalized and condemned as anti-liberal. Liberal democracy can neither value nor advance illiberalism in the modern world. Liberalism must stake final claims against illiberalism. Thus the war persists, though in hidden forms. Economic disparities belie the rhetorics, but counter-political and counter-religious orientations also cannot be fully legitimized, even though liberal democracy supposedly promises a space for all. If inclusivity functions as an exclusivity, the god term of inclusivity has become less godlike. In sum, final claims today are less about any physical war of all against all. Final claims are more hidden—indeed, they reside in the social contract, inside the democratic rhetorics themselves, where they are buried underneath layers of virtue. Their virtuousness, as I have said, exacerbates their violence. This new, more attenuated war is sometimes staged in courtrooms, where the conflicts under a sovereign are settled. Here the sovereign doles out both relief and violence. Rights claims are pitted against rights claims or freedom claims against freedom claims, and forbearance is shoved aside in favor of lawsuits. Thus inside the social contract lies the war of all against all—transformed into a ghost perhaps—but ever present. We might want to acknowledge that sovereign authority establishes its justice, in part, through its violence.[26]

I turn now to the second way that rhetoric is used in this text. The *universal elements*, as I suggested earlier, seem to have a generative force that results in our capture. That is, they are a set of rhetorical bear traps that are, for all practical purposes, inconspicuous and insidious. This insidiousness is inherent to language, I argue, for language is a clinching force from which our thoughts cannot escape—indeed, our thinking cannot *become thinking* without some sort of language (and this is true for mathematical language as well). But this idea of language being a kind of "clinching force"—a force that captures us without our knowing it and, further, distorts our knowing by generating a sense that we do know—does not match our initial intuitions regarding what language is and what it does. Speakers, and I am talking of those who are not consciously lying, initially believe that words enable us to make better sense of things and do not capture and cast us into the dungeons of not knowing. Indeed, to speak assumes a particular condition—namely, that a term terminates, so to speak, at the edges of its referent, and from that point on the referent exists independently, no longer dependent on the term itself. Of course, whatever the referent might be at that point—in all its wordlessness—is not particularly clear. What is the nature of its independent existence? But at least the words got us to those objects, persons, or ideas that lured us to them because we wanted those matters to become *visible* inside our own heads or those of our interlocutors.

At this juncture, I want to turn to an old text, Augustine's *De magistro*, written around 389 B.C.E.[27] I would argue that this dialogue between Augustine and his fifteen-year-old son, Adeodatus, anticipates modern, even contemporary, discussions in philosophy, rhetoric, and semiotics. The capaciousness of his argument illuminates the prior paragraph and allows me to explain better my understandings of the universal elements of rhetoric or language use as a generative force, a kind of *energia*, embedded in language. I believe that there is a doubleness in his argument worth discussing. First, the "law of speaking," as he calls it, describes how both speakers and hearers attend to the signifieds of their talk, meaning that the signs, which conjured up the signifiers in the first place, disappear, for all practical purposes, from their view:

> If I were to ask what part of speech *man* is, you could answer correctly only a noun. Accordingly, when *man* is found to be both a noun and an animal, the former is said in the sense in which it is a sign, the latter is said in the sense of the thing which is signified. . . . According to the law of speaking . . . as soon as the words are expressed, by virtue of that law

> which by nature is very strong, namely, that when signs are heard the attention is turned towards the things signified. (34–35)

This "law of speaking," which strikes me less like a law and more like a deception or seduction that captures us, illuminates my earlier comment about terms ending at the edges of their referents. He and I both mean that we attend not to the sign-nature of language but to the supposed reality of the signifieds—and we do it almost instantaneously. Stripped of its sign-nature, the signified quickly becomes other than sign. There seems to be nothing theoretical about this process. That is, Augustine's law of speaking seems to be part and parcel of how words work, how we experience words, a kind of phenomenology of language. The important point is that it belongs to the universal experience of words, and it may go far in explaining the sorts of magical properties that are attributed to naming. Consider, for instance, that the devotee invokes a saint's name on behalf of oneself or a loved one not because the name is a mere word or noun but because she believes that it is much more—namely, the being of the saint.[28]

Second, believing that Augustine's first point suggests that signs have a kind of illusion-making power that produces the appearances of signifieds misses what Augustine ultimately intends. His essential point is that signs have their origins in a deeper reality that produces both sign-making itself and the things of the world.

> Words possess only sufficient efficacy to remind us in order that we may seek things, but not to exhibit the things so that we may know them. He teaches me something, moreover, who presents to my eyes or to any other bodily sense or even to my mind itself those things which I wish to know. By means of words, therefore, we learn only words or rather the sound and vibration of words, for if those things which are not signs cannot be words, even though I have heard a word, I do not know that is a word until I know what it signifies. So when things are known the cognition of the words is also accomplished, but by means of hearing words they are not learned. For we do not learn the words which we know, nor can we say that we learn those which we do not know unless their signification has been perceived; and this happens not by means of hearing words which are pronounced, but by means of a cognition of the things which are signified. For it is the truest reasoning and most correctly said that when words are uttered we either know already what they signify or we do not

> know; if we know, then we remember rather than learn, but if we do not know, then we do not even remember, though perhaps we are prompted to ask. . . . Referring now to all things which we understand, we consult, not the speaker who utters words, but the guardian truth within the mind itself, because we have perhaps been reminded by words to do so. (46–47)

If the first quotation hints at contemporary social constructionist theories regarding the power of words to create the appearance of signifieds, then this second quotation shuts down such interpretations. That is, his theory may resemble today's theories of language inventing reality, but, ultimately, Augustine believes that God is the deepest reality, the source of all invention. God precedes the sign of God, indeed, all signs. Further, Augustine's God is a kind of secreted being outside the being that we think through language. Further still, God seems to be both interior and exterior—therefore a paradoxical totality: on the one hand, "the guardian truth within the mind itself" and, on the other, that which teaches the human soul not by words "but by means of the things themselves which God reveals within the soul" (50). This paradox that cancels locatability would suggest the ineffability of God, for both language and things would exist only at the threshold of God without being identical to or able to locate God's finality. Let me summarize the argument thus far: words create the illusion of signifieds, but there is a sustaining presence behind signs and signifieds. This sustaining presence means that words do not utterly deceive us and cast us into the dungeons of not knowing but begin to convey us toward an ineffable reality.[29]

What is the relevance of this analysis of *De magistro* to my understanding of rhetoric and its universal elements? My central point about these elements is that they have remarkable potency. They are generative forces that result in our capture. What do I mean by "capture"? Let me answer by returning to the democratic rhetorics. These are democracy's key terms (special topics) that allow us to do democracy talk. My point is that each one exhibits Augustine's "law of speaking." That is, hearers and speakers, as Augustine says, stop attending to the sign-nature of "equality," "freedom," "justice," and so on and start attending to the signifieds as existents. Thus stripped of their sign-nature, the signifieds have now become other than signs—and this process occurs instantaneously at the moment of language use. So what I mean by capture is that this law of speaking occurs outside of our awareness, and thus it captures us before we ever know of it. But it also captures through seduction. That is, these terms are virtue terms. They are saturated in virtue because, as I have been arguing, they are associated with the release of potentiality—and hasn't the modernist imaginary sanctified the realization of potentiality as an ultimate good or virtue? It is believed, for instance, that when we institutionalize the democratic rhetorics into public and private life, we become better people. Here is the moral justification of democracy—or so I argue at various times in this book. In sum, the democratic rhetorics capture consciousness daily, both at the linguistic level and the level of moral conviction.

I now move from special topics (the democratic rhetorics) to some universal elements of rhetoric and language use that help to buttress them. I point to six universal elements. The primary quality of each one is energy, the energy to capture.

Topoi as storehouses of social energy: "Storehouses" is a metaphor for social beliefs and memories (commonplaces) acting over a long period of time. For example, the democratic rhetorics, as I have been arguing, are topoi (commonplaces) that "store" virtue until the virtue is "released" at the moment of enunciation. To repeat the earlier argument, the "law of speaking" suggests that the topos "equality"—to name just one of the democratic rhetorics—loses its sign-nature and becomes equality as such. It becomes something more substantive or existent or real—not just a "rhetoric" or "sign" but something that ought to be and can be *materialized* through policies or social engineering from either the left or the right. If equality for a specific group did not have historical energy and virtue stored inside it, we would not hear "equality now" during a political protest. Further, if it were not an "existent"—if everyone simply agreed that it was a silly fantasy—no one would bother trying to actualize it economically or politically. The intensity or energy behind the uses of this topos suggests that it functions for some as both a "storehouse" and an "existent" quite independent of its "sign-nature." In sum, our longing for change can be likened to eagerly opened sails that capture the winds of the democratic rhetorics. We are pushed through history into whatever routes are suggested by the antinomy. (The antinomy here refers to the fact that the left or right can mobilize "equality" or any other democratic rhetoric on its behalf.) We are captured, and the different shores where we land remind us of prior shores. It is all rather repetitious . . . and yet this banal repetitiousness is another driving power source.

Storehouses have a special function—namely, they work inside the work of other universal elements. A very special universal element is what I call the "architectonic of *limitation* → *limitlessness*." (*Arche*, Greek: beginning, origin, ruler, first principle, source of action.) The prior paragraph ended on the notion of longing, which is where limitation → limitlessness begins. Essentially, both limitation and limitlessness are empty placeholders. They have no specific content until they are filled with specific topoi to steer them. What is it that the topoi are steering? The answer gets us to the heart of this architectonic: limitation → limitlessness refers to the rawest of emotions and desires, whether ethically positive or negative. In other words, we are in the realm of the passions, and topoi steer the passions. For example, oftentimes an emotion such as rage tends to be generalized until a specific topos, such as the hate of police and authority, focuses the rage. Now the person is ready to act. The topos has named the source of confinement or limitation—as the person perceives it—and this name in turn will help name the rupturing force, the limitlessness that will relieve the limitation. Upon naming the limitations that confine our lives, we have immediately available to us that which constitutes limitlessness because both are already paired as premises, propositions, and ideologies. In the case of hating the police, a person might decide to kill as many as possible and hopefully die in the process ("suicide by cop," a topos) and thus pass into a limitlessness now free of the burdens of limitation. Or a person may decide to lead a protest and then work with the city council on a package of police reforms. The larger point is that limitation → limitlessness represents the intensity of the passions that will inevitably seize pairings of specific topoi. These pairings function as a kind of commonsense providing us with names and conceptualizations to locate a specific limitation and what we hope to realize as limitlessness. We are within the frame of the conventional—that is, the horizon of the available topoi—even though we may be experiencing deep-seated turbulences. In sum, we need to think of limitation → limitlessness as a paradigm for understanding rhetorical movement: a perceived limitation is simultaneously an emotion providing motive to move oneself or a collective toward the phantoms of limitlessness, phantoms because what we know palpably is where we think we are (a limitation), but what we know less well is limitlessness itself for the simple reason that we are not there yet. Given the nature of desire, we will probably never arrive, and so limitlessness will remain forever a phantom.

Let me provide a fictional scene regarding immigration, a major concern of mine. This scene pulls together my discussions of the democratic rhetorics (special topics) and universal elements (topoi as storehouses of social energy and limitation → limitlessness), but also antinomies, escape routes, potentiality, final claims, and, more broadly, democracy as having a telos. Imagine a protest march for rights led and organized by *le sans papier*, or undocumented. In this fictional march, the undocumented and their supporters are chanting "equality now," "freedom now," and "open borders." That is, they want to be exactly and immediately equal to national citizens in terms of rights and freedoms. Among even more radical marchers, there is a desire to homogenize all rights and freedoms across every nation, which would, in effect, flatten different legal orders into a kind of radical global legal sphere or *nomosphere* (a term that I explain later) and begin to create scenes of free movement across borders. To the best of my knowledge, this exact march has not occurred anywhere in the world, but its possibility has already entered some pockets of world consciousness. Clearly, these marchers are aiming the premises of equality and freedom at a specific limitation—namely, the right of a nation-state to distinguish material presence from legal presence. The consequences of this distinction are dire: the deportation of those who are deeply present among us but without "papers." At any rate, the possibility of these protests was "stored" inside the democratic rhetorics at their historical moment of invention, along with their virtue, for the rhetorics are concerned with releasing individuals and collectives from their limitations and moving them toward limitlessness. Our fictional marchers, then, are unfolding the internal logic of the terms themselves. In this sense, they are pursuing what they think is the telos of democracy.

But standing along the periphery of this march are others muttering against the marchers. If we listen to them and compare their views to the marchers, we will hear antinomies. For those who mutter against the marchers are also mobilizing storehouses of social energy, that is, the same topoi of rights, equality, freedom, and what constitutes justice. The mutterers are sensing that the marchers are violating foundational premises of the nation-state. From the perspective of the mutterers, who are looking for escape routes, the marchers represent a limitation of life itself, and if the state gives in to the demands of the march, it will betray and abandon its "true and deserving citizens." The mutterers are starting to believe that they no longer live in a "true" democracy. Someone on the periphery says that the purpose of borders is to control the proliferation of movement. Too much movement of peoples results in the fragmentation of collective knowledge, a knowledge that enables informed decisions among the voting citizenry. "We will lose democracy and thus lose ourselves," says the person. "Is what they know really 'equal' to what I know? I was born here," the person growls. Someone else asks: "Who should benefit first when the nation distributes its resources? If the marchers were allowed to vote immediately, would they not pad their interests first? I would! And doesn't the state have an obligation to address the interests of citizens first, those who have lived here their entire lives?" Someone else mutters: "I don't like how they demand things all the time. I am starting to no longer feel 'free' in my own country." In these fictional rejoinders, democracy and its rhetorics seem to function like possessions that innately belong to one position but not the other. Indeed, both positions see the other as limitations that violate the limitlessness that belongs to the telos of democracy. Note that all the characters appearing in the last few paragraphs are subject to Augustine's law of speaking, and thus they fetishize and fixate the democratic rhetorics into self-subsistent realities. Furthermore, this process of "fixing" is part of the arsenal of making final claims.

Later in the book, I present actual arguments that sound similar to those of the aforementioned fictional characters. As we will see, the actual parties are deeply engaged with making final claims that capture what they think they know. This problem of knowing what something is, this sense of being captured inside our very knowing, is deeply complex and controversial. The problem deserves more than my truncated offerings here, but I at least want to hint at its scope and suggest connections to democratic life. With this in mind, I turn to a universal element that I call *ratio*. Broadly, a final claim, which is also a claim to know, denies the force of ratio.

For instance, the aforementioned fictional characters are not so much in opposition to each other or even on a continuum. I prefer to describe their positions as in ratio with each other. That is, their positions do not stand alone but exist as entailments of each other and other others. But the idea of ratio goes much deeper than this. My bigger thesis is that liberal democracy is in ratio or proportional relation with oligarchy. Consider that democracy legitimizes both vertical accumulation and horizontal distribution without ever resolving what proportion of the wealth should go into the hands of one or the other. Any given moment in democracy may represent a point of proportional relation, but even this might vary depending on different economic sectors. For instance, manufacturing at a moment of strong unions would represent horizontality, which can certainly coexist in the same city with a housing boom relying on day labor (vertical accumulation because of cheap labor). Ultimately, I place all democratic rhetorics under ratio: for instance, any act of justice must entail an injustice, meaning, for instance, that the conviction of a drug-dealing gang lessens the flows of capital in a neighborhood or causes the shifting of gang boundaries that raises homicide rates, which raises the suffering of the neighborhood. One can say much the same about transparency versus corruption. Perhaps the former ought to remove the latter, but, as I have shown elsewhere, in places such as Eastern Europe corruption represents a reasonable ethos for survival.[30] The larger point is that we cannot "know" democracy as being only associated with justice. The sovereign authority that maintains democracy must also be in ratio with violence, a point I suggested earlier. Thus the idea of ratio withers our confidence that democracy is about justice, pure and simple, and it should also wither our conviction that the democratic rhetorics are containers of virtue. Hence when we do not acknowledge proportional relation or ratio, we fetishize. Further, readers should note the connecting strands that hold together antinomy and ratio. As usual, the world that interests me is the rough-and-tumble of living that seems to erode the idealisms of the democratic rhetorics as having innate virtue. These idealisms try to function as limitlessness but must always be in some proportional relation or ratio to limitation.

The next three universal elements seem to be three parts acting in tandem: the *what-is-question*, *logical connectors*, and *presence* and *the arts of presencing*. All three help to establish final claims and a sense of knowing. I start with the what-is-question. Here is the beginning of ontological inquiry with the goal of knowing what something is as such. Both everyday and formal reasoning value this sort of knowing. The what-is-question, then, seems to be on the hunt for an answer that approaches the universal. Admittedly, idealists, Platonists, and Thomists will not agree with me, for I argue that the what-is-question is a kind of trick. The hunt to know may occur in a place where no final prey may exist. That is, to ask a question (what is the nature of such and such?) produces, syntactically, an internal momentum that takes us to an answer, but at the end of it all, there may be no clear answer. I argue that the question/answer structure is an energy form that may take us for a ride. True, my method is deconstructive, but please do not forget my earlier discussions of Augustine, who, I argue, laced his deconstructive tendencies with metaphysics and thereby pulled the two into ratio. I, too, argue for a ratio of not knowing and knowing.

Can what-is-questions be as easily applied to abstractions as to objects? I suspect not. Questions such as "What is equality?" or "What is justice?" are questions about abstractions. They presume that a kind of static "isness" can be located, and that it will have some identifiable quality or attribute, a "whatness." Now, asking what-is-questions of an object seems to be a different matter. "What is a house?" is easier to answer than "What is equality?," for, if necessary, one can point to a house, and its thingness will remain steadily visible. The question, I suppose, is whether locating the "isness" and "whatness" of objects is transferable to locating the "isness" and "whatness" of the democratic rhetorics. Do democratic rhetorics remain steadily visible? Apparently, the democratic rhetorics belong to another domain, but the what-is-question does not distinguish any domain shift. The English language does not make a distinction, and so the presumptions applied to objects and their objecthood are applied to abstractions. Further, the energy of the question, the pressure to oblige with answers that cannot be known except with, at best, the opinions and commonplaces at hand, exacerbates the problem. Suddenly, our lack of knowing—the condition of the commonplace—must take on the appearance of knowing, and this is particularly evident in public settings where substantive and expert answers are valued. The commonplace must enter the public arena wearing substantive clothing because it must show itself as an adequate reply to the universal implications of the what-is-question. To have clout on such a stage, we might want our abstractions to acquire the stasis of objects, an "isness" or thingness that is not ambiguous; we might want them to become entities with specific properties ("whatness"). The what-is-question then encourages us to understand the democratic rhetorics in the ways that we understand objects. If they can become object-like or objectified, then we have paved a path toward their instrumentalization in the form of policies and laws. Firm, unambiguous answers to what-is-questions grease the wheels for social engineering. Ultimately, what looks like an epistemological problem of knowing abstractions such as equality and justice reveals itself, in part, as an artifact of language structure and use. For whatever it is worth, my own sense of things is that what we know are the immediacies of some perceived inequality or injustice (the limitations that plague us), and what we invent, but do not know except as conjecture, are the phantoms of limitlessness that we think will correct our immediate confinements—and this analysis has serious implications for social policy.

In sum, the what-is-question is an energy form that encourages us to move from a state of not knowing (or intuition, perhaps) to a state of knowing. Is there anyone who would deny the value and virtue of moving from question to answer? But at some point, most people become attached to their answers, and the energy form loses its momentum. They believe that they have arrived at the end of inquiry, a belief that perhaps is an artifact of the law of speaking. The opinionated become authoritative, and if they should acquire genuine power, watch out! The what-is-question belongs to the arsenal of final claims.

Logical connectors also belong to the same arsenal, but their work may be more insidious. Again, idealists, Platonists, and Thomists will not agree with my deconstructive tendencies. They will shrewdly point out, for instance, that my deconstruction of logical connectors is so damn logical, and they will aim a second fatal blow: "Aren't you asking a what-is-question regarding logical connectors?" Yes, my analysis of the bear traps of language can itself be bear-trapped. Frustration incarnate! Would it not be grand to get outside bottomless casuistry—that is, outside linguistic entrapment, indeed, outside subjectivity—and enter a different space where words and thinking lose their rulership?

At any rate, these seemingly innocuous terms—*thus, therefore, if . . . then, either or, if and only if, not, nevertheless,* and so on—marshal considerable energy. They can take topoi (storehouses of social energy) and arrange them into persuasive propositions. Of course, the adequate deployment of logical connectors does not necessarily make for persuasion—even the insane use logical connectors—but clearly they have some sort of formal power to persuade. They enable the sequential arrangement of topoi and propositions, shaping a sense of causality, simultaneity, temporal movement, and so on. Indeed, they harness a sense of necessity that moves us toward claims regarding contingent and noncontingent truths. In one sense, they are mere signs among other signs and wholly internal to language. But, as Augustine might suggest, they, too, operate through the law of speaking. Perhaps at the moment of deployment we lose sight of their signnature and they become something other than signs. Indeed, it is a long-standing presumption that logical connectors are not just signs but evidence of some deeper principle through which everything comes into being. Such folks believe that logical connectors are, yes, human inventions, but that deeper still they are evidence of nonhuman logical relations and that mathematical language is their best incarnation. If logical connectors have some sort of prelinguistic state of being, then, presumably, causal, sequential arrangement orders all things, including the ordering in language. But in order to prove such prelinguistic states of being, one would need to explain away a contrary interpretation, Augustine's law of speaking, an interpretation that requires, unlike the other interpretation, no metaphysics. When we deploy logical connectors, their signnatures disappear from view, Augustine might suggest, for we are attending to their signifieds as if they were prelinguistic states of being. The thesis, then, that logical reasoning has transcendent origins has to answer the possibility that this transcendence is an effect of language use. I need not mention here how the conviction that one's propositions are logical, consistent, and so on is the scaffolding upon which we further build our sense of right that undoes other senses of right: *My* argument, not *yours*, contains the superior logic. Opinionatedness is the consequence of not knowing under the pressure to know. If our condition, indeed, is that of not knowing, logical connectors can hide that condition under shining logic and thereby enhance the firepower of the final claim.

I want to round off these discussions of the what-is-question and logical connectors by placing both inside the final universal element to be discussed—namely, *presence* and *the arts of presencing*. I argue that both the what-is-question and logical connectors are important in establishing presence, which is something that we have a deep longing for and, indeed, cannot live without.

At first glance, presence seems to be a property of being, and this is true at both the mundane and metaphysical levels. At the mundane level, we can speak of the presence of Lake Michigan affecting temperatures a mile or more inland beyond its shores. At the metaphysical level, recall that Augustine referenced a sustaining presence through which all things, including language, come to be. For Augustine, that presence belonged to a God that would always remain ineffable. For contemporaries, mathematics might be the presence of some deeper structure not yet fully understood and, therefore, still ineffable.[31] In the last two cases, metaphysics is being summoned. In the case of Lake Michigan, only physics is involved.

Presence and *the arts of presencing* are capacious terms that have implications for understanding the operations of conviction as well as the arts or techne for creating conviction. For instance, a verbal argument but also a statistic that persuades has *oomph* that rival arguments do not have. Such arguments have presence, meaning that they "stand out" or distinguish themselves from rival arguments. This "standing out" may dissipate with time as we come to know more, or its explanatory power may only appear after long study, or it may have *oomph* for only a small cult of believers. Hence this dependence on time and perception seems to suggest that presence is not solely out there. Still, that sense of presence when we are foundationally convinced of something points us outward. It feels *as if* presence is a property of something out there, a property of being, and not just constructed by the observer. In this sense, presence may be likened to a ghostly impression indicating that something even more true or real is projecting itself from somewhere behind the impression. Lake Michigan may be invisible one and a half miles inland, but its impressions are available to both the body and measuring instruments, and these impressions are not artifacts of language or the tricks of rhetoric. But even when the ghostly impression is the verbal argument, our conviction is not just a subjective experience or an artifact of representation but the experience of something projecting itself toward us. Even if, eventually, we decide that the projecting force was illusory, we will now sense that our skepticism is the new ghostly impression of something more true or real and other than the consequence of a perceiving subject and/or linguistic representation.[32]

At this juncture, I want to return to our two quotations from Augustine, for it seems to me that the two together shape a broad paradigm that roots this entire book and has much to tell us about presence and the arts of presencing. On the one hand, his law of speaking belongs to a now-well-established position in which language use has the ability to create the semblance of prelinguistic states of being. On the other hand, Augustine did not just deconstruct these effects of language but believed ultimately in a sustaining "real" underneath it all. As I phrased it earlier, for Augustine "this sustaining presence means that words do not utterly deceive us and cast us into the dungeons of not knowing but begin to convey us toward an ineffable reality." My interpretation is that Augustine is an early example of negotiating what appear to be contrary pulls toward both "linguistic philosophy" and "metaphysical truth claims." Now, these pulls need not be contrary. Indeed, they can exist in ratio, in proportional relation, particularly if one translates "metaphysics" into more contemporary terms.

Consider the contemporary theorist Mark Bevir. He inflects matters differently from Augustine but arrives at a similar conclusion: today's "extreme linguistic philosophers . . . [dissolve] philosophical problems simply by revealing them to be pseudoproblems that arise when we fail to grasp properly the way ordinary language operates." He continues: perhaps we should also "enhance our understanding of the world . . . rather than exhibit . . . the bewitching effects of language."[33] Bevir moves against linguistic philosophers who deconstruct the "metaphysics of presence" (e.g., Derrida's critiques of Husserl) and moves toward a different sort of language philosopher, Wittgenstein, and his interests in ordinary language. In Wittgenstein he finds, for instance, both the difficulties and the necessity to name the objects, institutions, and needs of everyday life. That is, Bevir argues on behalf of some sort of knowledge of the world that is common for "several minds," those minds, for instance, who share our form of life but not "every mind."[34] If Augustine wanted or needed the sustaining, abiding presence of a real God available to all minds, Bevir (and I) need no such thing. What we do need is a "real" or an existent, a sustaining presence that can hold our commitment and that is representable in ways that seem convincing because it contains a sufficient amount (not absolute amount) of objective knowledge. This knowledge is not utterly undone by a linguistic philosophy.

My own position, then, is that linguistic philosophy is in ratio with the implacable presence of a material world that must be attended to. In other words, language use and "the law of speaking" is simply one of the venues in which our living occurs. The abiding materiality of objects (temperature effects due to the presence of Lake Michigan) and the desire to materialize abstractions (the instrumentalization of the democratic rhetorics) in the form of institutions constitute other venues in which our living occurs. If I did not have an interest in understanding these materialities and living with them, I would not be writing this book. In sum, we seem to pivot between two poles: a generalized hermeneutics of suspicion (that sometimes spills into absolute denials of any objectivity) and an imperative to truth. In fact, the first is not the opposite of the second, for the first is a truth claim and also goads us further toward the second. We can undo a specific "truth," but we cannot undo the imperative to truth. So, it is this coupling, this ratio, this proportional relation that varies from thinker to thinker and era to era, such as we see with Augustine and Bevir. Finally, and even more importantly, please note the distinction between truth, which may defy inscription and access, and its presence, which is, in effect, its ghostly impression. The arts of presencing consist of the rhetorical techne that create conviction in an audience. Assuming that those wielding these arts are not bald-faced liars, they engage the imperative to truth, particularly if they want to be broadly influential. That is, they may never arrive at truth, but in their workshops they labor to create its presence, its ghostly impression that seems less ghostly the more it persuades. And certainly two of the tools most used in these workshops are the what-is-question and logical connectors, which earlier in the text I may have derided and deconstructed but now reveal themselves as implements that serve our longing for the rather magical arrival of certainty, one of the synonyms for presence.

What Are the Stakes of This Text?

This book does not treat democracy according to just its institutions. Institutional analyses have their value, but they also constitute a kind of professionalization of political science that informs the sort of managerial modernity that was taking shape during my stays in Kosova.[35] As I talked to representatives of the United Nations and the U.S. Department of State and read their many reports, it occurred to me that these professionals were managers of theory systems that had gone global. There was not much space in these theory systems for the sort of thinking that I was encountering during intimate conversations with my Kosovar acquaintances. As far as I could make out, the managers' guiding premise was the distinction between mature democracies that enforced private property laws and emerging democracies. Because most of the managers represented mature democracies, they had knowledge and know-how, and the Kosovars were their tutees. The tutees often reinforced this distinction during their meetings with the internationals. The Kosovars were in the uncomfortable position of knowing that they represented a "problem" on the international stage and that the internationals held "solutions." Thus the Kosovars were the bearers of how-to-questions and what-is-questions, and the internationals provided answers. Broadly speaking, these were the discursive divides present particularly during my early involvement in the Ministry of Health. "How does one create a national health insurance system?" "What does women's rights legislation look like?" The managers gave solid answers because they had to. What would it mean if they did not know? I did not believe that they did know. For instance, the internationals' plans for privatizing Kosovar social enterprises had led to a number of cases of political favoritism and to questions about pension fund distributions, according to local Kosovars. And lest we forget, this was the moment when a housing bubble was collapsing in the United States and spreading worldwide. These were also the years of the Iraq War. How complete, indeed, was managerial knowledge? Economic and political corruption in Kosova seemed minor in comparison. By the end of 2008, I had concluded that the international managers of democratic life oversaw a house of cards, a trump card away from exposing the thin line between mature and emerging democracies, and that the Kosovar politicians were even worse.

Over time, the fieldwork in Kosova began to mesh with my Chicago fieldwork. What I had been pursuing all along were the democratic rhetorics as replete with social energy. These rhetorics were key for the international managers (the walls of the ministry were plastered with posters announcing the value of equality, human rights, rule of law, freedoms, inclusivity, and so on), but the same rhetorics were also important for Chicago activists. The rhetorics appeared to be a driving force, a set of Burkeian god terms that almost everyone was eager to subscribe to. But why? I argue that these rhetorics represent a release of potentiality that fuels a kind of messianism and even "futurism" that underlies the democratic imaginary. I lay out much of this theorization in chapter 2. I argue that this release of potentiality in political terms is linked to other forms of potentiality stored in nature and technology. The eighteenth and nineteenth centuries are moments in Euro-America when one can glimpse these different couplings of potentiality. Today, we live in the wake of ideas and economies that rely on the potentiality of nature and of technology and machinic inventions for "civilizational advancement." These potentialities correspond to how the democratic rhetorics are also imagined. As one consequence, virtue gets smuggled into the democratic management of mass populations. I cut through this idea of embedded virtue by describing democracy as a "mixed system" in ratio with the "oligarchic condition." Indeed, all political orders are mixed systems that try to hold the competition between horizontal and vertical forces (the oligarchic condition) in some sort of ratio that cannot be predetermined. Constitutions, such as the United States Constitution, are documents that abstractly try to predetermine these competitions, but ultimately the determinations occur on the ground according to shifting imperatives. A similar fate seems to characterize all modernist communisms, socialisms, fascisms, and liberal democracies. Only anarchism—because it is a conceptual system and not one that can be easily, if at all, territorialized—seems to grasp the pervasiveness of the oligarchic condition. In sum, this book may have begun in ethnographic work, but at its core it is speculative.

Chapters 3 and 4 weave together ethnographic scenes and theoretical analyses in order to examine two broad issues embedded inside territorialized democracies. Chapter 3 examines the distinction between the citizen and noncitizen. I argue that this is a fatal distinction that exposes how democracy's inclusivity is constituted by exclusivity. I also argue that the citizen and noncitizen distinction exposes an antinomy in the body politic between what I call a "politics of mobility" based on deterritorialized fantasies of free movement across borders and a "politics of the stationary," which also invokes freedom on behalf of a national people. Broadly, modern democracies and nation-states have problematically inherited the ancient identification of a specific people "born into" a specific land—and so are not so modern after all. Thus democracy in practice collapses into its premodern forms that it never erased. The only resolution is the dissolution of nation-states, which is, at best, a distant pipe dream.

Chapter 4 addresses another matter that liberal democracy in particular cannot resolve—namely, property and how it simultaneously maintains social and private ownership claims. The chapter begins with fieldwork regarding urban gentrification, a major concern of my activist friends, but underneath gentrification is a far richer topic: ownership. That is, how do we claim to own land and, more broadly, how do we claim to own anything? One of my major conclusions is that the beingness of things is so entangled with the beingness of humans that modern laws of collective and private ownership are simply updates of the imperative to lay claim to an outside world in order to ensure survival. Hence a self (as in private ownership) or a group self (as in collective ownership) extends itself into a not-self and claims it as its own. These forms of appropriation are evident in such practices as eminent domain, private home ownership, community land trusts, and the practices of peoples claiming sacred lands. Ownership laws in every society are rationalized fictions—and nothing more—of what a society needs or wants, and every society holds in ratio an unresolvable tension between the practices of individuation and the practices of society as organism.[36] I conclude the chapter with a discussion of what I call the "deep commons."

←↥→

What's Up with the Form of This Text?

The book moves through a variety of textual strategies. Among these are parody, including self-parody.[37] There are also digressions sitting alongside major themes, and I have been known to mix paradox with social science realism. There are more strategies, but are these compatible with scholarly writing? Frankly, I consider all texts—including scholarly, scientific, and even mathematical texts—to be species of poetics insofar as all texts are hypotheses about the world attempting to overcome the hypothetical. That is, *poetics* is simply a term describing how words miss their marks and slide toward metaphor only to rise up and try again. So, for me at least, the deployment of multiple textual strategies produces a "thickened poetics." One strategy succeeds and fails, only to be compensated by the next one. Thus the form of the text displays the problem of argument and the problem of wording. At another level, however, I am also trying to suggest the contrariness and density of our living moment, our inability to find firm footing in a body politic shaped by antinomic complexities. Hence I cut one belief against the other, one assertion against another, one textual strategy slicing into another in the hope of exposing our predicament. Shifting textual strategies, then, mimics both an argument about texting and the densities of our living moment.

One of the early readers of this manuscript asked: What recommendations are you making to your activist, left-leaning friends, you who seemingly believes in politics and then gleefully unravels its possibilities? My answer is simple: continue to do what you are doing. After all, there aren't many practical alternatives. But cultivate that tragic awareness that you are deceiving yourselves. Unravel your own final claims, including the fantasies about the Other that you use to buttress your claims. Dare to feel a certain emptying out of conviction. This emptying, of course, requires more than what most people can afford. People fight to the end in order to hold on to their deepest investments. And so a question appears: Can we continue to act fullheartedly while withholding fullhearted conviction? To do so is a balancing act requiring never-ending self-scrutiny. It also requires a sense of radical egalitarianism between friend and enemy. Ultimately, I do not know if all this gets us very far. Maybe it is only a lark of a thought.

So goes the book.

2

Democracy Is . . . ?

Concepts forged by modern thought have either been progressively diluted, have become hazy, or have completely stopped functioning (the notion of "people," "nation" or "class," for example). We contend that the idea of sovereignty must be submitted to an increasing critique. . . . Globalization radically blasts away the set of old criteria of measure.
—Antonio Negri, *The Porcelain Workshop*

Some say that democracy is one of those concepts that is being blasted away. They point to a rise in "populist autocracy" that is making democracy shudder.[1] By my account, the members of the professional class who fear autocracy also fetishize democracy, while those who are turning to populism and autocracy are not so much rejecting democracy but, rather, seizing the populist strand that always exists inside democracy. And there is at least one more position: for the global populations who aren't well-off and who, for whatever reason, are suspicious of communism or of the "strongmen" (autocrats) who claim to be leaders of countries, democracy becomes a kind of emotional promise. The upshot is this: democracy takes on many meanings without a single, substantive meaning. People want democracy or their strong leaders to do all sorts of things—namely, solve their difficulties. Consequently, they often fetishize democracy, even when they claim to reject it. Moreover, they want the real deal, but no one knows exactly what that is or how to implement it. Part of the problem is that the term *democracy* is abstract and floats in the ether, meaning that it must become territorialized—that is, grounded in a particular scene with particular people. But when it becomes territorialized, its promise gets broken, for now numerous people start to wrestle over it and through it, trying to make it work to their advantage or conform with how they see things. Something will get lost because mass societies cannot be governed in ways that will foreground each person's expectations or dignity, and democracy, tragically, creates the promise that everyone's dignity will be recognized. When this recognition does not occur, people become hot and bothered. They cry out: "What democracy? You call this democracy?" And so they demean what they have, and they fetishize what they don't have. Now the well-off may not need "democracy" quite as much as the not-well-off, but they, too, fetishize it when they need to protect their goodies. Overall, I argue that there is a contentious Machiavellian or Hobbesian world beneath all the trappings of our democratic rhetorics. So I am willing in this book to blast democracy apart so as to reveal its ruses.

←↕→

I begin by turning to a specific photograph. The moment is a massive protest march in Chicago in 2006—250,000 people according to some estimates—on behalf of the legalization of the undocumented.[2] By May 1 of the same year, another march for the same cause drew between 400,000 and 500,000 people. But, importantly, these marches were not just about immigration law and the conceptual distinction between the citizen and noncitizen. They were also about the centrality of labor. One sign held amid the crowd, though not legible in this photograph, said: "We demand equal labor rights and legalization for all." The labor unions, for very good reasons, were major organizers of the protest—even if, historically, labor unions in the United States have also protected American workers against immigrants.

Clearly these protests were huge, perhaps the largest in the history of Chicago, and the photo indicates how the people stretched beyond the possibilities of the camera. I am somewhere down there supporting the marchers but also doing ethnographic fieldwork alongside colleagues from my university. Prior to the marches, we had been examining how they were being organized and talking to a remarkable, if controversial, figure: Elvira Arellano. Months before the marches, she had taken sanctuary with her son at a storefront church in the heart of the Puerto Rican neighborhood where I had been doing fieldwork since 2001. Her case, along with the passage of H.R. 4437—Border Protection, Antiterrorism, and Illegal Immigration Control Act of 2005, otherwise known as the Sensenbrenner bill[3]—had created a firestorm in Chicago's Mexican neighborhoods. The Mexican radio stations, which I often enjoy, could not stop talking about these and similar events, and indeed they were one of the galvanizing forces behind the marches.

This picture is a vehicle, an opening, a heuristic that seems to hold this entire book together. That is, this picture is all about the idea of the citizen and

1 | Protestors for immigrants' rights march east on West Adams Street in downtown Chicago on March 10, 2006. From "'La Marcha': March 10, 2006, Chicago's 'General Strike,'" *Substance* (April 2006): 6. Photo: George N. Schmidt.

noncitizen, as well as the importance of this distinction for the making of the nation-state and ultimately for what I call the *territorialization of democracy*; this picture is also about property, particularly the concentration of wealth in a global city's downtown as it looms over more "lowly" laborers; this picture is also about what I call the *democratic rhetorics* as they rise up in protest and the sorts of fetishizations that occur around these terms; finally, this picture, where I am both present and invisible, seems to hint at the larger matter of writing texts, whether ethnographic or not, that attempt to name and interpret the important issues of the moment—how do we do this in convincing ways? This last point takes us to the heart of rhetoric: for rhetoric, historically, has been about the problem of creating conviction; for the history of rhetoric, the problem has been the exchange between presence and invisibility. This picture, then, contains all of that.

The placement of the camera tells us something special. The height of the camera above the crowd reveals, both symbolically and materially, an unresolvable tension inside the democratic imaginary. Specifically, the photo points to the importance and legitimacy of vertical power in democracy—for instance, the right to accumulation—versus the importance and legitimacy of the horizontal distribution of power and accumulation. Consider that the massiveness of the protest clamoring for rights is a primary signature of democracy. The masses have been set loose, so to speak, and here is the politics of enthusiasm that emerges from a specific aspiration—namely, the possibility that a horizontal distribution of power might replace vertical or hierarchical accumulations of power. We can give horizontal distribution a more specific definition by turning to the Greek *demos kratos* ("rule by the people"—that is, the people are sovereign over themselves; *demos* also means "village" or "the body of Athenian citizens").[4] In this sense, protests of this sort are deeply predictable, particularly within the liberal democratic imaginary, because they continue the modernist desire to perfect democracy,[5] to overcome barriers (racial, patriarchal, etc.) and make democracy available to as many as possible. The argument here suggests that there is a kind of teleological impulse that moves through the democratic imaginary. This telos was not so much a part of the classical Greek experience of democracy, but it became ours during the Euro-American upheavals of the seventeenth and eighteenth centuries. Some have read this teleological unfolding transcendentally as the "end of history,"[6] but it also can be read more immanently and locally—for instance, the betterment of a here and now by enhancing "pluralism" or expanding "rights" and "access." Thus the tropes of reform and revolution as advocated in street protests perform the perfection of democracy and, consequently, structure the populist rhetorics of both the right wing and the left wing. Consider the iconography of revolution as it appears in the Tea Party (right wing) as well as in Bernie Sanders's Our Revolution (left wing).

But the irony behind this particular protest is that the marchers are arguing on behalf of those who are not authorized citizens. Hence the protest stages a particular problem: How do we construe the demos? Can noncitizens in some fundamental way act as and even be citizens? Can noncitizens "legitimately" protest for political rights?[7] Or, stating it as starkly as possible: Can the undocumented or noncitizens become sovereign over themselves within a political order that restricts sovereignty to citizens? If the horizontal distribution of power has always been foundationally exclusionary because the distribution can only be among citizens, the marches of 2006 seemed to arch toward some universal condition—namely, some inclusionary ideal that might grant the undocumented the right to protest (i.e., might equalize in the same space both the authorized and undocumented). It is not as if democracy as such can enable this equalization, for in all of its incarnations around the globe every country structures some legal hesitation regarding absolute and immediate equality between one's own and the foreigner. Interestingly, the Fourteenth Amendment to the United States Constitution, as we discuss later, has been interpreted as providing a certain set of equal protections for the undocumented, as seen, for instance, in *Plyler v. Doe*. Nevertheless, even in *Plyler* and similar cases, one can conclude that democracy rhetorically announces a "belonging" for everyone but always hesitates to do so in practice. According to international law, the nation has the right to *democratically* determine those who can and cannot belong.[8] So democracy in its current incarnations, no matter how permissive, does not grant a universal equality to citizens and the undocumented. Democratic states may benefit economically from the presence of the undocumented, but that is not sufficient to grant them the right to freely move from place to place or to receive all the benefits of the state. States always hesitate before granting the juridical condition of citizenship or the more profound condition of belonging. Therefore, the promise of a fully horizontal distribution of power—say, an equalization of the documented and undocumented—is no natural consequence of democracy. Consider how the philosopher David Miller frames it: political philosophy from Hobbes on has been "state-centric," meaning that it has been concerned with the "internal relationship between the state and its citizens," and the foreigner has been a challenging figure. Even today's universal human rights paradigm has been unable to trump the state's right to determine who belongs.[9] Hence I argue that democracy—because it is entangled in state-centric interests—cannot overcome for a variety of reasons this rather profound inequality.

Thus prior to all the political enthusiasm that runs beyond the limits of the camera, there is a vertical accumulation of power—in the form of a nation's right in this case—to foundationally determine who belongs to the nation and who doesn't. But consider this as well: the marchers in the photo are very much dwarfed and squeezed in by the buildings. In a sense, everyone is being herded through a chute. All other photographs that I have seen were taken from the ground, and thus they do not capture the verticality conveyed in this photograph.

In other words, against the reoccurring pleas to distribute power horizontally there is an ever-present and determining verticality. The vertical symbolizes the concentration of power and capital—and what better symbol of the vertical than the thriving center of a global city, for skyscrapers and such are themselves literal projections of capital accumulation. They are, in effect, the verticalization of property enabled by rules that encourage the concentration of capital and the ethos of ownership. If the distinction between the citizen and noncitizen is at the heart of the democratic imaginary, so are the laws guaranteeing ownership of property.

Let me summarize my argument thus far. At the heart of liberal democracy exist two foundational structures: (1) the citizen–noncitizen distinction and (2) the right to accumulation—that is, private property. Of course, one might expand the claim: At the heart of any political order are rights, rules, taboos, and beliefs regarding who belongs and who does not. Alongside these are rights, rules, taboos, and beliefs regarding possession: what is mine versus what is thine and what can be owned versus what cannot be owned. In other words, conceptual categories regarding citizenship and property—even if these specific terms distort the historical terms used in different linguistic communities—are inevitably important matters of local governance for tribal peoples, liberal democrats, socialists, communists, and so on. At some level, both of these conceptual categories are inclusionary. But by delimiting who or what is included, one also excludes. Indeed, what is outside defines what is inside. Hence someone's inclusion is someone else's exclusion. Call this the paradox of all political governance. Thus the felt sense of being excluded becomes the generative force of upheaval that can never be quieted.

Let me elaborate a bit by introducing a term, a heuristic—as opposed to a theory—that might capture the horizontal-vertical relation: *ratio*. Liberal democracy contains a ratio, meaning that the logics and desires for a horizontal distribution of power cannot be pried apart from the logics and desires for vertical accumulations of power. Like most forms of governance, democracy is composed of a wealth of truth claims and sensuous spectacles. It is thickly dimensioned. The photo, then, does not so much symbolize the horizontal-vertical relation but is its manifestation, since it is vertical accumulation itself that enables the camera to be placed high. In sum, the term *ratio* here means that, within democracy, horizontal interests are tightly related to vertical interests. One set of interests can never establish dominance—and perhaps this is liberal democracy's compromising genius and the source of a killing frustration for those who wish to stand on one side or the other, or name the essence of democracy.

Let us return to our earlier reading of the *demos* but this time through the eyes of the classical philologist Luciano Canfora. He points out that the word *demokratia* functioned not in a celebratory way, as we read earlier, but as a denunciatory term, "a factional term, coined by the higher classes to denote the 'excessive power' (*kratos*) exercised by the non-property-owning classes (*demos*)." Canfora replaces our earlier reading of *demos kratos* with a fine-grained analysis of the sociopolitical context: "Democracy was the term opponents of government 'by the people' used to describe such government, precisely with the aim of highlighting its violent character (*kratos* denotes exactly the violent exercise of power). For the opponents of the political system that was based around the people's assembly, therefore, democracy was a system that destroyed freedom."[10] The freedom of the elites, we might call it—the freedom to maintain, as I describe throughout this book, the oligarchic condition. At any rate, this tension between vertical and horizontal power seems to be the enduring paradigm. We cannot equate the term *democracy* with just the horizontal, for democracy also ratifies the vertical. They are in ratio. Indeed, if we wish to fabricate a political life that is constituted only by the horizontal, we would have to tear apart the texturing together of the vertical and horizontal, which ratio provides, and create something other than democracy as we have come to know it.[11]

So the buildings are signs of capital accumulation with the ability to endure and shape the life below while remaining nearly impenetrable—this is what dominates the photograph. Protest marches in the name of empowerment are dwarfed by the power that is already in place, and so marches are sites where the wrestling over the control of space indicates how vertical and horizontal powers never fully resolve their animosities. Anyone who has marched in a peaceful protest knows the extent of control: permits are necessary, routes are planned beforehand in conversation with the police, and protest marshals in constant contact with each other assure that the marchers stay in line and move forward. Even though such protests are challenging the state at some level, the state is clearly in charge, and it is the official permit that seals the contract. So, it could be said that the purpose of these formalities is to ritualize and neuter the raw character of the protest and dilute whatever bitterness and suffering may have given rise to the march.

And what if some of the protestors should break rank and run down one of the side streets breaking windows and destroying private property?[12] What then? Such an act breaks the original contract between protestors and police, and though the police in a democracy are always subject to rules of engagement, they now have greater leeway to use weapons and strategies that push toward the limits of lethality. So, how does vertical power interact with the horizontal? It dilutes its passion, whether of the right or left; it wrings out its raw character and transforms it, at most and if need be, into legislation. That is, if democratic legislation should absorb in some fashion the cause of the protest, it will have neutered the protest's potential for violence. Violence is horizontal power's most distinctive and ultimate possession. It is a transcendent possession because violence, as the last card to be played, aspires (or at least its adherents aspire) to absolute finality, but this does not mean, of course, that this transcendent possession has moral authority. Indeed, violence as an expression of horizontal power has become profoundly delegitimized in the context of liberal democracies. It is one thing when the tyrant says that violence against him or her is not legitimate. Everyone knows that the tyrant is lying. But democracy also delegitimizes violence. That is, violence has moral authority only when it faces tyranny, but once the tyrant has been overthrown (presumably by democratic forces) violence loses all moral authority. How did this magical transformation of violence occur? The best explanation appears, I believe, in Walter Benjamin. Benjamin explains that when violence confronts authority, including the authority of liberal democracies, the authority responds with equal or even more violence, not just because it is obliged to protect social order but because "there is inherent in all such violence a lawmaking character." That is, the state knows and fears that its laws are replaceable, and therefore "modern law [tends] to divest the individual, at least as a legal subject, of all violence."[13]

Of course, Benjamin's point about the law-making character of violence refers not to the production of any old law but a profoundly new law with the power to form a new world or institute a new order. The violence of a revolution aspires to such a law—and in more diluted and inchoate ways, so does a riot. And this analysis recalls my earlier talk of the antinomic and final claims. That is, violence seems to be the seizure of a specific escape route, one pole of the antinomy, one final claim that overthrows the existing final claim. This seizure, in effect, destroys all appearances of the antinomy because it strips the antinomy of its force and delivers it wholly to the other final claim. That is, the antinomy is backgrounded and the final claim foregrounded, and so the antinomy seems to disappear. But any violence that responds at some point in the future will be a dim recalling of the antinomy. We seem to be in a kind of circular pattern:

violence topples one final claim with another, but the reification of the new final claim is also violent because in both cases the antinomy is not allowed to live; the process repeats itself, back and forth, until, perhaps, the material conditions change enough that the paradigm becomes exhausted and a new paradigmatic antinomy starts to appear in a new present already caught by circularity. I honestly do not know if we are ever outside the antinomic.

It is crucial to note that this analysis of violence and its law-making character is applicable to more than tyrannical states. All states ruled by any political ideology fear this sort of violence. That is, Benjamin is amplifying Max Weber's famous notion that only the state can lay claim to a monopoly on the legitimate use of violence.[14] Thus vertical power, of any sort, must deny horizontal's claim to violence, must deny the desire for a new, world-forming law as replacement of what exists. In tyrannical states, horizontal interests may face incarceration, but in democracies horizontal interests face their own precarious situation. They cannot violently overthrow whatever vertical interests upset them. What they can do, however, is vote against them. Thus there is no such thing as a revolution against democracy. Hence horizontal interests in democracies must find some sort of accommodation with vertical interests, must suck it up, for the potentiality of violence that belongs especially to the masses has been craftily delegitimized, leaving them with not much else but the vote.[15]

Admittedly, the 2006 immigration marches in Chicago were about many things, but violent they were not. I have never before marched alongside so many baby carriages, so many families hand in hand, so many claims to being hardworking and worthy. These marchers aimed to create an image of respectability, while the white anarchists who marched beside them drew their disapproving stares. If we follow the logic of the prior analysis, the anarchists were ready to establish a new, order-instituting law, but the immigrant marchers, orderly and decent, were not. If anything, they embodied many of the values of vertical power. Many horizontally based protests claim an alienation due to some systemic injustice that must be righted while simultaneously affirming their moral worth. That is, the alienation must be severe enough to represent a danger if not addressed, but because the protestors frame themselves as worthy, as just like everyone else, the entire society will benefit if the wrong is righted—or so goes their claim.

And the 2006 marchers followed suit: they claimed an injustice, hence an alienation from the mainstream, while simultaneously claiming to be just as responsible and meritorious, just as hardworking and devoted to family as the mainstream. This was not an angry, alienated crowd at their wit's end but rather a crowd claiming cooperation with vertical forces and their willingness to be assimilated into its structures, for the crowd's merit was evidence of a de facto citizenship that ought to become de jure. Thus the prevalent orientation and hopefulness of these marchers were that current laws should be, at most, tweaked, thereby recognizing the marchers as already part of the textures of American democratic life. In sum, when existing law grants fairness to the deserving, it gathers moral authority, but if marchers choose violence, they are trying to replace existing law and gain the moral authority of a new law. The first summarizes the hopes of protestors, and the second the hopes of rioters and revolutionaries.

I want to insert more difficulty into my analysis by considering the importance and legitimacy of the vertical accumulation of power within the democratic imaginary. Vertical accumulation always represents a gathering up of potential, and this is why there is always a battle for it. It is the potential to do. Whether what is done in the name of vertical accumulation is negative or positive for one party or another is a secondary point. The primary point, that which cannot be vanquished—and therefore ought to be called a "primal necessity"—is the need to gather up potential in order to do, make, create, change, give shape to, guarantee, and protect. In this sense, liberal democracy can never just be a horizontal distribution of power, a vast equalization of power, but must also provide mechanisms for the vertical accumulation of power. Otherwise, doing, making, creating, changing, giving shape to, guaranteeing, and protecting become unrealizable. Of course, numerous mechanisms can be adopted. Socialism, for instance, is nothing less than vertical accumulation done horizontally in the name of mass society, and in liberal democracy vast protests in the name of the 99 percent against the elite 1 percent are also vertical accumulations through horizontal means. The state itself, whether communist or liberal, represents a form of vertical accumulation, but broadly speaking it is liberal democracy that wavers in its institutionalization of verticality, choosing socialist versions at one moment and privatized versions at others. But the larger point is the primal necessity of the vertical accumulation of power. So this accumulation—whether done in the name of communism or a deep socialism or the individual's unrestricted right to accumulation within a free market—represents the power of verticality to realize potential. Projects of scale require concentrations of vertical power, and herein lies the dangerous authority to gather up and realize the potential for doing, making, changing, creating, giving shape to, guaranteeing, and protecting—and this doing can be seen as either brutally negative or wonderfully enabling.

←↨→

The term *heuristics* indicates an "opening up of a line of inquiry" in order "to meet with" a "finding," a "discovering." In this section, I want to explore the term *ratio* as a heuristic. Logic, reason, and *ratio*nality seem to be built into the term *ratio* because, perhaps, the term is derived from the exactness associated with numerical reasoning. I want to apply all these connotations to matters that are political—and decidedly not numerical—in order "to meet with" a possible political truth that many of us intuit: liberal democracy is always in ratio with oligarchy. The two elements compose a mixed system, and the two cannot be pried apart.

The *Oxford English Dictionary* (*OED*) offers this definition of *ratio*: "a proportional relationship between things not precisely measurable." Important in this first definition is the idea that measurability is not precise, and yet our common understandings of *ratio* do not suggest ambiguity. Perhaps this is because below the first definition are some foundational undertones derived from classical Latin. That is, according to the *OED* again, *ratio* is linked to "reason," even the "faculty of reason," "calculation," or "guiding principle"—as well as, and of considerable importance to us, a sense of action and process, as in "the act of reckoning" or "the act of reasoning." (*Rat* is a past participial stem of *reri*, to think, perhaps originally to count, though of uncertain origin. And more provocatively, the *OED* says: "It has often been suggested that classical Latin *ratio* originally denoted 'account' and developed further senses especially in the language of rhetoric and of philosophy partly by association with" the ancient Greek word for *logos*, "as this word also denotes both account and 'reason.'")

Rhetorical theorists do not need to be told of the importance of logos for rhetorical theory. The term can mean "word," "reasoned discourse," "opinion," "ground," "logical appeal," "the principle of order and knowledge," "God's generative principle," and so on. The point is that moving through Greek and Latin is a relationship between *logos* and *ratio*, and these terms can have at some moments a sense of "counting" and "accounting," and at other moments a sense of the ordering principle of the universe. Thus *ratio* would seem to be an important term for rhetorical theory, but one that is rarely discussed. I want to make the term more available to rhetorical theory, and in order to do so I want to foreground its relation to mathematical reasoning as creating the rhetorical force of certainty, which can then be used in a variety of thought systems, such as economics.

The term *ratio* refers to the even older term *geometrical ratio* as a "relation between two quantities" expressed as "dividing the first by the second" (*OED*). Here is a mathematical technique that can serve the making of foundational or final claims, and Plato's privileging of geometry as exemplar of pure reasoning—uncontaminated by human reasoning (and therefore "certain")—is just one instance. Many today continue to believe that mathematical reasoning is the gold standard of logic. Consider how economics makes final claims regarding the ratio of government debt to gross domestic product (GDP). This particular ratio claims that there is some critical relation between a country's government debt and the totality of what it produces and sells in terms of goods and services. If the GDP is high, there should be a sufficient amount, seemingly, to pay debts back and thus refrain from taking on more debt. Thus this ratio can function as a universal template for comparing any set of governments (thus countries) at a particular point in time or to compare different eras of the same country. That is, the debt-to-GDP ratio can be used to discern economies of the past and present, and it can be used to predict a bit of the future. Insofar as the ratio can help to determine the economic health of a country or even the world economy, it would seem that it functions biopolitically. That is, this ratio can help discern the "well-being" of a macro economy and, hence, the appropriate policy actions, such as whether austerity measures need to be instituted or removed. Thus the ratio of debt to GDP is a technique that puts numbers into relation in order to reify an otherwise impossible abstraction, such as the "health" of an economy, and, once produced, an action or nonaction can follow.

However, many economists have argued that at the heart of these measurements is mismeasurement. That is, the ratio of debt to GDP presences exactness, but behind the scenes is inexactness.[16] We seem to have arrived at one of the cornerstones of rhetoric—the staging of proof, truth, certainty—while behind the curtain is uncertainty. If ratio is a type of mathematical reasoning while logos is discursive reasoning and both are attempting to make a case for certainty where contingency is likely to exist, then we are seeing how the visible and invisible are being used in the management of mass societies. That is, what is worrisome about modern mass societies is that they are ungraspable. For instance, all the economic transactions occurring at this very moment in the United States are invisible.[17] In calculating the debt-to-GDP ratio, we objectify (make visible) a thin slice of what is happening and construct a universal threshold where debt levels may impinge on growth, and this objectification is meant to replace subjective intuitions. Similarly, much of rhetorical argument is about the challenge of making contingent matters appear certain—even if the measurements and contingencies cannot be fully eradicated. Both numbers and words then play in the arena of making the invisible visible. They are forms of presencing, an artful bringing before the eyes.[18]

Still, despite all the qualifications that I have made regarding the term *ratio*, I want to summon the aura of conviction and certitude that is built into the term—that sense of getting at a truth derived from numerical reasoning—and to apply it to reasoning that is inherently enthymematic.[19] Political reasoning is always enthymematic because it depends on the commonplaces of a people, commonplaces that try to rise toward a kind of universalism ("democracy is good for all") but eventually fall back into the contingency that seems to haunt all commonplaces. Political reasoning cannot escape contingency, can never seize the universal—even though it tries to. Apparently, as we have seen, some forms of numerical reasoning can't do it, either, and yet its aura of arriving at certainties is impressive. Of course, the tension between certainty and contingency can be largely set aside when we allow something to be simply good enough. At any rate, I want to borrow this aura built into the term *ratio* and apply it to the key terms or commonplaces that serve as some of the "underlying structures" of liberal democracy (freedom, equality, rights, justice [including social justice], transparency, etc.) and put them into *ratio* with their oppositional terms.

Today, liberal democracy's opposite term is primarily *oligarchy*. Granted, there is also today a new oppositional term, a kind of religious absolutism that has solidified during our so-called war on terror and, supposedly, opposes "secular democracy." But, overall, we have seen that since the sixteenth and seventeenth centuries, liberal democracy has been in a face-off with a set of opposing systems (aristocracy, communism, Nazism, religious absolutism, warlordism and tribalism [particularly during the era of colonialism], and dictatorships). In my view, each of these systems, even religious absolutisms, are not just species of authoritarianism at local and larger scales; they also weave inside of themselves elements of the oligarchic condition. I am not interested in proving all the details of this last claim because my broader thesis does not depend on it. My central thesis is that liberal democracy is in ratio or proportional relation with oligarchy. So, for instance, if mathematical ratio means a relationship between two numbers regarding how much of the first is contained in the second, then the assertion here is that some amount of oligarchy exists inside liberal democracy and vice versa. But these amounts are not determinable. They are too massive for any single person to witness, and the proportions constantly shift across time depending on which side has the upper hand. They also differ at different scales. A national government, for instance, may exhibit one proportional relation, but a regional and local government in the same nation may exhibit a different proportional relation. Precision, then, in these matters is not relevant because with the term *ratio* we are heuristically trying "to open up a line of inquiry" in order "to meet with" a possible truth about political life that many of us intuit. And yet we want to couch our intuition with a kind of exactness, as if (metaphorically) we were engaging a kind of numerical reasoning.

Liberal democracy and oligarchy do not name stand-alone political systems as if they were two prior existents waiting to be named. Instead, the idea of ratio tells us that when we name one—and, moreover, try to institute it—it will contain the other as an entailment. Liberal democracy and oligarchy fornicate, and our beliefs about their separateness are some of their offspring. So we might think about each one as an idealism that can only function heuristically. That is, each one opens up a possible way to reason about governance but never achieves governance itself. Hence each one is ever present in the other and sits there as a line of reasoning just waiting to deconstruct the other.

In other words, polar habits of thought (dialectics)[20] operate in this way: they try to "perfect themselves" and their opposition, as Kenneth Burke suggests, by elaborating each other's essential premises until they make themselves into monuments of rational coherence and their opponents into monuments of incoherence. Their lives as ideas depend on this double invention. But as a further step in perfecting themselves, each one might strive to become and make the other to be more than a mere idea. Indeed, for many the ultimate goal of a political ideal is to shed its status as mere idea and to acquire more materiality, to become implemented, to achieve "thingness." Strong believers in liberal democracy, for instance, want their belief to be more than an abstract idealism. In this sense, liberal democracy aims to be in the world, somehow, and it uses law to get there. This state of "thingness" is important, for if the opposite is also a "thing," then it can be construed as a "real and present danger." After all, solutions invent themselves and achieve legitimacy via the problems that they identify and the cures that they produce. For instance, after the financial crisis of 2008, the Occupy Wall Street movement organized protests that seemed to shape a problem even as they offered their cure. I briefly participated in these protests, and I was particularly interested in how they rallied around the need for "more democracy." Among the signs the protestors held were those with cutouts so that the faces of protestors could be seen. Such signs would read "This is what democracy looks like." Thus they named themselves—and by extension the common person, the 99 percent. Hence the oligarchic condition may have been ever present as the object of protest, but it was also excluded from the being of democracy because it represented the "real and present danger."

Consider this simple design at the heart of representative democracy: the many → the few → the one. The arrows mean "give rise to," and "the few" is the prototype for representing the oligarchic condition. The design suggests that the one cannot represent the many, as claimed, because the many embody a level of difference that is unrepresentable. Thus the few step into the vacuum, and the few are indeed representable by the one. The few, more than likely, profit from their representation and have little incentive to represent the rest. Now the "few" could be anyone: trade unionists opposing bosses, bosses opposing regulations that favor the unionists, one faction of bosses opposing another faction. It is not as if the few can afford to give up their self-interest—particularly when their lives depend on it. If the few through their representative, the one, should compromise their self-interests, it is because the stakes of what they stand to lose are not yet high enough. Within the bowels of representative democracy, then, is a structural alliance between the one and a few that gives birth to one version of the oligarchic condition. Indeed, every political party, no matter its ideological orientation, is an oligarchy or the oligarchic condition melding respective legislators to a brand that attracts money and votes. As the economist Deirdre McCloskey states it: "Inherited political power allied to corruption is ancient. Political candidates in the Roman Republic routinely bought votes. There is nothing new about politicians and businesses and billionaires buying Congress for special treatment."[21] Or, as James Madison described it in Federalist Paper No. 10:

> The most common and durable source of factions has been the verious [*sic*] and unequal distribution of property. Those who hold and those who are without property have ever formed distinct interests in society. Those who are creditors, and those who are debtors, fall under a like discrimination. . . . And what are the different classes of legislators but advocates and

> parties to the causes which they determine? Is a law proposed concerning private debts? It is a question to which the creditors are parties on one side and the debtors on the other. Justice ought to hold the balance between them. Yet the parties are, and must be, themselves the judges; and the most numerous party, or, in other words, the most powerful faction must be expected to prevail.[22]

Furthermore, the oligarchic condition appears in every organizational structure,[23] and it is why anarchism, as a resistance to the sedimentation of any structure, endures. Of course, anarchism's refusal to oligarchize is part of its noble puritanism—and its failure. Thus its fate is to remain unrealizable, a manifestation of potentiality: negative, heuristical, performative. It cannot, by definition, govern.

←↕→

Aristotle did not fetishize democracy, much less liberal democracy, nor did he seem to disparage oligarchy.[24] Now, it may seem that much of Aristotle's analyses of the different political regimes of his day (kingship, aristocracy, and polity along with what he called their respective deviations: tyranny, oligarchy, and democracy [119–20]) are not particularly relevant for contemporary political theory. Nevertheless, he offers a few remarkable observations. First, his approach is diagnostic and uncommitted, and this is due to his belief that whatever predominates in a given city should determine the specific regime: "Where the multitude of the poor is preeminent, therefore, with respect to the proportion mentioned, there a democracy is what accords with nature. . . . Where the element of the well-off and the notables predominates in quality to a greater extent than it falls short in quantity, there it is oligarchy that accords with nature" (136–37). This approach is sobering. It does not fetishize. When he talks of equality, freedom, and justice, he does not associate these terms with the sort of ultimate moral rightness that seems to appear in the modernist versions of democratic revolution. The reason for this, seemingly, is that Aristotle believes that merit and virtue ought to be the rightful rulers over human affairs because these can protect us from the unseemly, that is, the more chaotic, unsuppressed, expressive tendencies of individuals and societies. Today's conservatives continue to speak this way. But the modernist revolutionaries—including the socialists, communists, and even liberals—were more willing to test the limits of social order via more absolutist versions of equality, freedoms, and rights. The reason why, perhaps, is because they believed in the necessity of releasing suppressed potential, both individual and social,[25] which if set loose would also release the potential of nature. That is, the modernist revolutionaries are imagining a transcendental progress that can sweep up the earth on behalf of a greater humanity once freed of aristocrats and monarchs. In time, the revolutionary sentiment moved from the poor to slaves, women, the disabled, and so on, and today it even has arrived on behalf of the nonhuman. Aristotle and the Greeks in general could not imagine such a thought as long as merit held sway over equality.[26] Compared to the cool, diagnostic temperament of Aristotle, the revolutionaries and postrevolutionaries lean toward the sentimentalisms of inclusion. In contrast, merit starts with exclusion, and inclusion only appears after one has proved one's worth.

But there is something more important in Aristotle's analyses of political systems. He lays the groundwork for understanding the "mixed system," the persistence of oligarchy inside other political orders. As Aristotle surveys the politics of his day, he eventually asks what system might be the best. The foundational danger, as he sees it, lies in the division of the well-off and the poor. The well-off "do not become habituated to being ruled even at school" and "hold others in contempt," but the poor are too needy and dependent and are "consumed by envy" (134). These factions tend to pull the city apart and governance results in bitterness. The only real cure is the emergence of the "middling," a kind of mean that reconciles extremities and thus points to the health of both an individual and a city: "The happy life is one in accordance with virtue and unimpeded, and that virtue is a mean, then the middling sort of life is best. . . . These same defining principles must also define virtue and vice in the case of a city and regime" (133). This middling, which we might call a proto "middle class," is best found among the Lacedaemonians, Aristotle says. He claims that some call their regime democratic and others oligarchic, and that is because it has features of both: "In a polity that is finely mixed, [the regime] should be held to be both—and neither" (132). (These ideas of the "middling" or "mixed system" echo, of course, the earlier discussions of ratio.)

Of deeper interest is that one of the primary signatures of oligarchy is the election of officeholders and overseers, but the primary signature of democracy is that leaders are chosen by lot. The idea of the lot is as radical as one can get, for it presumes a pretty thoroughgoing equality, a kind of substitutability of persons ("I am as capable as you are, no better or less"). Of course, given the administratively enforced divisions in the Greek polis, not everyone could qualify to be chosen by lot. Thus the idea of the lot as a method for choosing leadership may be ever present, but it is always denied—and probably for good reason. But let's focus more closely on what Aristotle says about elections. He claims that they characterize oligarchic political order: "It is held to be democratic for offices to be chosen by lot, oligarchic to have them elected, and democratic not [to do it] on the basis of an assessment, oligarchic [to do it] on the basis of an assessment" (131). His observations seem to presage a contemporary problem: today's political parties are, in effect, oligarchic structures filtering out those who can and cannot be elected to office. In contrast, the idea of the lot represents a kind of threatening equality that the oligarchic structure interrupts. As a result, a deep burning sometimes appears just below the surface of elections that are being managed by political parties. The population knows that it cannot be fully represented, but it wants to be, for it believes that its representation would be an acknowledgment of equality. When denied this route to equality, the population burns. Sometimes, the sort of radical equality represented by the idea of the lot, which cannot be instituted in any practical way, speaks narcissistically: "Only I can represent myself, and, because I cannot structurally do so, the system is suspect." If the divide widens between political leaders and constituents, the burning intensifies. In order to prevent the burning, political leaders must continuously bridge the inherent divide instituted by the oligarchic structure. Leaders turn to different ways to "identify" with their constituents. In doing so, the idea of equality becomes remarkably superficial. That is, the political leader must appear to speak like them, be like them, care for them. These displays may be trivial and narcissistic, but they represent the sorts of perverse routes that the idea of equality must take when burdened by the oligarchic structure of elections. Consider that during Sarah Palin's vice presidential run on the Republican ticket in 2008, her supporters sometimes said: "She is just like us." In moments like this, the mixed system reveals itself. Elections and political parties represent the oligarchic condition, while the lot—which can never be—represents a radical equality that has been structurally eliminated. Nevertheless, it burns through during raucous town halls, or during the enthusiasms that gather behind so-called movement politicians, or within populist politics in general. At any rate, democratically managed nations organize the competition among rival oligarchic forces according to political parties, which in turn try to channel different factions of the less-well-off under their orbits. But sometimes even those efforts fail—sometimes voters don't turn out, or they explode against the available oligarchs or party options—but at no point can the voters seize the lot and the totality of its symbolism, and in many cases they don't even want to because of the amount of radical effort necessary. Perhaps, then, the fetishization of democracy burns through as a response to the oligarchic condition that seems to be more in charge than the narcissistic claim "But I 'own' the government." Deepening the tragedy still further is that quite possibly the very claim of such ownership is itself an invention and projection of the oligarchic condition insofar as it keeps the meaning of the lot both in play and at bay. So that is one way to think about the emergence of the fetishization of democracy within the populace. To repeat, Aristotle's sober assessment of democracy contrasts with our own era, but his description of a mixed system holding together oligarchic and democratic tendencies—as if in ratio—seems to analyze the single most enduring political structure.

←↕→

The idea of the fetish is, of course, quite popular among modernity's hermeneuts of suspicion because it allows theorists to upend conventional notions of what is true or real. Essentially, there seems to be three historical strands that have made use of the topos of the fetish: (1) anthropology, particularly during its early years, as it tried to explain how traditional worship could transfer supernatural power into objects and make them animate; (2) Marxist theory, which used the idea of the fetish to characterize, among other things, money as a kind of divine power creating equivalence among unrelated objects but also extending what the individual human could not otherwise accomplish; and (3) Freud and his followers, including Lacan and Žižek, who, broadly speaking, have understood the fetish as a kind of substitution or obsession that becomes a reality via the power of anxiety, desire, and a feeling of lack. Dragging the reader through the details of these theories would consume an inordinate amount of time. I hope that it is sufficient to simply note that the fetish is an important modernist conception, for it seems to overpower the human capacity to see "what is really there" or "to think straight about something." In this sense, the idea of the fetish is negative because it indicates the impending loss of rational powers and clearheadedness. For instance, for the early anthropologist the shaman's fetishes were merely inanimate idols, not actants; for the Marxists, the bourgeoisie's fetishization of money and commodities hid the exploitations occurring on the factory floor, including the stolen surplus value or profit that rightfully belonged to the laborer; for the Freudians and post-Freudians, anxieties and obsessions emerging from conditions of lack and desire had the power to shape the world into forms (fetishes) that might satisfy the bottomless desires that haunt individuals and collectives; and so on and so on—the endless use of the trope of the fetish.

In sum, the importance of the fetish in modernist analyses is because it functions as a powerful reminder of one of modernity's major negatives: the loss of self as in self-control or the loss of judgment, which is nothing less than the loss of self- and collective governance. Consider how David Graeber, an anthropologist who has, in my view, one of the better descriptions of the fetish, phrases it:

> Perhaps the best way to describe the view of fetishism I have been developing here is to say that when one recognizes value in an object, one becomes a sort of bridge across time. That is, one recognizes not only the existence of a history of past desires and intentions that have given shape to the present form of the object, but that history extends itself through one's own desires, wishes, and intentions, newly mobilized in that very act of recognition. In fetishizing an object, then, one is mistaking the power of a history internalized in one's own desires, for a power intrinsic to the object itself. Fetish objects become mirrors of the beholder's own manipulated intentions. And in a way, the very notion of desire—at least, as I have been developing it . . . demands such fetishization."[27]

It seems, then, that theorists who use the term *fetish* are trying to describe some sort of misrecognition or false consciousness. But we need to be cautious regarding these assessments, for the fetish and misrecognition are also fantastically productive. In this sense, then, the fetish is not just negative but also positive—or at least ironically positive. That is, we act and think on the basis of our fetishizations, and thus we bring a world into being. For instance, as long as we fetishize money—indeed, as long as we grant value and utility to money—then we perform something "uncanny" by "rendering dissimilars [commodities] into species of the same." Indeed, this is a point that both Marx and Freud made regarding money.[28] Thus an entire global economy comes into being based on the productivity of a kind of fantasia[29] functioning as bedrock truth. (This deep link between fantasy and truth as well as the production of both material life and consciousness have been one of the central analyses underlying the entire corpus of a theorist such as Žižek but also a sociologist of the economy, Ole Bjerg.[30])

But beyond the fetish's negativity–positivity, there remains much to think about regarding the idea of the fetish. Because the concept occupies a central place in this book, I want to do some deep mining into the terms *fetish* and *misrecognition*. According to my count, there are three presumptions that we ought to address. First, a person who says that something is a fetish presumes that there is a sharp distinction between what most people believe and perceive and what the analyst sees. This distinction can be likened to Plato's favorite distinction between appearance and reality. That is, the fetish is a misrecognition because perceivers fail to look "beyond the curtain" of mere appearances in order to spy the "really real" that is otherwise hidden. The domain of this "really real," the place where it exists, can be succinctly summarized as somewhere "above-behind-beyond-below."

Now, ironically, the person who recognizes and therefore corrects the misrecognitions of others is, perhaps, being led by the nose through the work of these not-so-innocent prepositions acting as spatial metaphors. Consider the following analogy and thought experiment: here before me, without a doubt, is a curtain—and I also know, without a doubt, that there is something *behind* the curtain. But is this analogous to the events of my life being a kind of curtain behind which lies the certainty of a meaningful life shaped, perhaps, by a loving God? Traditional theologians and metaphysicians have been inclined to accept the analogy. Their arguments and reflections constitute a kind of *seeing* into the very core of existence. Indeed, they are in the long line of shamanic seers, who also literalize the above-behind-beyond-below, and their texts and bibles are their little fetishes. But the above-behind-beyond-below also applies to other kinds of theorists: scientists, mathematicians, economists, and so on. For the above-behind-beyond-below is a general heuristic that guides meaning-making—that is, the decipherment and distilling of voluminous information until one finds a pattern or structure below the phenomena itself. Voila, meaning and meaningfulness: the above-behind-beyond-below—these simple, spatial prepositions that when chained together reveal a general heuristic whose verbal mechanics create a make-believe that there are literal spaces that must be inhabited by really-reals, for, "as everyone knows," space is not empty but the natural container of things and thingness itself! However, I do not want to treat this heuristic sarcastically, for without it we do not arrive at DNA whose discovery depends on instrumentation capable of seeing the micro spaces behind the curtain of our limitations. Nor do we get mathematicians such as Pythagoras and the contemporary physicist Max Tegmark, who claim that there is a mathematical structure below the curtain of visible matter: "So the bottom line is that if you believe in an external reality independent of humans, then you must also believe that our physical reality is a mathematical structure. Nothing else has a baggage-free description. In other words, we all live in a gigantic mathematical object—one that's more elaborate than a dodecahedron [sly reference to Pythagoras]. . . . Everything in our world is purely mathematical—including you."[31]

At any rate, the vision of such specialists, by definition, is supposedly more complete and insightful than the visions of others. This sort of specialist—a kind of minor Plato—cleaves the world into its surface appearances versus its deeper meanings and structures. That is, we are compelled by desire, and, it just so happens, we have the vehicle of verbal mechanics that can drive us beyond contingency and toward the rock bottom that exists somewhere above-behind-beyond-below.

It turns out that the first presumption takes us to the second. In the aforementioned account, the fetishist can be of two kinds. She might be the person who misrecognizes because she accepts the appearance or surface as sufficient. "What is in front of us is enough," such a person says. "No reason to mobilize the above-behind-beyond-below. All this deeper meaning stuff is quicksand, subjective and esoteric," says the person.

But the second kind of fetishist trumps the first, demeaning all those who fail to or cannot see beyond the appearances. He mobilizes the full potential of the above-behind-beyond-below, believing finally that his conclusions represent, indeed, rock bottom. Thus this fetishist runs the risk of thinking that he has escaped fetishism.[32] Such a person fetishizes truth itself. He believes that he has found the really real, the rock bottom that lies above-behind-beyond-below. He believes that he has escaped misrecognition and replaced it with genuine recognition. If only it were so simple! Consider: rather than playing the game that we are the genuine seers and others are not, or rather than playing the reverse game that genuine seeing is always misrecognition (false consciousness) spinning out into a kind of infinite relativism, we might play the better game of always pursuing the imperative to truth while, simultaneously, dislodging an eager rush to absolutism by acknowledging that misrecognition is at least a minor, though probably not an ultimate, truth. Misrecognition is a minor truth and not a foundational one because those who delight in revealing misrecognition are themselves pursuing the imperative to truth. (The term *imperative to truth* signals compulsion toward the truth, not acquisition of the truth, and I talk about this later in the text.)

The third presumption regarding the idea of the fetish takes us to the heart of this book. My specific interests are in examining the presumptions that underpin democracy, particularly liberal democracy. A central thesis in this text is that we fetishize democracy, but what are the mechanisms that enable such fetishization? My claim is that we can reveal this fetishization by looking deeply at what I loosely call the "democratic rhetorics" (equality, freedom, liberty, transparency, rights, self-determination, and so on). These are universalist terms—and the problem starts here. These are also "god terms," as Kenneth Burke might say. He might also describe each one as a "title of titles,"[33] meaning that each one bears considerable heft insofar as liberal democrats grant these abstractions innate prestige in the hierarchy of values and virtues. The point is that they evoke universality because they radiate inclusivity. As an example, consider the presumption of inclusivity that appears at the beginning of the second paragraph of the American Declaration of Independence: "We hold these truths to be self-evident, that all men are created equal, that they are endowed by their Creator with certain unalienable Rights, that among these are Life, Liberty, and the pursuit of Happiness." The universalisms here are so familiar to the American ear that they have become banal: "self-evident truths," "equality of all," and "unalienable rights," including the "rights of liberty."

It should be clear that the universalist terms underpinning democracy, by definition, are inclusive of everyone. Hence we can ask the following: Is this presumed inclusivity that organizes universalist terms simultaneously a kind of exclusivity? Furthermore, if inclusivity is what endows these terms with virtue, can they retain their virtue if they are simultaneously exclusionary? They can, in my view, if we uphold the earlier arguments regarding ratio. That is, universalist terms are both inclusionary and exclusionary—"smarten up and just live with it"—but many people seem unable to bear such a conclusion. Instead, they fetishize the inclusive potential of universalist terms by occulting from their view their exclusionary potential.

My argument, I hope, is not just the standard cynicism used by the progressive left: "Our founding documents talk a good line, equality, but fail to walk the walk, fail to make me as well-off as you." For many critics, this argument is sufficient for exposing the disappointments and hypocrisies of democracy, and it encourages them to advocate, for instance, for an economics of redistribution—as if redistribution was synonymous with the inherent virtues of inclusivity. Or, to use the language of the Declaration of Independence, as if redistribution was a kind of "self-evident truth" or "unalienable right" that establishes the "equality of all." Indeed, some sort of economic redistribution was exactly what fueled some of the great radicals of the French Revolution, such as Gracchus Babeuf.[34] But for the American revolutionaries, *equality* meant merely the opportunity to equality. Thus they opened the door to the oligarchic condition, more specifically, to meritocracy, which is nothing less than stealth aristocracy and certainly not economic equality. Thus the governing norms of liberal democracy have always checkmated moves toward broad notions of equality. Consider that redistribution arguments from the progressive left that base themselves on universal terms, such as equality, are simultaneously exclusionary. They are "takings"—to use a term from legal theory—unless the rich are incentivized or choose to distribute voluntarily (and good luck with that). Some group must be targeted for exclusion if equality is going to do its work—even if such a group, for instance, can afford much higher taxes. Hence such a group will quickly seize merit arguments to trump equality arguments, and when that occurs, equality no longer seems to be a self-evident truth. The group feels singled out and desperate to escape the clutches of equality, and so it reaches for merit arguments as an escape route. Thus equality, from the perspective of such a group, looks more like an exclusion posing as an inclusion. One of my arguments, then, is that the progressive left continues to fetishize the inclusivity of universalist terms by occulting from their view mechanisms of exclusion. Hence they do not see below liberal democracy and the democratic rhetorics.

I want to deepen these arguments further, for it is not as if any politics or any economics can solve this matter. The problems that I am identifying are unresolvable because they exist at the conceptual level that gives birth to politics or economics, and so they cannot be erased by any version of social engineering. Consider that universalist terms announce an inclusivity that they cannot guarantee at every instance, and, similarly, they announce a totality that, in fact, is a particularity. By juxtaposing the conditions of inclusivity and totality, I hope to expose how the idea of infinity haunts universalist terms. My thinking goes like this: universalist terms attempt to name an inclusivity that has no boundaries and a totality that similarly has no bounds. That is, inclusivity and totality presume infinity. Universalist terms are besotted by conceptions of infinity. The conceptual predicament of universalist terms, therefore, is that we speak glibly of limitlessness (inclusivity, totality), but our speech can only occur from within our conditions of limitation, from our inability to actually inhabit limitlessness. After all, we are not infinite beings. However, we enjoy speaking like we are, speaking as if we were not chained to our earthly conditions of limitation. And so when we speak of equality, it is not as if we know what we are talking about—the rich, for instance, do not want to be equal and will not easily give up their distinctiveness, but the rest of us do not want it, either, for we ceaselessly watch each other, measuring the merit of this person or that. We are infatuated by our differences, our identities, and we fear the substitutability that equality presumes. So when we demand "equality now," we are actually expressing some particular bitterness regarding our experiences with inequality. What we know in very real and palpable ways are our felt inequalities, but equality, like God, is a mystification or fetishization good for organizing our aspirations but always latent with potential betrayal. To repeat: what we know are not the totalities that we speak but the particularities from whence we speak. Thus we do not speak as truthfully as we think when we speak those universalist terms that we so admire, those inclusivities and totalities that make us sound so deeply ethical. Hence my argument: the naming of a totality is actually the naming of a particularity. Finally, it is not that our universalist terms are meaningless or hypocritical or empty of signification. Indeed, they are drenched with more meaning and signification than we can possibly manage.

←↕→

In 1795–96, Thomas Paine wrote the following in his last pamphlet, *Agrarian Justice*:

> It is a revolution in the state of civilization that will give perfection to Revolution of France. Already the conviction that government by representation is the true system of government is spreading itself fast in the world. The reasonableness of it can be seen by all. The justness of it makes itself felt even by its opposers. But when a system of civilization, (growing out of that system of government) shall be so organized that not a man or woman born in the Republic but shall inherit some means of beginning the world, and see before them the certainty of escaping the miseries that under other governments accompany old age, the Revolution of France will have an advocate and an ally in the heart of all nations.

> An army of principles will penetrate where an army of soldiers cannot; it will succeed where diplomatic management would fall: it is neither the Rhine, the Channel, nor the ocean that can arrest its progress: it will march on the horizon of the world, and it will conquer.[35]

Compare this with a recent claim by Naomi Klein: "Climate change can be a People's Shock, a blow from below. It can disperse power into the hands of the many rather than consolidating it in the hands of the few, and radically expand the commons, rather than auctioning it off in pieces."[36]

Throughout the pamphlet, Paine uses the phrases *common fund* and *common property*, in ways similar to Klein's use of the *commons*, to talk about his economic proposal. He proposed to create a common fund that would compensate for the loss of the common ownership of land that—supposedly—constituted the state of nature before the arrival of agricultural states and landed property: "To create a national fund, out of which there shall be paid to every person, when arrived at the age of twenty-one years, the sum of fifteen pounds sterling, as a compensation in part, for the loss of his or her natural inheritance, by the introduction of the system of landed property."[37]

It is not that these two authors would agree on all counts, but there is enough overlap across three hundred years to see the general lines of a kind of messianism—hence fetishization—internal to the more progressive versions of the democratic imaginary. Paine's pamphlet understands the democratic revolution as being fundamentally right and ultimately on the side of history, as if a kind of transcendental righteousness were now guiding the unfoldment of human affairs. He can claim this despite the bloody chaos that France had fallen into just a few years before the writing of the pamphlet, and that had taken the life of Gracchus Babeuf, whom Paine describes favorably. Because the revolution is addressing the misery of others by liberating them from the clutches of hierarchy, "it will march on the horizon of the world, and it will conquer." There's the messianism: democracy moving across the planet's space and time as if it were a teleological force.

"People Shock," acting like "a blow from below," a many against a few, is Klein's way of describing the same force, but now the villain is not the aristocracy or monarchy but the extraction industries that are at the foundation of any expanding economy. The carbon emissions that come with that expansion and the concentration of wealth and political power that enables the expansion (and therefore is protected) represent for Klein the sort of tyranny that must be removed in the same way that Paine saw the tyranny of his day. The only thing missing between Paine's account and Klein's is—possibly—that the messianism underpinning democracy's righteous unfoldment across history may be more diluted. But it is their shared conviction in the rightness of democracy that makes one the voice of the other. Hence I want to argue that the target of the critique is the same: hierarchical concentrations of power and wealth. The difference consists in the names we use to label hierarchical concentrations. The aristocrats and monarchs of yesteryear have morphed into today's oligarchic condition. Just as interesting is that both Paine and Klein agree that the solution to the concentration of power is horizontal redistribution in the name of the commons. Thus the democratic imaginary seems to structure the same cure to the same problem across time.

One clear window for making sense of this critique of hierarchical concentration is to look briefly toward the power of lobbyists, for lobbyists are the representatives of the oligarchic condition that has replaced the monarchs and aristocrats. We can turn, for instance, to the economist Jeffrey Sachs's mapping of Senate votes on the Climate Stewardship Acts during the 2000s. Klein also rails against these sorts of political moves on behalf of concentrated power. The stewardship acts of 2003, 2005, and 2007 tried to introduce a mandatory cap-and-trade system for greenhouse gases. They failed each time. But it is Sachs's maps that reveal how the senators who voted against the acts represented states with significant extraction industries. The pattern is clear: the maps are "an almost-perfect fit" between those states with strong extraction interests voting against and those without such interests voting for, and "this is the case all over the world."[38] Lobby power steers legislation that favors the concentration of wealth. Of course, trade unions also steer lobby power for their benefit. These are all versions of the oligarchic condition in which, structurally, the few achieve representation.

Klein's solution to the tyranny of lobby power engineered by the extraction industries is to decentralize energy production. This notion of decentralization, which is nothing less than the horizontal distribution of power, is consistent with Paine's "national fund," even if he requires a centralized government to put it into effect. For Klein, then, decentralization or horizontalization takes the shape of social movements in Germany and elsewhere that are forcefully regaining, for instance, control over electric grids and rejecting private energy monopolies beholden to shareholders (96–100). Indeed, she holds more hope in populist social movements than in the entrepreneurs who lead "green capitalism"

(90). In sum, she calls for a bottom-up deep democracy consisting of citizen-owned utilities (130–33), agroecology instead of agribusiness's "Green Revolution" (134–35), and she suggests that indigenous ways of listening to the earth is a better ethic than our current ethics of extractivism (182). For Klein, a decentralized economy under local democratic control would be a democracy running so deep that it would represent a revolutionary ideological transformation, a veritable overthrowing of capitalism in the clutches of the oligarchic condition. I sometimes wonder if too many of us want democracy to be more than whatever is at hand and to deliver, like heaven perhaps, more than the life we know.

So for Klein, democracy can press its claims against capitalism. Ultimately, her argument is not as perspicuous as Paine's. Paine is also after a kind of deep democracy, but for him democracy is enabled by capitalism. Paine advocates common ownership, which he sets up as a national fund to compensate those who have lost their "natural inheritance," but at no point in *Agrarian Justice* does he deny the right to own property. For him, the revolution of deep democracy cannot work without the power of capitalism. Indeed, his common fund protects individual property rights, for those who have lost their natural share may at some point decide to purchase property. Klein, three hundred years later, is not as clear on this matter as Paine.

In sum, here is what Paine understands well: at the center of the revolution was the horizontal distribution of property rights, for here was the key for opening up the possibility of wealth-making on a much larger scale than was possible under aristocratic, monarchical privilege. Again, this is not the distribution of property itself. Gracchus Babeuf argued instead that private property is "theft from society" (54), and that only a "revolution in things" could complete the French Revolution (86).[39] But Paine's arguments about the establishment of a common fund on behalf of those deprived of property is more conservative, more in keeping with classical liberalism's defense of property rights, for, as already stated, would not monies distributed from the fund go in many cases toward the purchase of property? In Paine and others of like mind, one sees the paradox of liberalism: its method for realizing horizontal distribution is to allow everyone the opportunity to accumulate. That is, the vertical problem can only be solved by giving horizontality the right to be vertical. It cannot put substantial restraints on this right or on the amounts accumulated, for if it does so it runs the risk of violating not only its core principle of freedom but even more importantly the very modernist ideal of releasing human potential. Hence liberal democracy is innately litigious. Because it contains strong defenses of both horizontal and vertical interestedness without ever fully resolving which interest is most innate, it creates a vast boxing match that plays itself out in such arenas as inheritance laws, eminent domain, the courts, and so on. Klein has stepped into the boxing arena naively and, in my view, incoherently.

If this boxing match metaphor is valid, then we should pursue how and why it is so firmly in place. In other words, we have much more to talk about than just the ratio of horizontal and vertical interests that began this chapter. And Klein is only an exemplar of a larger question: Can we press a claim against capitalism by using democracy and its tropes? I doubt it: the reason why has something to do with "potentiality" and how it saturates managerial modernity and the many political orders that it has spawned. Consider that at different moments different political orders have claimed potentiality for themselves—that is, as embodied by and rightfully belonging to the individual (liberal democracy), or rightfully belonging to the collective (communism), or rightfully belonging to the state on behalf of the people (socialism), or rightfully belonging to the spirit of the nation (Nazism and nationalism). But also conceptions of nature, capitalism, technical innovation, religious conceptions of the afterlife, and so on find purpose and rationale due to their appropriation of that nearly magical term *potentiality*. A basic argument, then, is that potentiality functions as a god term and ultimately a master discourse to the extent that a belief system can identify itself with the sort of importance, even impeccable goodness and rightness that seems to belong to the idea of potentiality. When someone says that such and such has "great potential," do we not grant it status? This way of speaking, I believe, resides in the belly of modernity, and pursuing why is certainly one of my intentions. At any rate, the difficulty for Klein and the progressive left in general is that both democracy and capitalism represent potentialities that, inside managerial modernity at least, are stitched together. That is, they exist in ratio and cannot be pried apart. Hence when we create a face-off between the two, we stage, unwittingly, a murderous scene where no one can die because of the extent of the social loss. It is not as if these belief systems or even their notions of potentiality can be grounded in something other than presumptions, but this weakness does not dampen the ferocity. Indeed, it probably raises the ferocity. If a specific belief system cannot aim a definitive attack on its rival, then every system somehow endures, and, when the moment is right, it gathers up the available conviction, and with hell-bent assertiveness it makes, once again, its final claim.

Narratives of potentiality are the sacred texts of modernity. Many books have been written about these narratives without necessarily identifying the common strand—potentiality—that links them. My goal here is simply to name some broad outlines. My goal also is to locate a source of fetishization inside notions of potentiality. For instance, we fetishize liberal democracy because it warrants the "liberated" individual to pursue the actualization of his or her potential, or because it passes civil rights laws that warrant a specific group to also realize its potential. The latter move, in particular, acquires the name *social justice*, another fetishizing term. How did we get here? I want to narrow this analysis of potentiality to three key strands that over time have been placed so deeply into ratio with each other that today we cannot possibly pull them apart. The three strands have also become, I suspect, a thick rope that hangs us.

So managerial modernity envisions potentiality as operating in three key domains. First, nature, materially, is a vast storehouse of potentiality, but to get at it, nature must be scientifically dissected and even atomized. Nature, when imagined in more spiritual terms, also contains vast potentiality, but now, as with Kant, takes the form of the sublime.[40] These two envisionings of nature are not contradictory but compensatory. In both cases, nature contains a vastness whose potential reshapes human limitation and points it toward a limitlessness that can be either material or inspirational. Second, machinery and technology are the techne that directly address the potentiality of nature in order to make an actuality in ways that humans cannot. Essentially, they are muscle power or sensory organs multiplied a thousandfold until, today, they lift humans beyond the pull of the earth or stare at otherwise invisible galaxies and quarks. Third, the democratic rhetorics in the form of rights and liberties (particularly property rights that enable the ownership of nature and things) represent a potentiality on behalf of individuals and collectives. Consider that the United States Constitution, as one example, is a potentiality that moves toward an actuality when it is translated into laws—that is, a nomosphere[41] shaping the rules of accumulation. If the laws benefit the many, potentiality is widely distributed; if they benefit the few, it is vertically distributed. In both cases, it is the right to the accumulation of potentiality and its actualization.

The tight braiding of these three strands appears in the following quotations. We start with Klein's own words in her description of the improvement of the steam engine by James Watts in the late eighteenth century:

> As Britain's urban population ballooned, two factors tipped the balance in favor of the steam engine. The first was the new machine's insulation from nature's fluctuations: unlike water wheels, steam engines worked at the same rate all the time, so long as there was coal to feed them. . . . Steam engines also worked anywhere, regardless of the geography. . . . Coal's intoxicating promise of freedom from the physical world—a freedom that unleashed industrial capitalism's full force to dominate both workers and other cultures [made the steam engine into a] portable energy creator. . . . The promise of liberation from nature that Watt was selling in those early days continues to be the great power of fossil fuels.[42]

The economist Robert Gordon describes the next step after the steam boiler and, consequently, a sense of how innovation expands human potential: "When the electric elevator allowed buildings to extend vertically instead of horizontally, the very nature of land use was changed, and urban density was created. When small electric machines attached to the floor or held in the hand replaced huge and heavy steam boilers that transmitted power by leather or rubber belts, the scope for replacing human labor with machines broadened beyond recognition."[43]

John Maynard Keynes, in the throes of the 1930s depression, reflects back on the entire history of innovation, which at this point we might call the release of the potentiality of machinery as it attacks the potentiality of nature on behalf of the potentiality of humans—that is, the three strands of potentiality mentioned earlier:

> After the eighteenth [century], the great age of science and technical inventions began, which since the beginning of the nineteenth century has been in full flood—coal, steam, electricity, petrol, steel, rubber, cotton, the chemical industries, automatic machinery and the methods of mass production, wireless, printing, Newton, Darwin, and Einstein, and thousands of other things and men too famous and familiar to catalogue.
>
> What is the result? In spite of an enormous growth in the population of the world, which it has been necessary to equip with houses and machines, the average standard of life in Europe and the United States has been raised, I think, by fourfold. The growth of capital has been on a scale which is far beyond a hundredfold of what any previous age had known.[44]

So when Klein talks about James Watt's steam engine representing a "liberation from nature" or "freedom from the physical world" (173), she is, without saying it, juxtaposing two terms, *limitation* and *limitlessness*, and revealing both the release and direction of potentiality. Thus *liberation* and *freedom* are movements from limitation to limitlessness. Further, the movement of potentiality, as freedom and liberation, would seem to be embedded inside both the democratic rhetorics and inside machines and their actions upon nature. And is not Gordon's movement from human labor to machine labor nothing less than increases in efficiency and productivity, and are not these terms linked to "liberation" and "freedom," hence the release of potential? And when Keynes talks about innovation, "growth," increases in the "standard of life," and so on, is he not associating potentiality with a kind of biopolitical increase, a kind of social engineering or management of society that moves individual life from the limitations of disease, aging, wealth, and bodily constrictions toward a kind of limitlessness? Furthermore, is not the language of potentiality and its related terms deeply embedded within the imaginaries of the libertarian, liberal democrat and democrat, socialist, communist, capitalist, nationalist, and even anarchist?

My argument is that the belief systems just mentioned cannot afford to not appropriate the idea of potentiality for themselves. If they declared themselves antihuman, they would have a limited following. Hence they must sink their claws into different ways of imagining potentiality. Further, I would argue that there is no democracy as such, no communism as such, no capitalism as such, and so on. There are several reasons for making this claim. First, as I argue throughout this text, each belief system (e.g., democracy) cannot exist as an idealization or abstraction but must become "territorialized" to the needs of the nation-state and its managerial order, and this forcing down into territory denies each abstraction's claim to having a nature as such. If each of these belief systems lack a specific "nature"—that is, if they have no substance as such—then what are they? Second, here is how I answer that question: each belief system is, in effect, a different inflection of potentiality, meaning that potentiality is their master discourse, the thing that gives them truth-value. Tyranny, in contrast, lacks truth-value because it relies on the heavy-handed management of populations as opposed to releasing the potentiality of the "people." Thus Nazism, as the limit form of nationalism, cannot be described as tyrannical, for it saw itself devoted to the potentiality supposedly inherent in the "spirit" of the nation. Nazism, then, along with the other political orders mentioned, was attuned to the siren call of modernist potentiality. Thus the wars of the twentieth century that pitted the different political orders against each other were, in effect, a competitive struggle over the "true soul" of potentiality. Which system might best nurture it? By the late 1980s, long after the defeat of Nazism, the potentiality of Communism as territorialized in the state capitalism of the Soviet Union was also being replaced by the potentiality stored in the different nations of European democratic socialism and American liberal democracy.

Potentiality through a host of different terms incarnates itself into the arts, sciences, social movements, belief systems, political orders, and so on. Capitalist self-interest (*homo economicus*) and democratic rights as well as socialist equality are versions of potentiality. Indeed, making potentiality highly purposeful is the distinctive marker of modernity. The instrumentalization of nature's potentiality—that is, the harnessing of its powers through innovation and machinery—means that the idea of potentiality unifies the human and the nonhuman, the animate and inanimate. When Klein, then, talks about James Watt's steam engine representing a "liberation from nature" or "freedom from the physical world" (173), this is precisely what she is talking about—the potentiality of nature at the service of the potentiality of the human. The problem with Klein's thesis is that she cannot think outside the paradigm of potentiality that incarcerates all of us. She believes that potentiality is somehow natural to democracy, that both embody rightness, that democracy is self-evidently about potentiality, and that this is what makes democracy a universal paradigm. She sees in her arguments a kind of ultimate grounding for the building of a kind of progressive legal order, a new nomosphere in the name of the "people" in accordance with principles that transcend the merely human. The trouble is that her capitalist opponents are also advocates of potentiality but adhere to another one of its historical incarnations. So whether one belongs to the left or right, the idea of potentiality *constitutes* one's positionality. The conflicting paths, logics, and moralities that potentiality can take tend, in the case of Klein and her opponents, to cancel each other out—indeed, empty out the other. Their predicament, of course, is also our own: we are unable to arrive at the ultimate authority that the "god term" potentiality promises. One position or final claim becomes disgusted by the other because we hold so dear the truth that our version of potentiality is the correct one. We are caught in a profound vise in which our utter belief is pressed against our opponent's utter belief, and there is no further movement. In sum, potentiality seems to pour through all modernist political orders via coded terms such as *freedom* and *equality*—perhaps we have arrived at the ultimate antinomy.

←↨→

The commonplace or topos of the "people" is the primordial beginning of the democratic imaginary.[45] To invoke the "people" is to invoke a god term that legitimizes, even sacralizes, the release of human potentiality in the face of whatever is perceived as hierarchical authority. This release of potentiality, this sense of something within that must step forward, is as prevalent in liberal democracy as in socialism. The "people" in all their potentiality waiting to be actualized into their full beingness is, in effect, the movement from limitation—in this case, the vertical accumulation of power (tyranny)—toward a kind of limitlessness. Thus potentiality structures liberal democracy, socialism, communism, even anarchism, but it also structures economic aspiration. But when we look closer at these political orders, we see a kind of structuring absence. This absence, in effect, is that democracy, socialism, or capitalism is always in potential, waiting to arrive at some point in the future. The present, that is, is always incomplete and a little disappointing. In sum, liberal democracy, socialism, and capitalism are always eternally suspended in potentiality, always incomplete but moving toward a vague actuality. This condition of always becoming does not typically result in a critique of the ism itself. People continue to believe in the vast reservoir of its potentiality. Hence the future is always the holder of the ism's truth, meaning that we must look to the future as possibly resolving, or even transcending, the incompleteness of the present. All three, then, share a futurist outlook, a narrative of futurism. All are invested in reform; they are reformist, meaning that they are committed to the ceaseless movement of potentiality that never becomes an actuality but is always suspended as an infinite becoming. Advocates of democracy, whether of the left or right, talk about the necessity for "more democracy" or "deep democracy" and what it will bring; socialists talk about their commitment to expanding equality; free marketers, too, look toward an infinitely expanding future. Free marketers are enamored with economic growth—that is, the acceleration of innovation that will generate ever more expanding growth as measured by world GDP. Investors incessantly look for good return by calculating the potential of specific economic sectors. If returns go up, the sectors have started to actualize their potential. In this sense, the GDP is nothing less than the measurement of the movement from potentiality to actuality played out in economic terms.

Thus this notion of a "becoming" is another form of fetishization. In the broadest terms, democracy, capitalism, and modernity are futurist projects.

Liberal, libertarian, and socialist democrats represent democracy—and modernity as well—as open vistas for the realization, at some point in the future, of human potential. Liberal democracy becomes one of the major engines for pushing the world toward the realization of such potential. It claims that the present can overcome the past, and the future will be an overcoming of the present. The end result is an expansion of global wealth, global freedoms, and a global compression of space and time through virtual and transportation technologies. So the future is a site for the realization of a human potential believed to be innate to all of us, a liberatory condition to which we all have a right because through it we realize the depths of our beingness. The essence of the futurist narrative, then, is an overcoming of material limitation. Equality, freedom, liberty, and transparency (the democratic rhetorics) offer the hope of breaking the limitation by pointing toward some sort of limitlessness that is our birthright. A major question for our era is whether or not the futurist narrative is sustainable. Is it now an exhausted trope?

3

The Undocumented Among Us

> The freedom of movement remains the freedom of life itself, not merely the mundane necessity to make a living but the freedom to truly live. Deportation, as a more or less juridical, more or less arbitrary, exercise of state power, is therefore an exquisitely concentrated abnegation of that freedom, one more usurpation by the state of the sovereign power of humanity itself. The freedom of movement, as an inherently unpredictable and definitively open-ended precondition for human self-determination, can only ever be a perpetual and troublesome affront to the self-anointed sovereignty of state power. It manifests a restless and inassimilable alterity busily working both within and against state power's most cherished ideal: social order. Thus the freedom of movement supplies a defiant reminder that the creative powers of human life, and the sheer vitality of its productive potential, must always exceed every political regime.
> —Nicholas De Genova, "Theoretical Review"

The fetishization of democracy is on full display, I believe, in the relationship between the citizen and the undocumented. Consider: the citizen of a democracy is invited to see her own potentiality as due to the larger potentiality of her nation and, further, to see herself as the rightful recipient, even "owner," of whatever bounty the nation represents. Perhaps this citizen also sees democracy as granting her the right to determine through the vote who is to be included and excluded from the territory of the nation. If so, then who are the undocumented? The encounter between the undocumented and the citizen—for those who are strong believers in the ideological construct called the "nation-state"—is an encounter of unequals because one is perceived as rightfully belonging and, therefore, the rightful "owner" of the nation, and the other is not. Of course, there is another layer of inequality, the labor relation, which also represents complex sentiments. Here is a summary of what I have heard from undocumented individuals: "I am here looking for work because the labor in my native place does not suffice. I am here out of necessity; I have no choice, but, like you,

I, too, am worthy." I have always felt that these statements were humiliating, a kind of dagger sticking in the gut, because the speaker knows that the potential of their person and nation is always infantilized when compared to the abundance of the Other. "But am I not also deserving? And I will work hard to prove it." These statements seem to admit the infantilization even as, ironically, modernist potentiality speaks through the person. In some sense, the undocumented depend on the force of a deterritorialized democracy and its rhetorics of fairness, rights, freedoms, individual worth, and so on in order to justify their situation. Further, I have often heard the undocumented apologize for not being citizens and for not "properly" crossing the border, and I have heard them affirm their desire to eventually become good citizens. In other words, the citizen and the undocumented both value, typically, the nation-state form and, more broadly, ground themselves in the same democratic lingo because these function as a kind of "commonsense" argument machine.

2 | Mazatl, *Aqua Seguimos*, 2013. Engraved on linoleum, 80 × 60 cm. By permission of the artist.

←↨→

"Migration is life" and "All humans have a right to migrate. All migrants have human rights." These are the words on a variety of posters depicting the monarch butterfly, or mariposa, as it is called among the advocates of the sanctuary movement. For some time now, the mariposa has been a symbol for freedom and, in particular, freedom to cross borders.[1] Early in 2017, I was asked to take the lead in drawing up a statement that might circulate among both private and public entities on the north side of Chicago. We wanted to encourage them to declare themselves sanctuary sites. I laid out the framework and lawyers and others contributed changes.[2] There was talk that one of the lead institutions would send representatives to these entities to try to persuade them to sign on. If they agreed, the symbol of a mariposa would be prominently displayed, indicating that the undocumented could find at this site "freedom" or sanctuary from the Department of Homeland Security. The mariposa image trades on these "truths," meaning that it is an unconscious projection of a historical narrative of fetishization and deterritorialization that I have been tracking throughout this text. But Nicholas De Genova, one of my favorite immigration scholars, gives a more self-conscious analysis of the "freedom of movement" and "life" tropes. For him, these tropes are not tropes at all but a kind of essentialized human condition—namely, an "open-ended precondition for human self-determination." In acquiring the portentousness of a "precondition," the "freedom of movement" must exceed any state's capacity to contain it. In this sense, freedom of movement seems to be a kind of natural force, ceaselessly bubbling up from the depths of human being, whereas the state, in comparison, would seem to be mere artifice, a lesser thing, and thus incapable of restraining such vitality and potentiality: "The freedom of movement supplies a defiant reminder that the creative powers of human life, and the sheer vitality of its productive potential, must always exceed every political regime."[3] De Genova, whom I consider a friend, would readily admit that these "natural forces" bubbling up should try to lay claim to the state itself and to rewrite the nomosphere according to its precepts. Further, he would say that it is right to do so in order to make a more democratic world. But what if the same "natural," creative forces waving pretty much the same banners of democracy and freedom laid their own claims to the state? What if their writing of the nomosphere preferred state-centric interests privileging the "freedom" of citizens over and against the "freedom" of immigrants, the undocumented, and so on? Does "freedom" as argument machine produce "false consciousness" in one instance but not another? Chasing down an answer to this question is one of the goals of this chapter.

There is considerable variation in how freedom is mobilized in the different contexts that we have been looking at. The migrant who is compelled to move because of political and economic dislocations—for instance, the migrants from as far away as Brazil whom I met one day while helping out at a Catholic relief center along the South Texas border in the summer of 2015—does not talk about the "freedom of movement" as some sort of existential precondition of human being. They speak of raw necessity, of their need to move because of fears for themselves and families, and of their hopes of making a better life that might alleviate their difficulties. De Genova and the mariposa image would seem to begin, arguably, in these grounded notions as well, but then, simultaneously, they make abstract assertions ("All migrants have human rights" or De Genova's "freedom of movement" as a kind of essentialized human condition). They are compelled to make these assertions because, apparently, actions emerging from raw necessity are somehow not sufficient until filtered through more abstract, moral frames, a kind of higher law synonymous with the democratic rhetorics. But are the state-centric presumptions somehow not also democratic? Hardly. It is just that these democratic, state-centric juridical presumptions seem unable to address, at every instance, the raw necessities of people. And let's be clear here: we must be talking about extreme conditions, a kind of perceived dehumanization in which humans feel that they have been reduced to desperation—but a desperation that seems unable to gather up sufficient moral authority on its own terms and must instead be filtered through a higher authority beyond the juridical presumptions of the democratic state. And this is precisely what the sanctuary movement does—it looks toward some higher moral ground where some deeper "freedom" supposedly exists beyond the "freedoms" guaranteed through state-centric laws. In sum, the appeal is toward a democracy deterritorialized because territorialized democracy seems insufficient. The deep question is: Can territorialized democracy ever look like our imaginings of deterritorialized democracy? Perhaps at some point in the future. And is this why democracy is a kind of futurism, a species of potentiality looking to become actual in some not-now, not-here?

Or it can be phrased this way: these notions of a higher, moral authority that seem to be attached to concepts such as freedom, freedom of movement, and so on provide a measure of hope for solving the problems of raw necessity. They are utopian concepts, and thus they can rhetorically alleviate when things become burdensome, but they alleviate particularly if they make the rough passage toward becoming law, a passage that will inevitably compromise some of the utopianism. At any rate, the point is that freedom and freedom of movement are deceptively seductive because of the hope that they promise. De Genova and the mariposa image are persuasive to the extent that these seductions of hope have become commonplace. More broadly, this analysis also explains why democratic lingo, which is secular in its origins, can sometimes acquire spiritual overtones, even a kind of messianism, in which deterritorialized notions such as freedom and democracy move like autonomous forces rightfully across history, steadily liberating different kinds of marginalized peoples and changing in the process the "nature" of the sovereign state. Jean-Luc Nancy sometimes speaks this way.[4] But so does his absolute nemesis, Milton Friedman, whose *Capitalism and Freedom* asserts that "freedom" from centralized state power and the "freedom" of markets is the hallmark of advancing civilization.[5] Nancy and Friedman, of course, are stand-ins for the progressive left and libertarianism, respectively. They organize economic and political life differently, but they have a shared commitment to the metaphysics of freedom and democracy that can guide humans like a beacon beyond the raw necessities that govern everyday life. Nancy's "freedom" emphasizes the collapse of vertical accumulation so that the horizontal (the many) can rise up to their greater moral authority. Friedman's "freedom" emphasizes individual innovators (the few) and their rights to vertical accumulation that will lead to, for instance, an expanding GDP that will maximize the "freedom to choose" and thus over time supposedly solve the needs of the horizontal. Both look to freedom's and democracy's opening up of potentiality and the futurism implied therein. So this shared commitment to releasing potentiality—this something that lives within and must step forward—allows us to see the left and right as different shadings of the same thing, even as we admit the rage that these differences entail. For example, the left will argue for increased social spending so as to increase the potentiality of the horizontal, whereas the right will argue for deregulation and about the evils of national debt in order to increase the potentiality of entrepreneurial innovation and vertical accumulation.

Hence it seems to me that "freedom," "freedom of movement," and "democracy" are kinds of delirium, meaning that they do not exist as such but exist as enthusiasms belonging to metaphysical presumptions, which, like gods, address human needs. If this admittedly tendentious claim has some truth to it, then our political systems would be wise to reproduce these enthusiasms and its language as often as possible. In other words, another way to think about "freedom" is as an invention of managerial modernity that helps to firm up state power because it aligns the state to higher moral authorities. As Michel Foucault says, "We should not think of freedom as a universal which is gradually realized over time."[6] "Freedom is something which is constantly produced. Liberalism . . . proposes to manufacture it constantly, to arouse it and produce it, with, of course, [the system] of constraints and the problems of cost raised by this production."[7] Foucault in these accounts strips freedom, and by implication democracy, too, of any metaphysical telos. Freedom is now something produced.[8] Its production occurs through a variety of means. The culture industry ceaselessly produces freedom as a specific possession, as something, for instance, that especially marks the American nation, a kind of birthright, or as the consequence of an education, or even as something embedded inside luxury goods. If freedom is more of an arousal, then it would seem to lack a determinate meaning, and, therefore, it can be wielded by all sorts of contrary motives (e.g., Nancy's versus Friedman's). Freedom, then, as an arousal is a way of speaking produced by liberal democracies and other entities. Even when it becomes seemingly grounded in liberalism's institutions, as in the legislative production of laws and protections that are then tested by a Supreme Court's readings of the Constitution,[9] it remains fundamentally elusive and deeply fragile, always subject to repeal due to social emergencies and contradictory interpretations of other laws protecting other freedoms. If freedom is this dependent on shifting social conditions and how the state addresses them, then freedom's metaphysics is both rhetorically ever present, because the nation-state always produces it, and also never arriving, as if always waiting for someone's freedom to come into being.

Freedom is also produced by specific subjectivities that liberalism gives birth to: here freedom can become the profundity of what one is willing to live and die for in the name of the nation-state, or the triviality of what designers hope to suggest in the aesthetic surfaces of their creations. Freedom, then, is not so much a substantive condition or the telos of nature, or De Genova's precondition, but more particularly a response or an arousal to some prior condition of limitation. Managerial modernity has habituated us to think and speak of limitation and relief from limitation in precisely these ways. People are encouraged to say: "I have a right to my fulfillment or I do not deserve to be subjected to *X*." Indeed, we have become so habituated that even critiquing these sentiments and this language seems useless. At any rate, freedom is our era's argument machine for limitlessness, a desire machine that motivates. That is, liberalism has produced for our consumption both a vague referent called "freedom" that, nevertheless, determines decisions and a restless longing for something beyond the here and now. Sometimes, the nation-state, and even entities beyond the nation-state, are challenged when the "people" wield terms like *freedom* against them; at other times, these same entities claim the terms for themselves in order to maintain their moral authority, but in all instances we seem unable to satisfactorily territorialize all the meanings and hopes contained in all the deterritorialized imaginings of "freedom," "freedom of movement," "democracy," and so on.

←↥→

Borders mobilize both a physics and a metaphysics.
—Nicholas De Genova, "Globalization and Mobilities"

I want to go back to when the sanctuary movement was even more heated than it is at the time of this writing. In a prior chapter, I described Elvira Arellano taking sanctuary with her young son in a well-known storefront church in the heart of a neighborhood where I do most of my fieldwork.[10] She was an undocumented Mexican laborer swept up by Immigration and Customs Enforcement (ICE) during a raid at the Chicago O'Hare International Airport. She had been defying for some time a judge's deportation order. She was not hiding. The government knew exactly where she was, newspaper reporters had been documenting her story on a regular basis, supporters gathered regularly in front of the church, academics like me were constantly talking to her, and immigration restrictionists also gathered in front of the church to protest her actions. Behind the scenes, there had been considerable political maneuvering. For one, a Mexican had taken sanctuary in the heart of the Puerto Rican community, a maneuver that Puerto Rican activists embraced and even helped stage after some hard discussions. This church was in the Fourth Congressional District, represented at the time by Luis Gutiérrez, a Puerto Rican and perhaps the most important figure in the immigration fights in Washington. Arellano, then, was political capital for all the Puerto Rican activists interested in Latino coalition politics. Indeed, she had been one of the galvanizing figures for the rights of the undocumented, which had exploded just months earlier in some of the largest protest marches ever seen in Chicago. But even behind those solidarity marches, there had been considerable infighting among Mexican activists who did not like the fact that this minister and his wife had become so influential in the movement.

At one moment during a 2006 interview with Arellano, I turned to the minister of the church that was giving her sanctuary and asked a question about his encounters with immigration restrictionists. The publicity surrounding Elvira and the church had attracted a steady stream of protestors who opposed the undocumented and called for restrictions on legal immigration. As a result, he had to publicly reply on different occasions. The minister himself was a longtime activist, even a Maoist back in the day, so he was well prepared with both political and biblical arguments. As he answered my questions, he was interestingly respectful of the beliefs of the immigration restrictionists. I appreciated his magnanimity because I had been interviewing restrictionists at the time and had become familiar and genuinely interested, as was the minister, in their arguments and beliefs.[11] At one point, he said this: "The woman who came here from Mothers Against Illegal Aliens. They had to get her from Arizona. She said several things that were really very interesting. She said, 'My children won't have the same country that I had when I was a child. They won't have the same privileges that I had as a child, because there'll be all these other people that I didn't vote to let in and I want my child to have the same thing that I had. That's what I'm fighting for.'"[12]

The woman that the minister was referring to was Michelle Dallacroce, the founder of Mothers Against Illegal Aliens.[13] For a few years, her views on immigration restriction had some notoriety on Fox News and other venues. I realize that we are working with a quote of a quote, but it represents well Dallacroce and other restrictionists whom I have come to know over the years. One of the arguments that was central to their beliefs concerned democracy and how they thought that their positions were fully in keeping with democratic principles, and they even thought of themselves as democracy's strongest defenders. They did not make these arguments just for public show—rather, these were cornerstone beliefs of their entire position. Indeed, in coming to know their arguments, I had begun to rethink the standard progressive left analysis that restrictionists were only racists. Even if they were, I surmised, what if I took seriously their affirmations of democracy and how they were textured to the restrictionist position? What if I explored the consequences of their arguments for understanding democracy as a whole?[14]

In the quotation, Dallacroce, like other restrictionists, announces the theme of securitization, which also appears in a variety of permutations in United

States Supreme Court decisions. Her words are more paranoid and less nuanced than the Supreme Court justices' words. Seemingly, she wants only to securitize the country for future Americans who resemble her, and she does not say that others not like her or their children may come to resemble her in time. For her, their class and ethnicity seem to be fixed and reified, and it is against their permanency that she wants to secure the nation. But it is her turn toward the democratic vote that I think is interesting. Is she attempting to legitimize her position by invoking the vote? She seems to be looking for some finality that might exist at the heart of democracy, some trump argument or god term—in this case, the idea of the vote—that might buttress her opinion: "My children won't have the same country . . . because there'll be all these other people that I didn't vote to let in."

Let's return to De Genova's quotation that began this section: "Borders mobilize both a physics and a metaphysics."[15] I think he is correct, and Dallacroce's language is an example. Her invocation of the vote seems to be reaching for an ultimate value so thoroughly sanctioned that it can convince all of us. In sum, to the extent that metaphysical concepts evoke ultimate value, they become both appealing and useful. Moreover, Dallacroce's arguments from motherhood attempted to dislodge Elvira's equivalent arguments that mothers should not be separated from their children through deportation policies. Both women were trying to ground their positions through similarly ultimate arguments regarding some special status called "motherhood." And floating in the background of this almost carnivalesque but also tragic scene were the metaphysical arguments of freedom, as in the "freedom of movement," alongside the idea of sanctuary as "spiritually" protected space both inside and yet "free" of the nation-state's claim to space. All sorts of ultimate claims had sunk their claws into this small block of a Chicago neighborhood.

Dallacroce's attempt to locate some ultimate authority in the vote was another example of fetishization. The appeal of any fetish, of course, is how it corrals power and conviction. It is humanly impossible to seize any ultimate power—unless we seize a kind of magnificent violence. However, what is typically available is the evocation of the ultimate, and that is what she has tried to do with the notion of the vote. Seemingly, the vote here signals a kind of individual ownership over the country, as if all things occurring in social life ought to be brought to a vote, and once the votes have been cast, then some sort of collective, legitimate ownership will have been established. And that's key: the idea of legitimacy. The vote itself is a key mechanism for establishing legitimate rule in a democracy, and so Dallacroce by seizing the power of the vote, as trope, and linking it to her position is attempting to make her stance regarding the securitization of the country against the undocumented as legitimate as possible. And her thinking is not eccentric, for the idea of the vote resonates, indeed, with virtue, legitimacy, and a certain populist sense that the people "own" governance. "A government of the people, by the people, for the people"; "the people are sovereign"—are these not the nostrums that we hear all the time? Alongside this notion of the vote, she could have easily mobilized other populist legitimacies of the anti-immigrant stripe that were circulating then: "We are a country of laws" or the very catchy "What part of 'illegal' don't you understand?" These legitimacies are more like resonances, meaning that these conceptions borrow the quality of legitimacy without necessarily being "legitimate." But claims don't have to be legitimate in order to have public force. The resonance of legitimacy may be all that they need. Hence we are not talking here about institutionalized or correct understandings of democracy. We are talking, rather, about the resonances of democracy that seem to circulate nonstop. That is, democracy's associations with such qualities as legitimacy derived from the act of voting or a populist sense of justice can be deployed to buttress all kinds of claims and policies that may be in direct contradiction with each other.

Returning again to De Genova's quotation, what does he mean by "borders," "physics," and "metaphysics"? By "physics," he means the securitization of the border by increasing the number of agents and high-tech surveillance (literally a physics)—or President Trump's fifteen-foot wall that keeps climbing higher and higher. By "metaphysics," he is referring to a propensity to elevate the nation to such exceptional, transcendent worth that it can demand acts of sacrifice and devotion, a kind of guardianship over the nation that individuals ought to take. Thus Dallacroce, who once served in the Air Force, seems to fit the mold. In a number of public performances, she has indeed asked for enhanced securitization on the basis of her patriotic concern for the exceptional but vulnerable nation.

←↕→

Securitization, what Dallacroce is ultimately concerned about, represents the heart of the problem. I begin by asking a set of questions: What was Elvira Arellano subject to, and how did this subjection come to pass? Similarly: What is Michelle Dallacroce subject to, and why does she defend this subjectivity as if it represented a profound, existential question for her and others? How is it that Arellano's body could have a kind of double existence, a material being that is distinguishable from her legal being, which is a cleavage that only the state can make? Or, phrasing it a little differently: How could she be materially present alongside us but not legally present? How did the sovereign nation-state acquire this power? Has the sovereign, whether democratic or not, always had such power?

World order today depends on dicing the world's population into legally bounded geographies. This means that all peoples are territorialized—that is, placed under a sovereign rule responsible for managing each specific space. A series of obligations and benefits chain the sovereign to the people, and always on the lips of the people is the loaded term *justice*. What the people ask the sovereign to maintain are a series of securities or idealized stabilities. Among these are a functioning economy, one that provides sufficient income for many though not necessarily all; a functioning state, preferably democratic so as to soften, even if it cannot remove, the abuses of hierarchy; a nationalism that functions as a kind of spiritual glue underpinning both the nation-state and the democratic imaginary; a culturalism functioning through media and institutions, such as education, and overseeing the production of coherence; and, of course, protection from internal and external threats. If these stabilities weaken, then people move—often as political refugees or economic migrants—seeking the stabilities of another place; if these movements are significant, they cascade across the stabilities (which are, incidentally, never achievable) of other nation-states, raising fears among pockets of the citizenry about whether their own social contract can endure the new arrivals and, if so, how many can be absorbed. These existential doubts reproduce the stabilities themselves: "Are we losing our culture, our nation, our jobs, our democracy?" Note that cosmopolitan elites, who are also on the move, do not raise these doubts, for their investments are typically welcome.

Ultimately, migration points to a broad issue: the sovereign nation-state has become the naturalized, default condition as the primary organizer of global political order, but its conceptual origins lie in the problem of war. I am speaking of the long rise of the idea of the nation-state and how that idea became increasingly solidified across a number of events, including the settlement of the Thirty Years' War in 1648 and the Peace of Utrecht in 1713.[16] That is, the evolution of the nation-state through international treaties and laws has delivered to each nation the right to manage its own particular patch of earth.

Against its competitors, each nation-state struggles to maintain its powers of self-determination by cultivating, among other things, a military, economic sufficiency, historical identity, and cultural exceptionalism. These are tactics of securitization, and what is meant by managerial modernity, in part, is the deployment of these tactics so that the values of the sovereign nation are passed on to its product, the sovereign individual. Sovereignty as an idealization must be reinforced across geographies, institutions, and individuals if it is to establish its grip, but the struggle of the nation to form its being across all scales is most difficult. Consider the competition between states' rights and federal rights in the United States; the struggles over sovereignty in today's Iraq, Syria, Afghanistan, and so on; and the struggles in the EU regarding migrants, Russia, and financial bailouts for member states. For many, the creation of the appearance of sovereignty is the most that can be hoped for.

If the nation-state was born in war and from the need to securitize, then we should expect borders to be spectacles of occasional, legal violence. For instance, when the progressive left complains about the current militarization of the United States' southern border, they are correct to note that this is a relatively recent phenomenon. I know this firsthand because I grew up along that border during another era. But the complaint is also naive if it does not understand that the world apparatus of passports, alien registration, residency requirements, deportation rules, and, more seriously, refugee camps and detention centers belongs to the heritage of nation-state conflict. Hence the current intensification of the global movement of the undocumented is often interpreted as a kind of war in diluted form: low-intensity conflicts, as our better border theorists call it.[17] Because of the international right to self-determination, the nation-state creates a thin line between the appearance of abuse and the appearance of legal securitization. Consider the distinction between political refugees and economic refugees. This distinction has led to high rates of death in the Mediterranean after the so-called Arab Springs. Typically, only a miniscule number of applicants qualifies under the established rules for political refugee status.[18] Those who do not qualify flee on rickety boats, and if they are "rescued," they are often returned to the dangers that they fled. Or consider the internment camps legally established by Australia.[19] Or ponder the cash deals that EU countries have cut with North African countries to brutally police migration from the south.[20] It is hard to not see many of these instances as the legalization of abuse.[21] As long as we remain under the grip of the nation-state form, justice will remain territorialized despite our intuitions regarding a universal justice. In sum, the rights of self-determination and the imperatives to securitize mean, ultimately, that war and the regulation of migrants are consequences of the same conceptual apparatus—namely, the nation-state. Furthermore, the recent emergence of a populist, authoritarian nationalism as expressed in political campaigns in 2016–18 across Euro-America (Turkey, Hungary, Italy, and elsewhere) foregrounds culturalism, securitization, and national interests. We have seen this before: the territorialization of human populations is so naturalized that people "speak" their nation as something nearly primordial and not artificial. Again, these sorts of nationalisms and culturalisms are not alien to democracy but allow democracies to cohere and, further, to come into being, for democracy can only materially exist when it is territorialized.

In order to deepen further the theme of securitization, let us briefly survey the history of some of the naturalization acts and immigration laws of the United States. Since the founding of the country, the United States has been developing strong distinctions between citizens, legal aliens, and undocumented aliens. What is striking about reading the acts and laws from 1790 to today is the endurance of certain themes. Indeed, it is almost shocking to find that despite the great detail that characterizes contemporary immigration laws, the broad parameters were already well in place by 1790. How do we explain the endurance of these parameters? We could say that these shared themes reveal a foundational structure for imagining the nation-state through the lens of the citizen–noncitizen opposition, which distinguishes between those "born into" versus those who are not. At first glance, that distinction seems relatively banal, of no great significance. However, if those "born into" more "genuinely" belong to a specific nation-state, then it would seem as if the act of birth, which is nothing less than an act of nature, inserts into our concepts of citizenship—and by extension the nation-state—the idea of the natural. That is, the "born into" citizen would seem to be the most natural entity for shaping the nation-state, the natural grounds upon which to found the nation-state. And when talking about a natural condition or entity, we are also, more than likely, talking about its fetishization.

And yet we also know that in many instances these acts and laws are not determined by the idea of the natural. Sometimes, they simply reflect the political and economic push and pull of a specific moment in time. That is, immigration acts and laws, as with any rhetoric, are responses to time-bound perceptions of reality and have the specific intention to shape a different sort of reality. That is, through these acts and laws we can see the intricate machinations of managerial modernity.

This is De Genova's point when he describes how immigration law primarily produces the categories of legality and illegality at the behest of what is perceived as national interest.[22] If there is a need for an illegal laboring class, then immigration law and enforcement practices satisfy that need by drafting legislation that tweaks who may or may not enter the country. As a result, the nation historically has swung back and forth between the imperative to securitize versus the imperative to populate open territory or secure cheap labor. Under the force of these imperatives, both the citizen and noncitizen become flexible figures—relatively empty of meaning in one instance, rhetorically loaded in another. Something similar can be said for the significance or insignificance of our national borders. Although frontiers are etched plainly on a map, their porosity to migrants varies from one perceived historical reality to another. The larger point is that at one moment the citizen-noncitizen opposition raises existential questions for the nation-state, while at another moment these questions are trumped by the historical socioeconomic order.

Let's briefly consider the naturalization acts of 1790, 1795, 1798, and 1802, when the young nation first established the rules for converting aliens into citizens.[23] The shared themes here are straightforward: such converts needed to be of the white race, have good character, not be feeble, and be willing to declare loyalty to the Constitution and nation. Of course, these rules echoed what was already in place in the surrounding monarchies of the day. Indeed, contemporary social theorist William Walters makes it clear how ancient the "citizen-territory link" is and how it has justified historically all sorts of expulsions via exile, banishment, deportation, population transfers, and removal—as in the Act of Settlement and Removal of the poor in England in 1662.[24] That is, the sovereign, whether monarchical or democratic, has always maintained the special right of shaping who belongs and who doesn't within his or her territory.[25]

At any rate, the naturalization acts of 1790, 1795, 1798, and 1802 repeat the themes already mentioned but also repeat the need for citizens and aliens to be formally registered by an official of the state as well as the importance of residency. Indeed, residency requirements escalated to fourteen years in the summer of 1798 with the passage of the Alien and Sedition Acts. Also appearing forcefully in 1798 is the presidential right to deport enemy aliens, and the reason why, of course, is that the country was headed toward the Quasi-War with France. Our own era of amplified monitoring and control, exemplified in E-Verify practices, is rudimentarily present, then, in the much older insistence that port authorities, ship captains, and court clerks keep good ledger entries of entering aliens.[26] All in all, I think it can be said that deportation and citizenship function as ancient and therefore constitutive hallmarks of the sovereign right to determine inclusion and exclusion. And brand-new nation-states and democracies do not break this ancient right but only continue its heritage, which suggests to me the difficulty of arguing for more inclusivity in the name of democracy when, clearly, democracy, like monarchy, is not synonymous with inclusivity.

Now, there is one new thematic that appears in a pronounced way in the Chinese Exclusion Act of 1882.[27] In addition to the state's traditional interest in preserving what it names the "white race," the state now also becomes interested in the migrant economy. The intention of the act was to defend the wages of native laborers, particularly those in white unions that feared cheap Chinese labor. Of course, the underlying sentiments of the act had been simmering for forty years, but the point is that today's use of immigration law to shape local and national economies had already been in place by 1882. Compare this to immigration law after September 11, 2001. Today, there is considerable interest on the part of big business to quell incipient labor movements, and one of their tools has been immigration policies. Woodfin Suites, for instance, in Emeryville, California, fired hotel workers in 2006 for lacking valid Social Security cards, which had been a nonissue prior to 2005. In 2005, however, the workers along with city voters backed a worker protection ordinance, and within a year Woodfin Suites retaliated.[28] Or consider how the American meatpacking lobby has argued for some time about the dangers of undocumented migration in order to promote an expanded guest worker program for unskilled foreign labor in order to maximize the industry's control over an otherwise mobile workforce.[29] At other times, however, immigration-related law has served neither big business nor union movements, and a good example of this, perhaps, is the raid at another meatpacking plant, Agriprocessors Inc., in 2008 in Postville, Iowa. This raid, according to its eyewitness, Erik Camayd-Freixas, seemed to be a test-run for the possibility of future prosecutions under identity theft law, and in addition the raid jacked up arrest numbers that would impress Washington oversight.[30] The point is that by 1882, the paradigm is very much in place for wielding immigration law in order to shape an economic order. Immigration law, then, almost from the beginning, has cut across a host of interests: nationalist sentiment, securitization, foreign relations, economic intervention in the name of labor rights or capitalist accumulation—and more recently, resource distribution, state's rights, and electoral districting, among others.

Of all these concerns, is one uppermost? Securitization, arguably, underpins each concern from 1790 on as seen in loyalty oaths and in the need to secure whiteness. Indeed, all of the concerns listed earlier may be different manifestations of fear that can only be fully addressed through the attainment of some form of security. In this sense, the kinds of nativist and racist fears that underlie some versions of nationalist sentiment, as well as the need to shape an economic order through government intervention, are equally motivated by the need to securitize against some threat of impending sociopolitical disorder. In both cases, there is some underpinning fear or baseline anxiety that calls upon the rectifying power of the law.

For all their potency, the fears and anxieties may not be well founded. For instance, one of the rationales for current deportations from the United States is to rid the country of criminals, but, as Patricia Macias's ethnographic work inside immigrant courts in Arizona points out, these "criminals" are administratively created. They are not "criminal" in any commonly understood way but become so during court proceedings when a detained migrant chooses *deportation* over a *voluntary departure*. In these court scenes, the judge presents these puzzling choices to migrants who cannot possibly understand the distinction because they mostly lack representation and because the distinction itself is comprehensible only to judges and lawyers. Administratively, *deportation* means that the migrant is barred from reentering for ten years. In contrast, *voluntary departure* means that there are fewer penalties and includes the possibility of future legal migration. But voluntary departure often prolongs detention in order to complete background checks, and this extra time in custody oftentimes frightens migrants. However, when choosing the alternative of deportation, they put themselves, ultimately, at greater risk, for now they will be breaking the law if caught again—that is, they will be criminally prosecuted for the felony of reentry.[31] It has never been this way. The line between immigration law and criminal law has never been as blurred as it is today. In the past, border crossers were simply economic migrants who, if caught, were mostly charged monetary fines and voluntarily returned without consequences. Administrative restrictions to legal migration because of prior criminal prosecutions were rare. But today, immigration law has been mixed in with criminal law with very serious consequences. In short, these court scenes participate in a fantastically circular structure in which the national urgency to securitize by deporting criminals has produced—through the labyrinths of immigration law, policies, and crowded courts—exactly the sort of figure that satisfies the national anxiety.

The imperative to securitize is visceral, and so the need to securitize has been around from the beginning. So if the need to securitize is a kind of governing condition, and if, therefore, immigration law and naturalization acts belong to a broader securitization regime, then it makes sense that rights-based claims on the part of immigration rights activists continually butt heads against the principle of security. If we understand universal rights claims as another version of deterritorialization, then we can understand the territorializing force of securitization as tending toward a kind of evisceration of the universal. That is, securitization is the gravity that pulls down our inclination toward the universal—it territorializes the universal. The nation-state is the territorialization of democracy in the same way that securitization territorializes justice. The Constitution, as the lawful grounding document of the laws, is the territorialization of both democracy and justice.

←↕→

If securitization underpins immigration law, it should be evident in Supreme Court decisions on immigration. Legal theorist Linda Bosniak in *The Citizen and the Alien* does a painstaking job of summarizing what is at stake in the court decisions addressing alienage. Indeed, when she describes the "Constitution's commitment to protecting the rights of aliens as territorially present persons," she opens the door to exploring those moments in immigration law when the nation-state's imperative to securitize does not win the day.[32] The argument of her book is that the Supreme Court in a variety of decisions has declared that noncitizens, such as legal residents and the undocumented, have a variety of rights not commonly noticed, but she is also keen to argue that citizens themselves often feel rightless.[33] Her book, then, is a remarkable analysis of how the courts themselves have been a forum for the conceptual struggle over the rights of citizens versus alien persons. But her work also introduces the important terms *present/presence* and *personhood*, and this gives me a platform for exploring both the conceptual inadequacies and potential of these terms in legal theory.

One exemplar of the ambiguities in immigration law is the 1982 Supreme Court case *Plyler v. Doe*, which was decided on a five-to-four vote.[34] The importance of the case, which turned on the scope of the Fourteenth Amendment, is that it granted noncitizen children a public education. *Plyler*—and other Supreme Court cases that I will not be reviewing—says that a modest number of protections are granted to even those who technically should have no rights. I interpret this granting of modest protections to mean that there is a kind of incompleteness of the territorialization of the universal. That is, the nation's rights to self-determination are, on occasion, curbed but then, in a surprising reversal, are also given free rein. That is, *Plyler* seems to point to the simultaneous imperative to territorialize and the imperative to deterritorialize; to both securitize and universalize; to waffle between the nation's need both to limit and offer a sense of limitlessness. The nomosphere is antinomic.

In *Plyler*, the state of Texas claimed "that undocumented aliens, because of their immigration status, are not 'persons within the jurisdiction' of the State of Texas, and that they therefore have no right to the equal protection of Texas law" (210). Chief Justice Burger's dissent from the court expanded Texas's claim. The Equal Protection Clause of the Fourteenth Amendment may indeed apply to aliens after they have entered the country, he said, but it "does not mandate identical treatment of different categories of persons" (243). So, in Burger's view, what Texas brought to the court was the need to determine "whether, for purposes of allocating its finite resources, a state has a legitimate reason to differentiate between persons who are lawfully within the state and those who are unlawfully there" (243–44). Burger, in moments like this, acknowledges the right of Texas to secure its resources against the claims of everyone who may be present within its jurisdiction. Burger goes on: "The Equal Protection Clause protects against arbitrary and irrational classifications, and against invidious discrimination stemming from prejudice and hostility; it is not an all-encompassing 'equalizer' designed to eradicate every distinction for which persons are not 'responsible'" (245). In sum, Burger acknowledged the good intent of the Fourteenth Amendment but worried that the "Court employs, and . . . abuses, the Fourteenth Amendment in an effort to become an omnipotent and omniscient problem solver" (243).

Justice Brennan, who delivered the opinion of the court, agreed considerably with Chief Justice Burger. For instance, both did not think that there is some fundamental right to education, and both believed that the undocumented, including parents and children, are legitimately subject to deportation. In contrast to Burger, however, Justice Brennan emphasized that the state of Texas exaggerated the financial stress due to undocumented children in its public schools. But his central argument concerned the "specter of a permanent caste of undocumented resident aliens . . . [functioning] as a source of cheap labor, but nevertheless denied the benefits that our society makes available to citizens and lawful residents" (218–19). So Justice Brennan worried less about the deportation of children and more about the cementing of a "discrete class" marked by the "stigma of illiteracy," which would disable them from living "within the structure of our civic institutions" and "foreclose any realistic possibility that they will contribute in even the smallest way to the progress of our Nation" (223).

In sum, *Plyler* seems to be paradigmatic of Supreme Court decisions when it comes to determining the conditions of life for both legal and undocumented aliens. On the one hand, the courts have granted a certain latitude in terms of alienage rights. Under *Plyler*, for instance, schoolchildren who are undocumented immigrants can receive state-supported K–12 public education. On the other hand, *Plyler* also reinforced the vulnerability of aliens by stating that both undocumented children and their parents can be deported by the federal government. There are other restrictions, but the point is that for some time Supreme Court decisions have been both restrictive and permissive regarding the status and privileges of resident aliens and the undocumented. In some instances, the courts have defended some form of securitization; for instance, deportation in the case of both Brennan and Burger emphasizes, as argued earlier, the disposability of the undocumented. But in other instances, inclusion has trumped exclusion—or, at least in the case of *Plyler*, an inclusion that foregrounds an abstraction, "the progress of our Nation"—and is utterly ignorant of the law's role in creating disposability. Bosniak, then, writes within the wake of this impasse, for she wants to expand the privileges of aliens based on the Fourteenth Amendment's protection of personhood.

Consider, then, Section 1 of the Fourteenth Amendment, which seems to let loose these multiple interpretations appearing in *Plyler v. Doe* and more generally in American law: "All persons born or naturalized in the United States, and subject to the jurisdiction thereof, are citizens of the United States and of the state wherein they reside. No state shall make or enforce any law which shall abridge the privileges or immunities of citizens of the United States; nor shall any state deprive any person of life, liberty, or property, without due process of law; nor deny to any person within its jurisdiction the equal protection of the laws."

Does the Fourteenth Amendment draw a distinction between citizenship and personhood? For Linda Bosniak, there does seem to be a distinction: "This is a function of the American constitutional system's guarantee of rights to persons rather than citizens . . .—a state of affairs that has been forcefully defended by many scholars over the years" (94). For Bosniak and others of like mind, citizenship would seem to be our relation to the state whereas personhood would seem to be our relation to some broader, more universal condition. Within this paradigm, the idea of citizenship as a relation to the state does not seem to capture the dimensionality and breadth of our persons, meaning that personhood seems to stand above and beyond our citizenship. Now, the Fourteenth Amendment writers may not have been making such a strong distinction between citizenship and personhood. After all, the first line of Section 1 territorializes persons by emphasizing their nature as citizens when born or naturalized into a jurisdiction. So, contrary to Bosniak, one could simply say that Section 1 is pragmatically addressing post–Civil War conditions by casting personhood as a wide net that might protect former slaves from battered and bitter southerners who, if not accepting the term *citizen*, will be forced to accept the term *person* for the African Americans in their midst. So is Section 1 an expansive envisioning of personhood at the expense of citizenship, as Bosniak suggests, or is it a pragmatic maneuver meant to foreclose all the dodges that rebellious white southerners might cleverly concoct? The stakes today are very real in the sense that, as we have seen, Supreme Court cases can turn on interpretations of personhood, but in a more grounded sense immigration rights marchers invariably carry signs saying, in effect, "We, too, are persons," suggesting that in some fashion personhood as some sort of universal has become part of everyday rhetoric.

Still I am having trouble getting my head around this understanding of personhood—even if I deeply sympathize with its program of granting more privileges to the undocumented. If securitization underpins the long history of immigration law, Bosniak, nobly, wants to retrieve from the Fourteenth Amendment and a variety of Supreme Court cases the notion that personhood has a special standing that, at least in some instances, ought to overcome the imperative to securitize. If Bosniak is correct about the conceptual power of personhood, we need to examine the logic upon which the concept rests. For instance, does personhood stand above and beyond our relation to the state—deterritorialized as it were? Probably not, for at first glance personhood would seem to be a conceptual artifact put into motion from within the legal theories of the state as a counterweight to perceived limitations or reductions inherent in the concept of citizenship. It is as if there is a deep intuition within legal theory that citizenship is not a sufficiently universal condition—therefore, it must invent the universality of personhood as compensation. Indeed, citizenship can only be parochial, for it must be limited to a specific nation and culture. Hence legal theory performs a kind of self-correction of this limitation by inventing something more limitless (namely, personhood), because it fears the consequences of the law treating us as something less (namely, mere citizens or noncitizens). Personhood, then, directly addresses the inadequacies of the law as embodied in the concept of citizenship. The irony, of course, is that the law cannot articulate a genuinely universal condition external to the law. Like citizenship, personhood also names a state relation, albeit a special kind of state relation, one that tries to transcend the inadequacies of the state itself. Ultimately, perhaps, personhood reveals that neither citizenship nor the entity that citizenship embodies, the state, are sufficiently universal—both are parochial—but personhood also reveals that there is some underlying imperative on the part of the state to make itself out to be something more fully universal and just. To my mind, what Bosniak and others of like mind have missed is the function of personhood as a rhetorical cure to the real insufficiencies of citizenship and the state.

Let me reframe it this way: the law, as an expression of state authority, must limit and restrict its subjects within reason (as Supreme Court justices say) while at the same time providing subjects some sense of limitlessness. The first without the second translates to tyranny, but the incorporation of both may establish legitimacy (always an infinitely difficult project) across the minds of individuals in a mass society. The larger point is the following: the distinction between the citizen and the undocumented means that only one kind of presence (the citizen's presence) really counts, while the presence of the undocumented does not legally count. This distinction means that the undocumented are inside the law's restrictions and limitations but outside its sense of limitlessness. Remarkably, the world's populations have been habituated into imagining national spaces as legitimate spaces, as spaces that rightfully deny the undocumented the sense of limitlessness that also undergirds the law. This "rightful" denial is another instantiation of how utterly convincing the nation-state form has become. What might otherwise seem abusive—as if the life of the undocumented had become disposable—can be reframed as legal once we accept the legitimacy of national space, hence the legitimacy to pull apart the copresence of citizen|undocumented.

Perhaps an artful summary of the arguments thus far will help clarify the stakes of the game. I will put words into the mouths of some of the figures that we have encountered. The voices are Bosniak, me, Dallacroce, Justice Burger, and Arellano, and they will theatrically encounter each other on this constructed stage.

BOSNIAK: I extend equal rights of personhood to both citizens and noncitizens because this is a natural outcome of liberal democracy's theory of equality. Securitization too often violates personhood.

CINTRON: Liberal democracy's theory of equality is an idealization, even a deterritorialization, or one of the democratic rhetorics. It helps mass society habituate itself to a specific condition—namely, the lack of a viable path to reducing the disposabilities due to inequalities. So equality, on what planet? Rather than trying to establish the substantive dimensions of personhood, let's inquire into how such a novel idea as personhood gets produced in the first place, how it comes into being and why. Hence from this perspective, the universalism of personhood seems to be a compensatory move, an invention that attempts to cure—and exposes in the process—how nation-state citizenship is necessary but inadequate. Mind you, I do not like how securitization trumps personhood, but I understand how securitization acts as an imperative in national consciousness.

DALLACROCE AND OTHERS OF LIKE MIND: Citizenship is the internationally accepted signifier for determining the right to a specific political community. For me, a political community is not abstract but more like a gut feeling of belonging, unconsciously shared, while personhood, in contrast, may be an irresponsible construct that ignores the traditional and rightful authority of any nation-state to construct its own people. We must obey the imperative to securitize our culture, our safety, our American democracy, our economy, our way of life—and all nations need to do the same for themselves—for if we do not obey this imperative, then we lose the exceptionalism that a national people offers to the planet. What we offer the world is our American way of life, a beacon to the world that shines with safety, wealth, freedom, hope. We are the exemplar of democracy.[35]

JUSTICE BURGER: The law over time becomes a rationally tuned instrument that tries to maximize restrictions and protections for the creation of a reasonable as opposed to an idealized justice. In this sense, citizenship is a historical and workable mechanism for determining the political community, and personhood is an important legal theory emerging from the Fourteenth Amendment. My major concern is with the potential overuse of personhood as a kind of court-based mechanism for equalizing all kinds of social conditions, including the distinction between citizens and noncitizens. Justice Brennan and I in *Plyler* tried to negotiate the fine line between whom we should include and exclude. I believe that the rights of nations and states to control their jurisdictions, including their economic resources—the right to take care of our own—takes precedence over an equalization of persons. We ought not make meaningless the important distinction between citizens and others. Our first allegiance is to our own citizens.

ARELLANO: I am a loyal worker. I believe in the goodness of the American nation and its people. I have a son. My country is poor and cannot offer him enough. It is also dangerous. I fear for my life and my son's life, that we may be targets for those who want to do us harm. I believe in God. I believe that God does not want us to be put into danger, and that he does not want to separate me from my son. How could he ever want such things? The American nation should speak with the same righteousness that God speaks. It is sad that in today's world nations cannot speak this way. Do you think that God looks at his children as persons or citizens?[36]

For Dallacroce and Burger, Bosniak's personhood is simply too expansive while my speculations on the production of the law and the inadequacies of citizenship seem to seriously miss the practicality of citizenship as a legal mechanism for stitching the nation to the state. Arellano speaks with a voice that appeals to some higher order framed as God, while De Genova in the two earlier epigraphs frames a higher order as the freedom of movement. The "higher order" argument appeals because it is always synonymous with justice. That is, we are most drawn to higher order arguments when we need to dampen the seemingly arbitrary injustices of everyday life. Hence Arellano and De Genova, through their respective religiosity and secularism, argue on behalf of a higher principle, or perhaps even a natural law.

←↕→

Within the democratic nation-state, particularly the United States, personhood and citizenship address each other from within legal theory. Personhood implies, but cannot prove, that both citizenship and the state are limited and limiting forms. Citizenship conceptually and practically helps to securitize the nation-state, while personhood is a legal device that tries to rupture these sorts of confinements. In this sense, citizenship is the territorialization of personhood.

But we need to go deeper than this. We need to enter into the internal logic of citizenship to understand why it is so psychically compelling for someone like Dallacroce, but for others, such as Justice Burger, it is more like a useful, administrative device that orients both democracy and the nation-state. Let's consider Étienne Balibar's *We, the People of Europe?*, which makes clear throughout that citizenship is the institution of institutions.[37] What does he mean? For him, citizenship is the institution that enables all other institutions; hence the officialdom of the nation-state, for good or ill, rests on demarcating the citizen from the noncitizen and more deeply the undocumented. In other words, citizenship founds the political community, and it is then, and only then, that the political community can begin to actualize the potential of democracy. That is, prior to determining who is and is not a citizen, democracy remains inert, an ethereal idea full of potential perhaps, but not an official, bureaucratized body politic that can set into motion what it wants to be. In this sense, citizenship marks the beginning of all the practical decisions and existential questions that a body of people must raise. When a democratically ordered people put all this into motion, then democracy itself ceases to be just an idea. But, simultaneously, democracy ceases to be a species of universalism, for now it shrinks to the parochialism of the nation-state. It becomes territorialized to the nation-state, so that one becomes the citizen of a specific democracy but not of democracy as such. Thus the nation-state territorializes democracy. Of course, many might reply, and rightfully so, that citizenship is not the founding or inaugural moment. Civil war is—or better, revolution is—followed perhaps by a constitutional convention that will, then, constitute the people.[38] I won't argue against any of that. My point is simple: citizenship is the first institution because it severs the included from the excluded. Now the character of any inclusion is to simultaneously exclude, and this is precisely what happens under citizenship. Citizens, who are the included, have the official capacity to determine the institutions that will protect and govern them; the excluded undocumented do not so determine, and this is so even if the excluded live in their midst and otherwise fall under the jurisdiction of those same institutions.[39] It is in this sense that citizenship is the institution of institutions that enables the nation-state to actualize democracy by limiting the limitlessness of democracy.

Like a pit bull that enjoys attacking the Achilles heel of a concept and biting to the bone, I now turn to the next thing worth biting into. It seems that there are two modes by which modern territorialized democracies—territorialized by the nation-state—imagine the acquisition of citizenship. In our era, the most common ways of becoming a citizen are through natality and through naturalization. We saw those two terms earlier in Section 1 of the Fourteenth Amendment. Through natality, one is "born into a community"; through naturalization, one is "ritualized into a community." As a point of comparison, legal residents and the undocumented are merely "present in a community" but are not full members of the community. "Born into" and "ritualized into" have legal weight and standing, while "present in" lacks equivalent standing. "Born into" and "ritualized into" are devices that enable securitization; "present in" lacks the markers of "born into" or "ritualized into" and thus represent manifold, potential threats for those who believe strongly in the need for security.

So what is the meaning and importance of birth that cannot be replicated but can be ritualized? What does "born into" amount to? If we can answer these questions, we will start to understand why citizenship is so psychically compelling for someone like Dallacroce. "Born into" is the most privileged condition, the most natural and genuine; naturalization, certainly a revealing term, tries to imitate the natural (or at least compensate for the lack of a natural). "Born into" presumes that we are so porous to our national people that we somehow absorb them until we become ourselves such a people, but naturalization depends on bureaucratic ritual—the declaration of loyalty, the acquisition of minimal amounts of national language and knowledge—to compensate for all that remains missing.[40] "Born into" is ultimately an archaic concept, and to illuminate it we might turn to early articulations by someone like Aristotle, who in so much of his work seems to straddle the archaic and modern and thus reveal the longevity of ideas. As is well known, Greece had its own rules of citizenship that depended on natality.[41] And when Aristotle reflects on birth in his *Politics*, he makes the point early on that any person, by nature, is preceded by the city she is born into. Indeed, the essence of the person is not so much a kind of individual self-realization but a self-realization in more communal terms: "He who is without a city through nature rather than chance is either a mean sort or superior to man; he is 'without clan, without law, without hearth,' like the person reproved by Homer. . . . The city is thus prior by nature to the household and to each of us. For the whole must of necessity be prior to the part. . . . That the city is both by nature and prior to each individual, then, is clear. . . . Accordingly, there is in everyone by nature an impulse toward this sort of partnership."[42]

I would like to take up that last term, *partnership*, or κοινωνίαν in the Greek. Translators of the term have avoided the English word *community*, claiming that it conveys political connotations that the Greek had not acquired. Other possible translations are *communion* and *association*. This range of meanings for κοινωνίαν suggests that the πόλις (city) is a type of "partnership," "community," "communion," "association," which as a "whole must of necessity be prior to the part"—that is, prior to any individual. So partnership precedes us, according to Aristotle, and we find our individualness, purpose, meaning, and beingness as we enter into partnership.

We might also take note of the teleological thinking that characterizes so much of Aristotle's work, where the essence of a thing gets revealed when the thing comes to completion. We hear some of that in the phrasing "everyone by nature [has] an impulse toward this sort of partnership," but we hear it more clearly elsewhere: "What each thing is—for example, a human being, a horse, or a household—when its coming into being is complete is, we assert, the nature of that thing" (37). Now for Aristotle, there was also the notion that this movement toward completion is the realization of a thing's goodness. The larger point is the archaicness of what it means to be "born into." If Aristotle reflected the tenor of his times as well as the still more ancient world that preceded him (a big if, perhaps), the idea of being "born into" is not about the cultivation of individuality coupled to an economics of self-interest, as it is today in the United States, but more about human potential actualizing itself inside kinship, partnership, or political association. (Let us not forget that the prior chapter emphasized a ceaseless dynamism that Aristotle and other Greeks understood well and that we artificially label with our boundary-making terms: potentiality → actuality, which gives birth to a new round of potentiality → actuality.) Somehow, the newborn in all of its porosity gathers over time the character of her community, takes it in until he becomes a version of it, and this simultaneously is her self-actualization. The community transforms raw nature into human nature. To not undergo that transformative power is to be inhuman, that is, a wild animal (θηρίον) or a god (θεός), as Aristotle phrases it. In this sense, "born into" enables not a mimetic reproduction of the community but certainly its continuation, which over time might solidify its difference, its exceptionalism.

What I am suggesting here is the archaic expression of "born into" but also its modern expression in birthright citizenship. It is perhaps unfair to both Aristotle and Johann Fichte, the German philosopher, to compare 350 B.C.E. to

1808 C.E., but Fichte in his *Addresses to the German Nation* adds a love of nation and religion to Aristotle's sense of communal partnership. I juxtapose them because beneath both texts there seems to be an enduring sensibility—namely, that the self cannot find its beingness except within the community structures that one is "born into." "This is his love for his people: at first he respects, trusts, rejoices in it, takes pride in his descent from it. The divine has appeared in the people . . . [and so] he is active, effective, sacrificing himself on behalf of his people. . . . Permanence is promised to him only by the independent perpetuation of his nation; to save it, he must be willing even to die, so that it may live and he live in it the only life he has ever wanted."[43]

The persistence of the archaic inside the modern suggests that birthright citizenship is psychically compelling, for at least some folks, because it is more than a bureaucratic rule. In this sense, "born into" occurs at a visceral level where people recognize the singularity of their community or nation-state and believe that such an entity outlives their human frailty. Jacqueline Stevens calls this the move from finitude to infinitude,[44] or what I would call limitation to limitlessness, and it is visceral, a sense that one's distinctive individuality is structured by a commonality that is largely invisible but ever present. Vigilance regarding the life of one's nation gives one purpose and permanence. The person becomes possessive of their communality in the most disastrous ways.

Now this archaic view, which remains strongly buried inside concepts of citizenship and nationalism, needs one more element to be fully understood, the notion of place, that is, a demarcated patch of land.[45] People make claims on the planet either through rigidly determined borders, as with nation-states, or softly determined ones as in earlier times. The point is that groups tend to essentialize themselves—that is, make themselves visible to themselves and others—by pointing to their cultural difference as well as their geographies. Of course, only geography is genuinely unique and truly visible, much more so, anyway, than cultural difference that undergoes constant morphing under the pressures of transnationalism. At any rate, the modern passport and birth documents marking today's bordering of the earth represent the astonishingly ancient sensibility of fusing a people to a specific geography. Borders, increasingly, can no longer keep people stationary, but the extent to which they do so enables the fixing of difference. One cannot be born into a community without being born into a place, and this has led to all kinds of possessive sensibilities, such things as mythologies of land and community that become homelands, sacred lands, heartlands.[46] The psychic stuff of community leaks out into specific landforms and fuses them to the community's ultimate values. But all this cannot happen under conditions of too much mobility; hence we have seen the rise of a politics of mobility resistant to borders, which in contrast is hooked to a broader politics of the stationary that I labeled earlier as "managerial modernity."

In sum, spatial boundaries demarcate a place where the community can emerge by cultivating a common psyche, a culture, if you will—or so goes the thinking. A bordered place becomes identified with that psyche, enabling such and such a people to become the specificity of who they are. So this culture has its special place on the earth, is rooted to a place. "Born into" and "ritualized into"—archaically at least—signals a person's acquisition of a community that is like no other because it has its own carved-out place. Our idea of the citizen with its notions of "born into" or "ritualized into" seems to maintain some sort of archaic metaphysics, echoing back to De Genova's opening quotation, in which distinctive communities rooted to their special lands, which today are geographically fenced and internationally recognized, attempt to reproduce in each new person some particular attribute called national character or exceptionalism. Here is the stamp of who they are, who they really are, a people identified with their patch of land, which if they endure acquire a heritage, a certain beingness worth preserving. Perhaps this archaic metaphysics is not self-evident beneath the practical imperatives of managing a modern democratic nation-state that must determine its rightful voters, its rightful recipients of protections and benefits. After all, the distribution of limited resources and benefits, as Justice Burger told us earlier, is a legitimate concern that must be determined somehow. But the argument here is that these practical imperatives of modern democracies have absorbed into their operating structures something of these archaic sensibilities; for instance, the fact that democracies, in order to function properly, depend on a certain cultural coherence, even patriotic nationalism, that endlessly reproduces the values and value of the nation.

And this, at last, brings me to a major point: citizenship in the forms of "born into" and "ritualized into" reveals not just the nation-state's ancient sensibility but also bridges toward Balibar's provocative notion that citizenship is the institution of institutions for any democracy. What better emblem, then, of the melding of the nation-state to democracy than the common term that they share, *citizenship*? As I suggested previously, we do not live in democracy; rather, we live in some nation-state that territorializes a version of democracy. Citizenship is the territorialization of personhood in the same way that the nation-state is the territorialization of democracy. Such a notion runs directly counter to most left-leaning arguments that advocate for the rights of the undocumented by demanding that the country become truly, or at least more, democratic. Such advocacy fetishizes democracy, for citizenship, which underpins both the nation-state and democracy, represents that ancient hesitation to acknowledge the beingness of the Other. Democracy as we know it cannot dissolve this hesitation; it only preserves it because its "nature" is to distinguish between citizens and noncitizens. After all, democracies must determine their knowledgeable and proper voters from those who are not, if democracies are to ensure their continuance. Let me be clear: I am not a strong defender of democracy. Rather, I offer a diagnosis and critique of how democracy works. My activist friends engaged in immigration rights work critique the current system as not being sufficiently democratic. I think their critique is shortsighted. "More democracy" might relieve certain abuses emerging in the United States and elsewhere concerning, for instance, the narrowing of what counts as a legitimate asylum claim, but no amount of democratization can, finally, remove the fatal flaws of democracy.[47]

I have sketched thus far a kind of archaic metaphysics that underpins contemporary beliefs about the value of community, the importance of birth and belonging, and that establishes rituals of incorporation and grants a sovereign the right to create rules of incorporation.[48] These beliefs and practices serve an important assumption: a person cannot realize her personhood except through association, partnership, communal ties, and so on. But even if modern citizenship continues some of these archaic ideas, we should also note that it is a reasonable bureaucratic device—and I think this was Justice Burger's point. Conceptually, citizenship resists, and rightfully so, the romanticization of inclusiveness. In contrast, those who prefer the conception of personhood are resisting, and again rightfully so, the parochialism of citizenship. Whether they also sense the archaic residue that persists in citizenship, I do not know, but I do suspect that they sense how personhood is more modern conceptually. Modern personhood begins by critiquing and shrugging off the shaping hand of community in order to establish the innate worth and independence of the individual person. Modern personhood is established by summoning a difference between oneself and others and between oneself and the community one was "born into." This sort of person is buttressed by a whole panoply of negative and positive rights, including the rights of suffrage. Personhood here aspires to its own metaphysical positioning through notions of universal rights. This personhood claims that there is something more precious—the individual person with innate worth, dignity, and so on—that precedes the community. In sum, both positions invoke a certain metaphysics or a priori truth—the truth, on the one hand, that a person only comes into being via community versus the truth, on the other, that the person is not identifiable by community alone but is more than any community. The point is that both positions are in ratio inside each other, and so it should not surprise us that laws and Supreme Court decisions waffle, depending on the particulars of the case, between preserving the values of citizenship and "political community," on the one hand, and then, on the other hand, rupturing them with the so-called higher values of personhood.

←↨→

I want to introduce a thought experiment based on the presence of the immigrant as opposed to the rights of the immigrant based on personhood. I call it a thought experiment because our here-now offers, with the exception of Bosniak's theories and those of her allies, little legal standing for immigrant presence. Our here-now, our status quo, is utterly defined by both the right and left through rights-based discourses. But rights-based conceptions are hooked to liberal freedoms that are anchored to individuations, individualisms, and egocentricities, or what might be better called "singularities." The result is that a kind of commons of the citizen|undocumented becomes invisible and unthinkable. Consider that the rights of individuals, of private property, and of the nation-state seem to belong to the same ideological nexus that can grant rights to embryos and fetuses because these, too, are on their way to becoming singularities—namely, singular persons. In my view, personhood claims—and rights claims in general—are a mixed bag capable of producing a social order hyperfocused on atomizing the world into singularities.

But today these notions of securitizing and privileging singularity seem to be existentially threatened. A world of increasing mobility—indeed, a politics of mobility—seems to be taking shape beneath the weight of the nation-state and its politics of the stationary. I am talking here not just of the incessant mobility of the undocumented as economic refugees but the specter of something much more catastrophic for the future of the nation-state and its democratic principles. I am speaking of environmental refugees emerging from areas of increasing desertification and from flooding of low-lying coasts.[49] Today's bordered nation-state—the singularity that manages human populations—will lose its rationale if it loses its ability to control the accelerating movements of people. If the bordered nation-state represents, at its darkest, the heuristics of war, nationalisms, and a politics of the stationary, can it adapt to a quickly emerging politics of mobility? I doubt it. The modernist game has always centered itself on expanding its metaphysics of freedom by fetishizing democracy and inclusivity, but that game unravels if and when climate migrants have no place to go except detention camps, the supreme symbols of war as securitization.

So assuming that at some future date there will be a massive presence of bodies facing us from the other side of the border, each one claiming the rights of personhood, and assuming that at that precise moment the citizens of wealthy nations will "democratically" choose to protect and securitize "their persons" at the expense of others, it is then that the fetishization of democracy will no longer be possible. The ruse will reveal itself: Inclusivity has never been inclusive; it has always also been exclusive. Here is the war that democracy always said it was not. Assuming all that—a huge assumption to be sure—I launch this thought experiment as a foray, an adventure to see what parts of its theorization might stick before the future manifests.

The idea of the "present in," their presence among us, occurs in some remarkably trivial passages that keep reappearing in immigration law and Supreme Court decisions. In the first section of Arizona Senate Bill (S.B.) 1070—three of whose provisions were preempted in *Arizona v. United States*[50] while a fourth provision was upheld—a reference to "presence" is made: "The provisions of this act are intended to work together to discourage and deter the unlawful entry and presence of aliens and economic activity by persons unlawfully present in the United States."[51] The goal of S.B. 1070 was to make "attrition through enforcement the public policy of all state and local government agencies in Arizona."[52] That is, the goal is "self-deportation," wherein the state bears down until the undocumented "voluntarily" leave.[53] So the undocumented who are "present" among legal Arizonans, according to S.B. 1070, are both inside and outside the law. They are inside the law to the extent that they are incorporated into the long history of a deportation structure that Supreme Court decisions have commented upon numerous times, but they are also outside the law to the extent that the law produces their condition as being outside the rule of law and, therefore, as subject to deportation. Establishing those who are simultaneously inside and outside the law is, historically, the central apparatus through which the political community binds itself against radical alteration. Echoing some of my earlier language, it is simply the political community securitizing itself through the definitional power of the law. That is, the political community of Arizona acknowledges the physical presence of the undocumented and legislates against their institutional recognition—indeed, aims the law against them—in order to do away with their presence, thereby securing itself against alteration.

I want to describe and theorize presence as a certain brute condition regarding the undocumented. If we think of *citizen* and *citizenship* as referencing habitation—in its old sense, habitation in a city and, further, the rights and privileges of a "freeman" as inhabitant of a city—then we see its ancient dialectical pairing to "present in," those who are present alongside the "freemen" but not with the same standing. In other words, "present in" has been there all along. Because it is different from the conditions of the "born into" and the "ritualized into," it has remained more vulnerable to banishment, exile, and deportation. The first act of governmentality seems to start when the sovereign distinguishes between material being and legal being—that is, between those who are materially present but not legally present (the undocumented) versus those who are present in both senses (the citizen). Hence the birth certificate that notes the first minute of life of those "born into" makes utter sense as the persistence of the archaic in modern terms.

Presence, then, in contrast to personhood, refers to that other archaic condition that has always faced sovereignty. Today, it is a brute condition, a kind of implacability that the democratic imaginary must address—and this, indeed, is precisely what Supreme Court decisions on immigration, such as *Plyler*, have wrestled with. I would like to describe this bruteness as a type of "pre-political" condition that democracy must draw into itself, must absorb and transform, if it is to maintain its integrity and self-understanding.[54] Of course, the term *prepolitical* is a term of art, for in the United States and elsewhere everyone has at least some sort of political standing no matter their status.[55] (Notice that I am trying to distinguish the term *prepolitical* from De Genova's freedom as *precondition* for human self-determination, which I consider bordering on the metaphysical. If De Genova had also said that *precondition* is a term of art, we might have found ourselves on the same page.)

So *Yick Wo* (1886), *Wong Wing* (1896), and *Plyler* (1982) seem to confirm a broad point—namely, that the corporeal facticity of the undocumented faces the democratic imaginary and asks, essentially, if democratic justice, which presumes a kind of global, universal equality, can bear to be territorialized. Of course, justice is always territorialized, but even this fact is not sufficient to erase the force of the universal that is embedded in and acts upon human conceptions of justice. No matter how pragmatic and necessary our territorialization of justice, its residual universality continues to call. So there is always a strain between justice as territorialized and justice as universal, a strain that cannot be erased.

I use terms such as *implacability* and *brute condition*, then, to make the following truth: Democracy is the political order that invents the very idea of the political, for politics prior to democracy is essentially war among elites. Democracy changes that condition by introducing into this war a new population, which over time expands horizontally. These new populations, which in their day were ignored or brutalized by the elites, represented a "prepolitical" condition aching for vengeance or at least incorporation. Democracy, then, is identifiable with the slow transformation of prepolitical conditions into the political—this is its signature, its historical and ontological character. This is what gives democracy its forward motion, its relentless invention of the future, the idea of a better future for all, and why we fetishize it. *Yick Wo*, *Wong Wing*, and *Plyler* answer this call—granted, in minimal fashion at best—but the point is that it answers it. Similarly, the Fourteenth Amendment, as discussed earlier, answered this same call even as Justice Burger tried to resist its impulse to equalize everything. The prepolitical, then, always sits implacably in front of democracy as if it were its conscience. The call will come, and the undocumented today are simply one of the next groups uttering the call.

Now, I am aware of the stubborn problems that my argument represents, for my special interest is in presence as something weightier than personhood and weightier than agency. And yet all the legal theory that we have seen thus far has spoken through the trope of personhood. Why, therefore, defend presence? I address that stubborn problem further as the chapter progresses. For now, I want to conclude this section with the assertion that presence can sit in stillness and never act, for the facticity of its prepolitical condition is both democracy's creation and the brute material upon which it must act—and this is what makes it weighty. If democracy refuses to pull the prepolitical into the political, then, frankly, we exist in another political order. Democracy's self-definition, self-understanding, self-everything cannot do otherwise, and this is why the presence of the undocumented, in all their prepolitical condition—itself democracy's creation—can sit in front of democracy as an implacable force.[56]

I turn to the Dominican Republic (DR) and its relation to the Haitians in their midst. The DR represents an extreme version of the territorialization of human populations as a sovereign right of the nation-state. This fact means that events in the DR reveal with clarity the essential paradox of democracy—namely, that democracy looks in two directions, backward and forward. Its backward look is its dependency on the ancient metaphysics of citizenship that fuses a specific people to a specific place, while its forward look is its vanguardist metaphysics to expand the franchise of equal personhood to all and to upend limitation itself. So it is inevitable that this expanding metaphysic would eventually upend even the idea of freedom in order to make it truly vanguardist: a freedom of movement across nation-states, à la De Genova. Democracy, in sum, is constituted by its paradoxical tensions that always exist in ratio, for it is both territorialized and deterritorialized, a limitation and a limitlessness—these have been the themes of our discussion, and events surrounding the DR are further instantiations.

The facts are these: the DR—through a series of official acts that include the passage of the General Law on Migration in 2004, the 2010 Constitution, and a September 2013 Constitutional Court ruling—has changed the status of Haitians who, over several generations, have been born and raised in the DR. This subjugation of the Haitians continues into 2019 without any foreseeable end. Since at least the 1940s, many Haitians had the right to work in the DR if they had official papers from their employers. The children born to this largely menial labor class (sugarcane cutters) were considered citizens under the guarantees of jus soli (right of the soil) once the parents presented their documents to state authorities. Internationally, jus soli grants nationality to those born on the land with a few traditional exceptions, such as those who are *in transit*. The DR constitutionally had been interpreting *in transit* as ten days or less, and so it seemed that the children of Haitian laborers under jus soli guarantees were constitutional citizens with their many decades of residence. Indeed, with their official birth certificates and national identity cards, they fully belonged to the political community of the DR. However, at the same time, some civil registry officials, without legislative backing, interpreted some laborers to be *in transit* and that, therefore, their children could not be granted jus soli citizenship status. The result was the growth of a multigenerational class of undocumented Haitians. That is, two groups existed side by side: those of Haitian descent with citizenship status and those without. What they shared were years and years of residency. In 2004, the General Law on Migration overturned jus soli guarantees in favor of the *in transit* condition. From this point on, the DR, through constitutional changes and rulings, began to reinforce *in transit* over jus soli. The government of the DR has been applying *in transit* retroactively and asking for a review of all documents, even those that used to guarantee national citizenship, effectively threatening both groups of Haitian descent with statelessness. These decisions of the DR were brought to the Inter-American Court of Human Rights. Its ruling, according to the Open Society Justice Initiative, seems to capture what is at stake—at least for the global rights regime: Dominicans of Haitian descent are being discriminated against because the *in transit* condition does not have "a reasonable temporal limit" and because the "migratory status of parents" cannot be applied "to children born on a national territory" and cannot justify "depriving a person of their right to nationality."[57]

How does this wrestling match between the DR and the international order reflect the idea of democracy looking simultaneously backward and forward? Here are three observations. First, when international courts insist that there is a right to nationality, they confirm that the territorialization of peoples into geographic spaces is fundamental for both global order and the betterment of daily life. As I have argued, both the nation-state and citizenship are practical entities and mechanisms that territorialize both democracy and justice. That is, they make democracy and justice possible—indeed, this is the only way to "know" justice—but the very act of territorializing means that the nation-state and citizenship are revealed as profoundly incomplete compared to the deterritorialized imaginings of democracy and justice that many people hold so dear and even fetishize. This incompleteness is potentially productive, meaning that it can motivate groups to "perfect" by rupturing the ancient justice that they have so that it looks more like the justice that they want. But "perfected" justice, of course, can be horrifying—there is no guarantee as to where it might end up.

Second, the right to nationality, as argued by the international courts, also illuminates in a precise way the curious balancing act that advocates of a universal justice must negotiate. On the one hand, they speak against the structures and consequences of too much state sovereignty. On the other hand, they want to reinforce the structures of sovereignty until they become sufficiently strong to enforce the global rules that the advocates prefer. Indeed, they want all the sovereignties of the world to conform to those rules. So in their desire to have a better justice and more of it at a global level, they must erode sovereignty so that they can build it back up. In this sense, they are constantly negotiating their dismissal of and belief in sovereignty itself. The global rights regime seems to look to a future of relatively weakened sovereignties as far as the eye can see, each one reformed according to the global rights agenda.[58]

Third, the political leadership of the DR is facing what they know to be true: there are many Haitians in their country who know themselves only as Dominicans. How does a government dislodge this fact—this powerfully internalized sense of "born into," which the Haitians born in the DR clearly have—so that the authority of long-term residence means little? *In transit* is an honest legal term, but expanding its timeline so that years of residency no longer count betrays the DR's racism and classicism, which has existed for centuries. Dominicans have traditionally identified themselves as belonging to European stock and identified Haitians as Africans. Thus the political leadership fears a Haitian or Africanist takeover. It must expand *in transit* in order to securitize the DR. By distinguishing their own "born into" from the "born into" of Haitian experience, the DR pulls inward to secure the hegemony of their own. But isn't the term *in transit* marvelously revealing? It can only do its legal trick if it contains what it opposes as part of its conceptual structure. That is, residency must be conceptually embedded inside *in transit*. This embedded residency contains an enormous power that *in transit* had to reverse in order to gather its own power. Over decades, Haitians were "born into" the DR, and it was their facticity, their implacability, their immovability—that is, their long-term residency—that had to be delegitimized by transferring the power of their actual condition into an equally powerful, opposite term: *in transit*.[59]

I want to think a bit more about the relationship between residency and "present in," "those present among us," that this discussion of Dominicans of Haitian descent seems to illuminate. As I have argued, the planet is today utterly territorialized, demarcated into nation-states or other legally recognized units that typically contain a "people" who are understood to be their collective "owners," their rightful inhabitants. Here is another instance of the totalization of the law across the planet, the nomosphere. The law, which in every instance invents its objects of governance, is thus artifice because the law, if need be, could invent other objects. Artifice, then, produces the distinction between legal residency and the undocumented. Does this understanding of the magical properties of the law—to produce one thing as opposed to another—have any consequences for interpreting the undocumented who are "present among us"?

I argue that "present in" is as conceptually important as "born into" or "ritualized into" and, indeed, does have its legal correlations. For instance, one of the universal prerequisites for being "ritualized into," acknowledged, seemingly, in the immigration laws of all nation-states, is some designated length of residency. According to the United States Naturalization Act of 1790, "Any alien, being a free white person, who shall have resided within the limits and under the jurisdiction of the United States for the term of two years, may be admitted to become a citizen thereof." What is the significance of residency, whether that be two years or fourteen years? Residency seems to place a high value on the experiential quality of living with others, a kind of gathering into oneself over time the ways of another people, including their symbols and meanings. Because it is experiential, it can substitute for "born into," which is experiential in a more complete sense. World law seems to acknowledge that naturalization processes must contain this experience of others over a period of time. True, the left can regard residency requirements as forms of patriarchal acculturation that are meant to erode otherness and secure the hegemony of the nation.[60] But my point is simply technical: there is little difference—experientially at least—between legal residency and undocumented residency. Consider that the undocumented Dominicans of Haitian descent have come to know themselves experientially as belonging to the DR and not as a separate people *in transit*. Their undocumented residency is just as powerful experientially as legal residency. In this sense, legal residency is not substantively different from undocumented residency when it comes to experiential qualities. It is not as if legality guarantees a more genuine experience. The difference seems to be not substantive but normative in the sense that legal residency recognizes the rights of a community to determine its rules of belonging. Normative dimensions are exceptionally important, but the undocumented residency of those who are "present among us" accomplishes the same experiential necessity that is so important to naturalization law.

In 2015, Amnesty International documented some of the Haitian experiences in the DR. One of the Haitian interviewees said: "Without papers, I am no one."[61] The quotation echoes Arellano's double existence—that is, the split between material being and legal being. The Haitians are so materially "present in" the DR that they consider themselves Dominicans after living among them, for generations in some cases. But the phrase "no one" seems to contradict their entire experience. What is the strange profundity of "legal being" so that if you do not have it you are "no one"? At moments like these, the law seems to reveal its artifactual nature at odds with the deepest of experiential realities. Only the state performs this kind of cleavage. Is this a form of abuse made legal due to the rights of self-determination on the part of the nation-state every time it looks "backward"? If, as argued, the experiential quality of living with others does indeed initiate a transformation of the foreigner, then something more "forward" could be written into law. After all, a commons between citizens and noncitizens is the outcome of both "ritualized into" and "present among." The law creates its objects of governance, and so it could be rewritten to better acknowledge the difference and sameness between "ritualized into" and "present among."

←↕→

What happens to a thought experiment when it encounters ethnographic work? It gets demolished. Or at least this has been my experience over and over. It is as if ethnographic work erodes theoretical presumptions and forces the rewriting of our theories. Thus I present another dimension to my thought experiment: What happens when others think through their own versions of the undocumented "present among us"? I could represent such moments through a number of instances drawn from my ethnographic work, but here is the one I choose because of the complexities and ironies that it offers when juxtaposed to this moment of writing in 2019.

It is April 2010. I am in a small Puerto Rican restaurant on Paseo Boricua in the Humboldt Park neighborhood of Chicago. There are five others with me: the storefront minister who had housed Elvira Arellano and her son during their sanctuary stay, two other Puerto Rican ministers, and a Puerto Rican political activist well known in Chicago with ties to grassroots progressives in Latin America. We are joined by the guest of the day, Enrique Dussel, the Argentinean exiled political philosopher now living in Mexico City. He is one of the best known theoreticians of liberation theology and author of numerous books.

I am hearing still another version of a politics of presence, one that I am genuinely ambivalent about. The discourse is thick with a politics of mobility that is thrilling to hear, but simultaneously there are echoes of ethnocentrism. As the speakers swing through their ideas, I rapidly take detailed notes. It is not easy to label what they are saying. It seems, however, to be a kind of "cosmological politics" or even a "post-Marxist futurism,"[62] and because of its futurism, it is a species of modernist potentiality. Before I explain these terms further, I want to highlight that at moments like this Paseo Boricua becomes a self-consciously transnational space that theorizes about and acts upon the conditions of a local poor. The leaders of this space see themselves as belonging to a several-hundred-year-old progressive tradition, that is, as actors in a world-historical process. They do not use the language of deterritorialization and modernist potentiality as I do, but in many ways I have come to these ways of describing things because I have been a member of so many of these conversations. And the fact that Dussel is here speaks well of the activist reputation of this otherwise poor barrio. Many people like Dussel are constantly dropping by to better understand the accomplishments of the political activists along Paseo.

These discussions are not detached from the available structures of political power. Former representative Luis Gutiérrez of the Fourth Congressional District as well as members of the Latino political caucus, which includes Illinois State senators and representatives and Chicago aldermen, occasionally sit in on conversations just like this one. The ideas flow back and forth, with the elected officials measuring what they can pragmatically adapt into policy and law. In a sense, these political figures try to territorialize these high-flying ideas. At any rate, the hubris in this little part of Chicago is ridiculously large; the material successes are encouraging but always compromised; the failures reveal the enduring fragility that underlies even the material successes.

Today's conversation foregrounds the migrant of any nationality living in the United States. Of particular interest, however, are the migrants from Latin America. Ultimately, the speakers are interested in the entirety of *alla*, including its politics. *Alla* means here the massive presence of Latin America as an underbelly that is separated from the United States by the wisp of a river. Dussel was invited to tour Paseo Boricua to see firsthand the fruits of its political work and to offer further insights about alla. The ministers are particularly interested in discussing with him the meanings of migration as well as concrete strategies to persuade other churches, both mainline and Pentecostal, to join their cause. The pastoral tradition of Christianity, as one might imagine, is a natural defender of rights for the undocumented, particularly when families become split by citizenship status. So this is not just a theoretical conversation. For instance, the storefront minister who housed Elvira will later this day fly to Arizona to help organize church support to resist the growing popularity there of anti-immigrant sentiment, and he wants concrete arguments from the pastoral tradition that might enable him to further the cause. He is hoping, then, that Dussel will flesh out his version of liberation theology this morning.

Dussel is animatedly tying together different strands of the contemporary scene. Because it is 2010, his focus is on Obama and Evo Morales. However, today, in 2019, an opposite cosmological politics based on nationalism and closed borders—the politics of the stationary—is on the world stage. The juxtaposition of these two dates reveals the thematic ironies of this book.

Cosmological politics often relies on the trope of the "people" to establish legitimacy, and it finds signs in the world that confirm the unfoldment of a deeper, vaster movement—a metaphysics, as De Genova called it—on behalf of the "people." Because the left and right access the trope of the "people," they use the same bait and fetish. At any rate, Dussel says,[63] regarding Obama and Evo: the Americas have elected recently two presidents who represent oppressed communities, Obama for the Blacks and Evo for the indigenous of Bolivia. But these two are more than leaders of countries, he continues, for Obama's popularity stretches to Africa and Evo's to all the indigenous. What is happening in the world? Is this a new momentum, he asks, a sign of a deepening redistribution of power? The Americas are in a great experiment today. America's missed opportunities are now a source of great potential. Look, he says, the EU and China have formed blocks of regional power, but the United States is still haunted by its sense of superiority, its arrogance, toward Latin America. The Americas together are logically one political bloc, but what has happened instead? The history of exploitation and manipulation, he continues, its persistence in the eleven U.S. military bases that surround Venezuela,[64] is like a sword hanging over the head of the United States. That sword does not threaten Venezuela—it threatens the United States. As long as the United States remains captured by its history of manipulating Latin America for its own self-interests, it cannot adapt to the new world that is emerging, a world that might redeem the United States.

And who are these migrants from Latin America, he asks, small waves here and there, but behind them is something that cannot be resisted: the huge presence of Latin America. This is the future that is coming, he says: a larger America, an alliance of the Americas, a redemption of the past and present of what the United States has been so as to point to what it must become. It must both absorb Latin America and be absorbed by Latin America, he says. The United States may not want to, but it has to—the pressures of capitalist competition say so. The economies of the Americas must grow together if they are going to stay an economic power, he concludes.

His vision is one of economic regionalism that will inevitably stitch together rival hemispheres. Those gathered here all share a sentiment: "Get ready, United States, the times are a changing." The figure of the Latino migrant, those "present among us," is being reconfigured by these speakers as something more than migrant, as a transformative power changing the Americas, the tip of a lance, so to speak. Those who want to hold on to American exceptionalism as

Anglo-driven would have trouble hearing this discourse. But do migrants really think of their hopes and dreams in this way? Or are they being framed in a politics of ethnocentrism, an ethnocentrism that Dallacroce also wields but on behalf of white Americans?

In my view, a wild, romanticized hubris is on full display. Dussel is reading the "signs" of the current moment, the meanings, as it were, of Obama and Evo, who appear pregnant with meaning, as if they were flares shooting up into the night sky and spelling out a future. The speakers nod in agreement, for this type of discourse is familiar to them. What are they recognizing here? Is it the theme of redemption? They are mostly ministers, after all, but how does anyone imagine the redemption of a nation? Is there some sort of ultimate justice (deterritorialized, as it were) that reveals the wrong of an entire nation (a territorialization, as it were) but at the same time does not abandon that nation and in time provides it with the opportunity to change direction—as if a plan were in place? But maybe Dussel means much less than this sort of transcendent justice. Maybe he means only that the socioeconomic imbalances need to change.

I find all discourses of redemption, no matter their origin, worrisome. In this particular case, the underlying ethnopolitics—that sense of a Latino collectivity functioning as a tool for redemption—reminds me, as it has before, of Fichte. Fichte launched a cosmological politics in the name of the German nation. I call it "cosmological" because of its spiritualization of struggle. That is, for Fichte the struggles of a national people demanded movement toward freedom as a foundational condition that must be pursued. Freedom, then, as the release from suffering—that is, suffering as limitation in need of limitlessness—could occur through the self-recognition of the German people. It was their collective soul that they needed to recognize—and it was under the sign of the divine. If the construction of Germany as a response to French invasion seemed like a liberating act in 1808, today, in our own era of mobility, the nation-state is not a sign of liberation but a politics of the stationary. So Fichte's cosmological politics has lost some of its force. Or, rather, it has morphed into post-Marxist futurism, meaning that the spiritualized qualities of Fichte's nation have been replaced by the spiritualized, borderless multitudes of Michael Hardt and Antonio Negri.[65]

Let me be clear: I am not satisfied by these theories articulated at this table or the more polished versions that circulate in academia. Nevertheless, they vibrantly articulate a politics of presence at its farthest edge. These articulations seem to take note of the strain between the national and the transnational. Or, speaking more theoretically, they articulate the strain between Fichte and Hardt and Negri. Fichte thought the nation to be a sign of spiritual liberation, but in our own era of mobility borderless transnationalism is the sign of liberation. For Hardt and Negri,[66] liberation is the name of the game. Their sense of liberation must break free of the nation-state and become the freedom of transnational movement, the freedom to pursue labor. And this is also what the speakers eating breakfast this morning on Paseo Boricua want. They, too, are questioning the older rules of jus soli as well as jus sanguinis and broaching the possibilities of legalizing a kind of global *in transit*. There is a tentative real-world example: the EU has, in fits and starts, legalized a certain amount of internal transit within its borders, but this comes to a halt at its bordered edges. Moreover, right-wing anti-immigrant political parties have been on the increase across Europe.[67] So jus soli and jus sanguinis will not be erased at their foundations any time soon in the EU—nevertheless, they are being conceptually altered.

At any rate, what is circulating among these speakers is a kind of increasing realization regarding the politics of presence, a sense that the undocumented "present among us," who may be "just" menial laborers living in the shadows, represent nevertheless a deeper meaning—they might be the transformative muscle to change the face of a nation that has been historically oppressive to Latin America. They, coupled to their kin who remain alla, might become the conduit to the vast potentiality of Latin America. That is, together they might engineer an economic and spiritual redemption of North America. In my view, what is circulating here is a kind of spiritualized ethnocentrism that may be essentially archaic, as I have argued. However, when coupled with a politics of mobility, it becomes ultraprogressive or vanguardist. This coupling of a conservative ethnocentrism to progressive mobility does not mean that the first hollows out the second. Rather, it means that only as abstractions do contradictions have essential natures. In the cauldron of real life, ratios are made from the heat of necessity. I find this particular ratio disturbing.

Let me return briefly to my earlier analyses of "born into," "ritualized into," and "present in" or "those present among us" in order to reveal some of the disturbing ironies within the discourses of our speakers this morning. My central claim is that "born into" roots a politics of ethnocentrism, an ancient metaphysics, as well as a politics of the stationary. As we saw, "born into" seems to be psychically compelling because it is the way of nature, the most natural way of belonging to a family, or a community, or a nation, or, for that matter, an ethnicity. And "ritualized into," in the case of a nation, is, of course, an artificial solution when the real deal is not available. "Ritualized into," then, overcomes its deficit of authenticity through rituals that enact a kind of simulacra of "born into"—and this simulacra we call *naturalization*, a revealing term to be sure. It would seem, then, that "born into" and "ritualized into" are part of the substrate upon which the edifices of citizenship and ethnocentrism are built. Today, most people think it is "natural"[68] to cut the planet into nations or ethnicities, and most think that the most viable way to belong to both is to be "born into" them. Most people also think that a politics of the stationary is a practical and effective means for maintaining the integrity of nations and ethnicities. Hence it is ironic to link ethnocentrism to a politics of mobility—but clearly not impossible.

So our speakers this morning, eating breakfast at a small restaurant on Paseo Boricua, are dismantling the edifice of American ethnocentric politics with an ethnocentric politics rooted in Latin America. They are attacking the current structures of "born into" and "ritualized into" citizenship insofar as these help to construct a conservative politics rooted in American whiteness. Those structures were ready to deport someone like Elvira Arellano, who clearly was "present among us" and living with her son, who, ironically, was "born into" the United States. And so she took sanctuary just two blocks from here. And again in 2017, on behalf of this same group, I wrote an even broader statement, as described earlier, which tries to apply the idea of sanctuary to entire neighborhoods. But beyond these instances of sanctuary, what interests these speakers is the massiveness of Latin America, its sheer presence as production and consumption. Elvira's *presence* spoke for the whole of it. The vision here is that of multitudes as a transformative force pressing against the underbelly of English-speaking North America, not so much in physical rebellion but simply waiting out North American monopolization of capital. In their view, Latin America is rising as an inevitable future, shifting the scales until it swarms across both Americas and rewrites the English-speaking identity. Ultimately, the speakers want to see the evening out of inequality, but they do not trust that such efforts can come from the English-speaking Americas. It can only come, they believe, from Latin America amassing its own capital, its own lending banks, its own version of the International Monetary Fund.[69] Meanwhile, the tip of the lance, ever growing in the United States, will shift voting power until domestic policy gets rewritten to favor the likes of Arellano in the same ways that it grabbed power in California and was signed into law by Governor Brown.[70] Presence here, then, is being conceived as a kind of mythic unity harnessing sheer numbers even as it harnesses capital. What animates these speakers is literally not the position of asking, or even demanding, from the position of underdog but of simply flipping hierarchical relations because one's numbers just outnumbered the opponents. They relish the sweet, silent vengeance of it all—as I do.

But I am not fully convinced. The future that these speakers project is an artifact of the subjugations of colonialism. They need not name colonialism with all its words like Spain, the United States, foreign banks, lost wars and snuffed rebellions, NAFTA, CAFTA, or neoliberalism, for colonialism today has no exact referent. Indeed, for those around the table colonialism even goes by the name of gentrification, which has sent the Puerto Ricans in Chicago into local migration more than once. So the term *colonialism* is multireferential—or better, a kind of nameless dull haunting that links past to present. The speakers want to redeem this haunting that organizes so much of Latin America, and so they project Evo and Obama as flares of liberation. But then the flares return to Earth, and we are left with ceaseless hope that never seems to achieve completion. And then, seemingly, a flare not representing a politics of ever-expanding mobilities but, rather, a politics of the stationary shoots President Donald Trump and Nigel Farage into the 2017 night sky, and it, too, claims to be a politics of world-historical change with cosmological overtones in the name of the "people."[71]

Why isn't there more skepticism regarding the liberatory capacity of the multitudes and of the messianism that seems to underlie these sorts of historical narratives? Sadly, I suspect that those who will write the rules of this emerging future of integration that Dussel talks about will be the transnational network of the rich, a constituency already fully formed. And already they sneer at transparency, and they sneer at the slow-moving bodies of menial laborers *in transit*, for the rich, in contrast, are the educated who move capital electronically and hide it when they need to. Nor do I believe that the rules of jus soli and jus sanguinis and all the practical organization of populations that nation-states enable can be easily discounted. Citizenship at its heart does, indeed, divide a nation. But to fight against citizenship's territorialization of justice in the name of some broader universal justice fetishizes the idea of justice. Justice can only ever be territorialized, meaning that someone's dream of inclusion will be someone else's exclusion.[72] Moreover, our speakers seem to have a certain enthusiasm for a militant *latinidad*. The term mobilizes a unity of language, culture, and color at a transhemispheric level and in so doing gives the likes of Dallacroce permission to mobilize language, culture, and whiteness in the name of the United States. Further, latinidad may conceptually erode attachments to specific nations, but it reestablishes attachments at the transhemispheric level. Conceptually, then, jus soli and jus sanguinis remain intact inside the idea of latinidad. As for the ideology of "born into," it is as applicable to ethnocentrism as it is to the nation. Hence the problematics of these terms have not been eliminated. They remain alive and kicking underneath political positions that want to do away with them. Perhaps because of my own residual resentments, I share the speakers' desires to see the hegemony of the English-speaking Americas overrun by Latin America, and yet the deeper one reflects on the methods and motives (an ethnopolitics) that might create such a future—given the long, endlessly repeated history of such things—the more worrisome it becomes.

Are there ways to not fall into the liberatory-messianic narratives, the narratives of ethnopolitics or militant latinidad that were born as responses to the colonialisms of racial, political, economic, and even spiritual subjugation? A theory of ratio suggests that these militant narratives, as necessary as they may be, are always already structured by the discourses that they wish to break. Hence even at the moment that the militant narratives try to liberate themselves from those discourses, subjugation in some form persists somewhere in the "new" conceptualizations. Thus a theory of ratio suggests that a deeper break never arrives. For instance, I have been arguing that the structures of "born into" and "ritualized into" shape the nation-state and its notions of citizenship and help to bring into being a politics of the stationary. But these same structures—functioning, admittedly, at a different scale—also underpin the narratives of ethnopolitics and militant latinidad. How and when might we break with "born into" and "ritualized into"?

I have tried to argue on behalf of a "present in" or "present among us." Perhaps it will never have the political or legal force of "born into" and "ritualized into," but it should be acknowledged somehow. After all, the "present among us" are substantively performing what legal residency rules require, but they cannot be awarded legal standing under a more rigorous politics of the stationary. The "present among us," as far as I can tell, represent the need for a deepening of a politics of mobility and freedom. They are among the consequences of globalization, which means that they are simultaneously "present among us" but also present elsewhere, shaping the economies of both here and there, alla and *aquí*. Perhaps a new geography, driven largely by undocumented laborers, is indeed pressing up and into the current geography of the bordered planet, and perhaps over time this new geography will profoundly alter the politics of the stationary.

My complaint for the time being is that the speakers at this little restaurant in April 2010 continue to fetishize cosmological politics and its trope of the "people" sallying forth with righteous truth in their breasts. I no longer believe this. The "people" do not represent righteous truth—or, better, whose righteous truth do they represent? Nigel Farage's or Enrique Dussel's? My suspicion is that both the right and left make use of a sentimentalized rhetoric posing as ontological truth. The idea of democracy legitimizes the trope of the people and vice versa. I prefer to empty these god terms of their power to convince.

In January 2011, Dussel was once again in Chicago, delivering lectures at Northwestern University, DePaul University, and the University of Chicago. The DePaul lecture went into more detail about the importance of the messianic, and he and I talked after. This time, he was making the significant point that messianic time is the moment of suffering. In this sense, Latin America's history has been embedded in messianic time insofar as it has seen a succession of oppressions: the indigenous at the hands of Spain and after the revolutions of independence, or all Latin American peoples under the colonial boot of Spain, the United States, and, more recently, the financial markets. In the United States, politics functions differently, he continued, for democracy here does not function messianically, that is, as a rupturing of current conditions, but rather as the struggle to further the prevailing conditions. The messianic moment creates the messianic leader, and here is the person who "receives the call of the people to risk one's life." Without this risk and danger, there is no messianism. During an engagement with myself and others, I claimed that messianism might fetishize the goodness of the people. I also asked, "Who are these 'people' who supposedly speak on the side of goodness and right? Do the people hold a coherent ideology, an essence, that is representable by the messianic leader?" I am afraid that I sounded like a cynic. Dussel replied that "the natural place of power is the people," and that the "first principle to be affirmed is the life of the people." In this sense, "power becomes ethical, and the people ethically limit power." Such talk inspires a commitment to altering the suffering of others, and so it seems that the cosmological politics of the visionary left that I have been trying to distinguish here presumes a kind of essential goodness in the "breasts of the people." Guaranteeing such an essential goodness is, of course, most difficult. But still at another level, how do we make sense of this implied cleavage in which the "people" come to represent not the entirety of the "people," as its very definition seems to say, but only the segment that cannot participate in that entirety and perhaps who are intentionally blocked from participating?

Cosmological politics founds itself on this segment, on this cleavage in which the "people" cannot refer to the whole but only a segment of the whole, the segment that suffers—and so it is that these "people" have right on their side while the others are in the wrong. Sometimes cosmological politics claims a historical unfoldment in which this segment, rising up in the name of an essential goodness, puts balance back into the world, rights the illegitimate concentration of power in the hands of the few. In the presidential campaign of 2016, many of those who supported candidate Trump identified with his call to the "forgotten man," which is another way of speaking cosmologically to the liberation of the "people."[73]

In contrast to this cosmological politics is the work of the political theorist Robert Michels and his claims that there is no politics of the right or left that does not become oligarchic.[74] The move toward oligarchy is a consequence of organization. Michels, who saw this up close in the working of socialist parties and trade unions, claimed that whatever essential goodness might exist in the breasts of the people will become altered as they encounter the pressures of organizing effective mass movements. Leaders and cliques (oligarchies) will arise, sacrificing some segments and preserving others in order to establish coherence. In short, on becoming organized politically groups lose their innocent goodness; hence there is no unfoldment of a righteousness that will put an end to the profound wrongs that power can create. Rather, we have the "wrongs" of power moving cyclically from one set of hands to another.

4

Property and Its Entanglements

A protest sign can sometimes say more than what a protestor first imagines. One day in 2015, I was searching the internet for protest signs. I was looking for themes that supported rights for the undocumented but also themes defending immigration restriction. Among the immigration restrictionists, one sign caught my attention:

> This Is America
> Get Off
> My Property

Small American flags were drawn in strategic places. The sign was obviously handmade. The protestor was with a larger group of protestors whose nearby signs made "love for the USA" especially clear. But this sign suggested something more than standard nativism and patriotism. How did the ideas of property and ownership get into the conversation? How did a defense of America also become a defense of property? The protestor was naming America as their property, their possession, as if individuals like this person had some sort of ownership over the nation. Hence the sign suggested that the undocumented, such as Elvira Arellano, are trespassers. Regrettably, a few years later, when I tried to get the reproduction rights to the photograph, the internet had lost track of the website. But to this day, the protestor and the sign strike me as revelatory. A host of metaphors seemed to be swimming together. What enabled them to swim inside a single thought?

In this book, I've been trying to get at the deep common sense—the naturalized rhetorics, as it were—through which people hear and speak utterances that few pay attention to because they seem to be part of the air we breathe. This common sense begins as a set of presumptions that are native to the democratic imaginary, but a closer examination suggests that the presumptions go deeper than that. I am thinking particularly of the long-standing distinction in Euro-American politics between active and passive citizens. Given the various strands that compose this distinction, it might be best to think of it as a kind of psychic world that has historically preferred the active citizen over the passive citizen.[1] That is, the active citizen, at a practical level, is a law-abiding, taxpaying property owner who invests himself in his polis through deliberation and the vote. These practices help to establish merit, but more deeply they are practices that enable self-realization, autonomy, and political freedom (as Kant might argue). Consider that being law-abiding—that is, being legal—may have special standing, for legality maximizes the potential to act, and legality grants the freedom to act fully. (The "fully" here, of course, refers to permissible freedoms according to the law and not absolute freedoms.)

So if we frame the protestor in the picture through the psychic world of the active citizen—the protestor is, after all, an activist protesting—then perhaps we can begin to understand what goads the person. I argue, ultimately, that the distinction between the active and passive citizen establishes inequality at the heart of citizenship, a concern that worried Kant in his political writings. By mobilizing the rhetoric of inequality that exists at least psychically within this distinction—and therefore within citizenship—the active citizen eagerly separates himself from other citizens whom he does not consider equal to him, and even more so from others who are not citizens. But the relationship between equality and inequality is even more complex than this. Who really wants to be equal or substitutable with some other? Indeed, no one lives her life according to equality. Every decision that is made, from the most important to the least, from whom to choose as a lover to the mundane choices that constitute how we spend the day, is based on preference and not the equality of choices or the equality of people or the equality of things that we want. So equality—on its face—would seem to be a conflicted ideology. As theory, or deterritorialized concept, it seizes our imagination, but as practice we hesitate because we do not know how to fully territorialize it, or live it—and when we don't live it, we become guilty, or not. The distinction, then, between the active and passive citizen reveals an ambiguity that haunts the ideologies of equality.

Are we again inside a conundrum, an unresolvable antinomy? On the one hand, merit seems to be something that many people aspire to, or, like the protestor, they use it as a bludgeon as they measure others. The protestor seems to read the citizen privileges honored by nation-states as a form of merit, "rightfully" justifying their superiority. On the other hand, equality is also an opposing psychic imperative that many people also run toward because it is more forgiving and accepting. Recall in the previous chapter that I argued that the undocumented "present among us" share the same polis as the "born into" and the "ritualized into," and together they shape a social and economic commons, which is a type of equality. The undocumented that I have known are typically eager to enter this polis and to establish their accomplishments as equal to that of any citizen. That is, they are eager to establish their merit through hard work, the paying of taxes, and the ownership of property, and rather often they accomplish just that. Still, whatever genuine merit they have gained, or whatever commonality with citizens they have established, can be shockingly and quickly dismissed as irrelevant when the state decides to honor first its citizens. Hence whatever merit the undocumented have gained does not count in the eyes of those who may favor the psychic world of the active, legitimate citizen, because from that perspective "illegality" does not represent merit. In sum, the rhetoric of merit—and here I include the ideology of meritocracy[2]—is rather eager in many instances to denounce the rhetoric of equality, to obscure any notion of a commons, indeed, to destroy it because in the last instance merit and meritocracy can identify deeply with inequality.

Thus I turn to the idea of property, more specifically to the psychic world of property rights and legal protections of ownership that encourage people to really believe that they own the things of the world and can thereby separate themselves from others. That is, I am tracking a host of metaphors supplied by democracy. Each metaphor is a denial. One metaphor (private property rights) denies that there is a commons that links citizens to noncitizens; another metaphor (ownership) denies that all economic relations constitute a remarkably dense commons that makes it difficult to cut and dice the world into mine versus thine. Hence "get off my property" belongs to the psychic world of a people devoted to commerce in the same way that the privileges of the citizen belong to a psychic world of nations. Both these psychic worlds hold the idea of the commons at arm's length.

←↥→

I want to let this protestor and his sign "speak" a bit more. "This Is America—Get Off My Property" seems to hold two conceptual structures or logics that are vastly important to modern democracies: the sovereign individual as holder of property rights and the sovereign nation-state. If the individual "owns" property, does the nation's citizenry "own," by extension, the nation-state? And if both are owners, do they have a similar right, on the sole basis of ownership, to refuse the presence of another? Or, phrasing it a little differently: Is the sovereignty of a private property owner similar to the sovereignty of a nation-state? How does one make these instantaneous conceptual leaps, or are they not leaps at all but part of the easy air that we breathe? Rhetorically speaking, the arguments in the poster appear to be thickly clustered enthymemes[3] that depend on the idea of ownership functioning as a kind of commonsense. That is, *ownership* as a term is referentially open, and so, if one's common sense allows it, the word can easily float beyond concepts of individual ownership and attach itself to entities at another scale, such as the nation-state, if the idea of sovereignty links the two. The ability of a term to move across different scales, or even domains of discourse, might be called *rhetorical resonance*. Rhetorical resonance could not occur if there were not already in existence a commons of shared belief—in this case, a shared belief that relies on the privileges of sovereignty.

In this chapter, I examine individual ownership versus a commons that cannot be individually owned. At times, I call this distinction a "politics of individuation" versus a "politics of the organism." These two politics are in ratio and cannot be pried apart. My conclusions regarding ownership emerged over many years of watching gentrification move through the city of Chicago. More recently, I have become the president of the board of a nonprofit affordable housing agency. That position has provided a front-row seat from which to think further about gentrification. Such agencies typically attempt to mitigate the negative impacts of gentrification by offering otherwise "displaced" peoples the opportunity to stay in those neighborhoods where they have lived for a long time. Still, trying to name gentrification as purely negative is as difficult as trying to grab air. There are many not-well-off owners, for instance, who bought when prices were low and thus profit later from gentrification. Furthermore, just below the gentrification that I was seeing there seemed to be a conceptual problem that deserved analysis—namely, the idea of property that can manifest itself either as private ownership or ownership by a commons. In sum, I have come to understand gentrification as the capitalization of poor communities in which low-valued private property functions as a kind of speculative futures market. Or, borrowing Marx's language, a home becomes imagined more for its exchange value than for its use value. But underneath these definitions are numerous intricacies that defy easy analysis and, indeed, resist many of our political and moral dispositions.

So I return once again to the poster "This Is America . . ." in order to amplify the earlier point about two kinds of sovereignty: the sovereign individual as holder of property rights and the sovereign nation-state. Might we understand these sovereignties as discrete, bounded entities making claims over discrete, bounded land? I want to argue that the rhetorical resonance moving implicitly through the poster is that of private property, the nation-state, and the individual, and that each of these is being imagined as discrete, self-contained entities. In other words, each of these is similar, but they occur at different scales. Broadly speaking, these autonomous, singular entities are important operations in today's managerial modernity. Indeed, we might say that managerial modernity has produced a politics of individuation consisting of sovereign singularities such as autonomous selves, demarcated property, and bordered nation-states. Consider that for Kant, rational judgment and moral action depended on the autonomous individual;[4] similarly, the autonomous state for Adam Smith was the proper entity for the emergence of a rational and ultimately moral economy that might benefit the nation's citizens.[5] Autonomy as rulership over one's proper domain[6] links these entities of different scale. Additionally, in order to protect the autonomy of the individual and, by extension, the nation-state, we have developed a list of negative and positive rights. And certainly one of the more important of these protected, positive rights is the right to own private property. In other words, liberal democracy, in particular, emphasizes a carving of the world into a set of ownership claims. Thus the things of the world become distributed to many owners, who make legally protected claims over entities that are now formally theirs. In sum, the evolution of managerial modernity has placed considerable emphasis on the cultivation of rightfully protected autonomy at different scales. The result is, as described earlier, the nomosphere, which, among other things, provides clarity for managing the world.

Consider further that one of the central concerns of the democratic imaginary is the need to release human potential. Hence through property rights, the modern, democratic state tells its citizenry that each individual has the chance to make and keep wealth—and in so doing better herself.[7] Further, the individual ownership of a geographic space becomes mirrored at a larger scale in the bordered nation-state through pretty much the same reasoning. Bordered and segmented land overseen by either individuals or nation-states seems to be foundational within modernist logic and rhetoric, so much so that a cornerstone of any development project in any part of the world today starts with the establishment of property rights alongside the rights of individuals and, more broadly, minority group rights, which is another "individuation" in my view. All this occurs because the emerging nation-state must shore up its competency by establishing a set of protections and laws that will enable the prosperity of its domestic population. According to international liberalism, the ultimate goal for such emerging nations is to become free and equal among the family of nations. Indeed, I witnessed this consistently in the various ministries of Kosova as the UN and other international bodies engaged in nation-building. Here, then, is the field of resonance. Each term of autonomy (the individual, private property, the nation-state) is a kind of "spatial capture" sanctioned by law and thus considered a "just" way for partitioning the world in front of us.[8] Hence autonomy echoes or resonates across these conceptual apparatuses, reinforcing a thoroughgoing politics of individuation functioning at different scales despite the fact that these autonomous entities, in practice, are less autonomous than the sociolegal order makes them out to be. Indeed, the politics of individuation and the autonomy that it attempts to guarantee cast a shadow over the commons and communality until the commons becomes difficult to see.

←↕→

A "politics of individuation" is significant for the manufacturing of what I have been calling "managerial modernity." It behooves us at this point to take the long view by asking: What was property prior to being put to use by managerial modernity? For instance, what was land before it became property? What did it look like before it became individuated according to modern ownership rules that might enhance the release of potentiality? Those are daunting questions that cannot be fully answered here because they span too many millennia and too many locations. Nevertheless, I can provide a quick sketch. The anthropologists C. M. Hann and Alan Macfarlane provide hints to the answers to those questions. Hann starts us off:

> But what exactly is meant by greater individuation as far as land is concerned? The popular modern sense of property may be foreshadowed in Roman law, which allowed for the ownership of slaves as private property; but in fact the great bulk of land in the ancient world was farmed by peasant small-holders and transmitted within their communities according to custom. Most historians would argue that the same was true under feudalism. In a formal, legal sense the land was ultimately owned by the

> king, who granted land to lords or "tenants-in-chief" in exchange for services. These in turn granted plots to "mesne" tenants, who might or might not be the actual cultivators. At each level the tenant acknowledged obligations to provide services in return for the rights devolved to him. The peasants had exclusive rights to use particular plots of land and to transmit them to their heirs; but did English villagers of the thirteenth century view their land as a commodity that *individuals* could own and transact on a market? According to George Homans, the concept of private property in land was not yet a central principle of social organization. Villagers were a "social organism" rather than an agglomeration of individuals.[9]

The idea of private property as land that can be exchanged on the open market is a consequence of numerous transformations. Macfarlane elucidates many of these in his studies of early Europe and Japan, but at least two transformations in particular, an ideological one and a material one, seem to capture the general spirit of his argument. I will take up the ideological one first. According to Macfarlane and others, thirteenth-century England already had an "individualistic form of land tenure . . . linked to England's later development into industrial capitalism."[10] These systems of ownership were bound up with layers of rights and obligations overseen more by common law than Roman civil law, and it is common law that seems to point toward the development of capitalist markets.[11] For instance, can land be infinitely divided among heirs, or is land indivisible but the rights to it infinitely expandable? Roman civil law was more associated with the first notion and common law with the second.[12] So under Roman civil law, maintaining the integrity of a single piece of land over time is legally difficult, but under common law, land retains a permanent character while the rights to it can be exchanged. In this sense, common law allows for more flexibility. Macfarlane argues along with many historians and anthropologists that, ultimately, property is a "relationship between people in relation to 'things.'"[13] But the flexibility of common law allowed for the idea of land to become less of a social relation and more of a *thing* whose rights over it, eventually, could be swapped during market exchanges.[14] That is, the deep rules of social relation that provide a tenant farmer with cultivation rights over a piece of land that can be passed on to an heir but always with obligations to a local lord gave way, in time, to exchange rights in the marketplace. Perhaps it can be described this way: land had to become free of its social relations, such as customary obligations. Land had to move beyond the social and become more abstract—that is, become a more flexible entity subject only to exchange rights in the marketplace. Economic anthropology has long claimed that every society has an economy, but only a few of these create economies that function more abstractly, like an individuated sphere free of social relations.[15] In sum, those economies marked by self-interest and the drive toward efficiency become more abstract, less captured by social relations, and therefore can encourage pure accumulation. All this is what Macfarlane means by ideological transformation.

In contrast, material transformations, Macfarlane argues, concern the strength of the state. Property rights tend to emerge as challenges to the centralization of power, but at the same time, like other rights, they require the power of the state for their enforcement. That is, the state needs to be sufficiently strong to prevent one's neighbors from becoming Hobbesian predators against one's property but not strong enough to resist the emergence of ownership claims from the classes challenging the king's claim as ultimate owner. In other words, for the idea of private property to emerge the state cannot be absolutist; otherwise *it* becomes the Hobbesian predator. Under constant foreign siege, a state may well attempt to become absolutist because it needs taxation to finance its wars and standing armies to dissuade domestic rebellion. In these contexts, individual ownership claims can be destabilizing. Conditions of peace, then, are also helpful for the evolution of property rights, and it is through this lens, finally, that Macfarlane looks at that other island nation, Japan, and finds similar sociopolitical conditions. Ultimately, then, the idea of individual property ownership is not just about the ideological transformation of social relations into market exchanges. It is also a story about power relations[16] in which the self-interested state accommodates the self-interests of individuals under its domain.

Thus even though the state, holding absolute power, has the capacity to dominate its domain, it behooves the state to fragment that power into smaller powers and to construct a world of horizontal distributions. By decentralizing power and placing it into the waiting arms of all sorts of individuated, semi-autonomous entities, power now feels more distributed and thus more liberating. Whether a more efficient, just, and better world emerges due to such innovations is not pristinely clear—though, clearly, the belief that a better world does emerge has become naturalized among most conservatives, liberals, and libertarians. That is, celebrating the rise of individual selves; declaring these selves to have positive and negative rights; dividing land according to the authority of such individuals acting in a marketplace; establishing nation-states as management systems for property claims for the sake of releasing the capacities of its citizens and the nation's resources; and dividing such a state even further into smaller, more local control in order to make the system ever more efficient and productive—are these not strategies that characterize liberal democracy's version of managerial modernity? The logical apparatus behind these strategies resonates across a variety of discursive fields. According to federalism, for instance, decentralizing the burdens of management leads to less subjugation and enhances efficiency. Decentralization becomes a code word for greater freedom, more individual creativity, and more democratic experimentation. Here is the democratic imaginary and its commitments to individuation and autonomous entities that conservative, liberal, and libertarian dispositions have come to accept. That is, through decentralization and related ideologies and practices liberal democracy becomes that type of managerial modernity that expands its rulership by obscuring the completeness of its rule.

But this historical, legal, and sociopolitical analysis of property and the rise of individuation and autonomous entities have also led to the rise of certain visceral reactions that underlie public discourses around property and the nation-state. The poster "This Is America" and its rhetoric of "myness" totalizes the idea of possession by extending notions of private property to the scale of the nation-state. When I did fieldwork with the Illinois Minutemen (immigration restrictionists), this sense of "owning" America and even "owning" democracy was central to their ideology. (Recall my earlier discussion of Michelle Dallacroce.) Their idea of ownership was visceral. They imagined ownership as something constitutionally guaranteed to them and therefore protected by such democratic mechanisms as the vote, rights discourses, and such hoary and ultimately poignant nostrums as "The people are sovereign."[17] I say "poignant" because "myness discourse"—the discourse of possession—seems to expand the self over space and things, and this expanded self, inevitably, can only be fragile. Fragility or impermanence may be the condition of everything, but it is also intolerable as a state of existence. In this sense, "myness discourse" attempts to answer the problem of fragility by declaring to others that this is mine and not yours, and in so doing alleviate the fragility. One way to securitize one's space and the things in it is to expand one's domain of accumulation and to provide such a person with the "right" to do so. "This Is America," then, through my interpretive lens at least, articulates something more than racism. It articulates an immigration restrictionist's fear of losing national space that, in turn, resonates with a property owner's fear of losing wealth to taxes or declining property values. And behind all that, I believe, are long-standing political and economic narratives in which the values of individuation and autonomy encourage the rise of inflated selves in an atomized world.

In sum, behind ideologies of autonomy lie existential problems: How do we face the infinitude of all that is before us with such fragile, insecure bodies? At one historical moment, apparently, the idea described earlier by Hann of the "social organism" answered unconsciously that existential problem. Today's liberalism provides another unconscious answer. It says that the individuation of the self with rights to property and citizenship rights to a nation-state is the best way to securitize our existence. Parables of collectivity have been replaced by parables of individuation. We cut and border the world. We create autonomous entities at different scales and make them even more real through legal means. We defend these new parables with great ferocity. It is mine, ours, not yours. In order to legitimize the ferocity, we build a labyrinth of guarantees, laws, and rights that will allow us to go before deliberative bodies and stake our claims. The individual self becomes almost inviolable, as does private property and the nation-state.[18] The idea of autonomy further justifies itself to the extent that it is seen as an efficient mechanism for maximizing the acquisition of needs. At the same time, the constellation of laws that protect and expand these individuations begins to shape an understanding of justice as something that rightfully ought to preserve autonomy across as many domains as possible.[19] Thus a field of resonance gets established in fairly thoroughgoing terms. The poster "This Is America," then, taps these resonances of autonomy that today compose so many of the values and practices of managerial modernity, which, in turn, composes much of daily life. Or so goes my argument.

←↨→

I want to continue developing this narrative on property by exploring a contemporary scene that seems to illuminate how the idea of property and property rights does indeed aim to protect against an existential world full of fear and insecurity. The scene is the so-called Arab Spring. Not surprisingly, the economist Hernando de Soto and the French philosopher and communist Alain Badiou have opposite interpretations of the same events, and in their conflicting interpretations ones sees a politics of individuation in a death struggle with a politics of the social organism. De Soto encourages an international expansion of liberalism centered on the idea of property and property rights, and thus defends a politics of individuation as a remedy for much of the world's informal economies. He assumes that if this remedy can be institutionalized at a global level, then the potentiality of both individuals and nations will be released. Badiou disagrees.

It is generally agreed that the catalyst for the Arab Spring was the self-immolation of a Tunisian street vendor, Mohammed Bouazizi. Bouazizi had been unable to get a license to sell his vegetables at the market, and so he sold his goods informally. But the last straw was the confiscation of his scales, the destruction of his cart by civil authorities, and, finally, a humiliating slap in the face by a female officer. In despair, he set fire to himself in a public square. Many still consider him a martyr. But he was not pursuing any rhetoric of martyrdom. Martyrdom uses the body as ultimate evidence, or what might be called an "inartistic proof" in the rhetorical tradition of Aristotle and Quintilian. That is, martyrdom is delusional for those who do not believe in the cause; however, for believers, self-sacrifice transforms a truth claim into an indisputable truth outside all the artifices and manipulations of language, the pure presence of truth stripped of any subjective interpretation. Self-sacrifice exists at the extremes of humanity and thus may slip toward the more than human, the truth incarnate. This is how martyrdom persuades. But no, Bouazizi's self-immolation was not an example of the rhetoric of martyrdom. It was more akin to the expressive rhetorics of abandonment and despair, for he was not defending some abstract principle but succumbing to the fact that he had no solution to his humiliation (or *hogra*, in the Tunisian dialect) at the hands of civil authorities.

What does De Soto make of all this? In his film titled *Unlikely Heroes of the Arab Spring*, he argues that the best method for increasing the wealth of the poor is to strengthen their property rights.[20] This argument is consistent with his earlier work among squatter settlements.[21] There he made the case that squatters should be given rightful ownership to the structures that they have built and the land on which the structures sit. Granting rightful ownership to poor squatters, he claimed, would enable them to convert their effort into collateral, which then could be used to get small loans that might lead to modest capital accumulation. His analysis of Mohammed Bouazizi's role in the Arab Spring, then, is one more step in his broader argument that the structures of liberalism have not become liberal enough if they have not fully incorporated the poor. That is, De Soto has always favored the formalization of the extralegal economy, believing that such a move legalizes the otherwise hidden assets of the poor. Ultimately, he believes that the globalization of property rights on behalf of the poor will inevitably challenge local oligarchies and the favoritism that they receive from corrupt governance.

De Soto's economic theories lean to the right. Indeed, he belongs to a tradition in economic theory that has written extensively about the virtues of property rights and their legal enforcement as synonymous with life betterment.[22] This tradition leans to the right because it favors the distribution not of property but of property rights along with all the legal protections that bolster the iconic individual of liberalism. Thus De Soto defends the interests of the poor, he says, by offering them legally enforced ownership claims that can protect their tools and possessions from confiscation by government authorities and other elites. After all, if the authorities continually denied Bouazizi a license to sell in the marketplace and then attacked his "informal" practices by destroying his means of livelihood, what channels were open to him if he had no formal means of redress? His livelihood had been destroyed along with his relations with farmers and clients. De Soto argues that the oligarchic classes do not wish to defend ownership claims on behalf of someone like Bouazizi because elites are trying to stifle competition from below. Elites are too interested in preventing rival accumulations of wealth.

But addressing the problems of the poor from another tradition are the French radical theorists of the eighteenth century, such as Gracchus Babeuf and later Marx and Engels. For them, a distribution of rights was wholly inadequate compared to the actual distribution of the thing itself—namely, property. A contemporary voice in this latter tradition is Alain Badiou, and in *The Rebirth of History: Times of Riots and Uprisings* he addresses the likes of Mohammed Bouazizi in the various riots of the Arab Spring. Now, Badiou and De Soto are equally interested in the poor and just as suspicious of oligarchies, but Badiou, in contrast, wants to see the overthrow of Western ideologies of wealth-making so as to establish what he calls "movement communism": "The uprising possesses in a very pure form—no doubt the purest since the Paris Commune—all the features of what must be called a movement communism. 'Communism' means here: the creation in common of the collective destiny. . . . The Tunisian and Egyptian people are telling us this: to rise up, construct the public site of movement communism, and defend it by all possible means while inventing the successive steps of our action—such is the reality of the popular politics of emancipation."[23]

Badiou in his short book is interested in theorizing his notion of the event and using the idea of the riot as a case in point. Ultimately, he is arguing that these riots are not signs of a coming Western inclusion, as the European media at the time interpreted the riots, but as signs pointing to an "exit from the West, a 'de-Westernization.'"[24] "Basically, our rulers and our dominant media have suggested a simple interpretation of the riots in the Arab world: what is expressed in them is what might be called a *desire for the West*. A desire to 'enjoy' everything that we, the drowsy, satiated inhabitants of the affluent countries, already 'enjoy.' A desire finally to be included in the 'civilized world.' . . . In so doing, Westerners wrapped in the flag of Right forget that their alleged power to state the Good is nothing but the modernized name for imperial interventionism."[25]

What De Soto and Badiou share is an attack on the oligarchic classes and an absolute commitment to the expansion of human potentiality to marginalized classes such as the poor. Their interpretations are clearly opposed, but they share the deep bones of the same argument—namely, that modernist political solutions of whatever stripe share a moral urgency to expand potentiality. Thus Badiou's solution sees among the Arab poor a rejection of global capitalism; De Soto sees among the same poor a need and desire to enter into global capitalism by instituting a property rights regime that has been unfolding for hundreds of years. De Soto, in promoting this vast transformation of the world's extralegal economy into a legal economy, is, in effect, defending the globalization of liberal democracy's version of managerial modernity, particularly its legal structure, on behalf of the poor. This expanding legal structure in which every inch of social life becomes occupied by liberalism's version of the rule of law is, using David Delaney's term again, the *nomosphere*. De Soto sees nothing oppressive about this spreading nomosphere—indeed, for him, the globalization of the liberal nomosphere will result in a social upheaval leading to betterment. That is, De Soto argues for the release of potentiality stored inside the creative abilities of everyone, such as Bouazizi, against the institutionalized self-interests of elites. From De Soto's perspective, a variety of Marxisms has failed to accomplish this move from potentiality to actuality. On the one hand, De Soto wants to relegate Marxism to the dustbin of history; on the other hand, Badiou wants to relegate De Soto and others like him to the dustbin of history.

Badiou, to be fair, does not talk much about property in his account of the Arab Spring, but when he does, property is a negative institution.[26] Is his general silence about property a dark hole in his theorization? Is the ownership of property, whether the emphasis is upon collective or individual ownership, the central issue for life maintenance? If so, then doesn't every radical account of political and economic change demand its own ontological account of property? Without such an account, does property become an enigma and the proposed social change directionless? For instance, Badiou just might initially agree with De Soto that Bouazizi and the Arab poor in general need to have legal clarifications and protections that would grant ownership rights over the means of livelihood and shelter. He might agree because he shares De Soto's interest in the release of potentiality against the abuses of elites, and court-protected ownership claims become one vehicle for the gathering up of potentiality. But then would such moves imply increasing liberalization and democratization, and, therefore, Westernization? At some point in his evolving argument, Badiou would have to have an opinion about the role of property in *emancipation*, one of his key terms. For instance, socialist democracies and liberal democracies provide individuals with legally protected ownership claims, but are these sufficiently emancipatory systems by his account, or does Badiou demand some other, more emancipatory organization of property rights? Again, my argument is that property rights establish relations to land and things, and thus social relations. Thus the beingness of things becomes entangled with the beingness of humans—that is, these rights are the material foundations by which we imagine *potentiality*, a term that Badiou would link to emancipation. But without an account of property rights, Badiou's program of "movement communism" has no way to articulate its difference from De Soto's liberalism and indeed may replicate it—and if that is true, then Badiou's theory skewers itself.

And what about De Soto? Consider that the granting of private property rights leads to a future that cannot restrain an ever-advancing accumulation of wealth. I talked about the irony of this problem earlier in the book: liberal democracy in particular promises the horizontal distribution of power and money by granting everyone the right to vertical accumulation—thus instituting a kind of ceaseless, "creative destruction" of elites—but then it cannot rightfully cap how much an individual may accumulate. Socialist democracies, in contrast, can rightfully cap through very high taxation. At any rate, consider the following: if Bouazizi were given strong ownership rights that could be legally enforced, he might expand his business by replacing his cart with a truck and thereby expand his purchases and thus his number of clients. He might expand further and open a grocery store and then several stores, and his descendants, through generous inheritance laws, which also belong to a strong private property rights regime, might purchase entire farms and expand into fertilizer production. They might become monopolists and even oligarchs, hooking themselves to the political establishment to protect their investments as they try to crush both rival elites and forces emerging from below. De Soto's liberalism is an investment in the release of potentiality, and when it starts to curb a kind of excess of potentiality by encouraging high rates of taxation and regulation, and discouraging the rise of monopolies, it begins to encounter its own contradictions.

I return to an earlier point: property rights are one of the cornerstones of a particular envisioning of the economy. There are many types of economy, but market economies are engaged in a specific struggle to overcome an array of social obligations that tend to limit possible efficiencies, mobility, and accumulation. That is, market economies struggle to become their own entity, an independent sphere of activity that cannot be fully determined by the "social organism." Of course, market economies do not so much erode the social obligations that restrain them but, rather, cultivate another set of social obligations that help to release the potentiality of markets themselves and in the process shape a different kind of social organism. Stating this more broadly, we can say that "a politics of individuation" is in ratio with a "politics of the social organism" and that De Soto and Badiou are examples of that ratio. In a sense, they try to pull that ratio apart in order to establish the truth of their politics. For instance, De Soto emphasizes the politics of individuation as a cure for the poverty of the Middle East. Under his regime, Bouazizi and others like him might start thinking of themselves over time as rights-bearing individuals whose interests can be protected in the courts, and this consolidation of an ethos of individuation would strain against an ethos of social obligation. Badiou, presumably, would call this "Westernization." Further, would De Soto's solution exacerbate the rise of elites and oligarchs that De Soto tried to solve in the first place? Badiou, in contrast, emphasizes some form of a "politics of the social organism," as evident in his term *movement communism*, but in not specifying how his solution addresses the problem of property he may simply be rearticulating liberalism.

Ultimately, the idea of property is a confounding notion. It references a historical invention that marks a transformation from "thing," such as land, into something else. More broadly, it references a materiality that is also a potentiality upon which the potentiality of the human depends. This is why the material things that humans are in contact with become encoded with taboos, rituals, and, in more contemporary times, laws. Taboos, rituals, and laws thus contain ontological presumptions regarding what things and humans are, as well as the relations between them, but they are also signs of crisis, for without these "things" in our midst we may cease to be. Hence the urgency behind taboos, rituals, and laws is the need to guarantee the persistence of things that will enable the release of our individual and group potentiality. Thus our political, economic, and even spiritual systems are bound up with the urgency to guarantee the continuation of potentiality. The needy subject must be given permission to both be with things and to transform things. Ultimately, De Soto and Badiou are articulating paradigms—individualist and collectivist, respectively—for doing just that despite the fact that each paradigm is filled with contradictions that it probably cannot escape.

←↨→

Now, De Soto's paradigm requires a particular legal and political subject and subjectivity to come into being. That subject often goes by the name *homo economicus*. The emergence of this subject and subjectivity is what Macfarlane, as discussed earlier, was also trying to describe. That is, in the European context a politics of individuation along with its legal guarantees, according to his account, slowly altered an older subject and subjectivity based on the social organism. Badiou still has affinities to that older subject, but the slow emergence of homo economicus or economic human gave individuals increasing permission to seek their freedom from the limitations of social obligation.

Homo economicus has been famously analyzed by Foucault and many others, but the term, of course, has had many incarnations. The economist Joseph Persky has documented many of these. During the nineteenth century, for instance, the term was most often used pejoratively to rail against John Stuart Mill, who, interestingly, did not use the term. The debate concerned ownership, and here is how Persky, reading it into Mill, phrases it: "The more divided the laborer from ownership, the less industrious the laborer."[27] In other words, the notion of homo economicus, long before its articulation by Foucault, mobilizes many of the assertions that I have been making throughout the text—namely, that the ownership of property represents within managerial modernity a maximization of potentiality. To the best of my knowledge, Foucault does not apply the term to laborers. For him, the term marks the emergence of the self-striving entrepreneur, but with the help of Persky we can see how the term was applied to the gradual, nineteenth-century transformation of the anonymous laborer into an increasingly autonomous and egoistic individual. Perhaps the subjectivity of the middle class owes much to the evolution of the politics of individuation coupled with homo economicus. In other words, is the emergence of the middle class due to a political and economic evolution that moved from the anonymity of laborers and peasants to, finally, autonomous individuals claiming freedoms, political standing, and financial status? And was the outward sign of this status ownership, which became in due time homeownership? At any rate, homo economicus, through its many incarnations, seems to signal the emergence of the self-realized agent who realizes herself through and because of the economy. For Foucault in particular, "homo oeconomicus is someone who pursues his own interest, and whose interest is such that it converges spontaneously with the interest of others"; "he is the man of enterprise and production."[28] "So we are at the heart of the problematic of the invisible hand . . . that kind of bizarre mechanism which makes *homo oeconomicus* function as an individual subject of interest within a totality which eludes him and which nevertheless founds the rationality of his egoistic choices."[29]

To return to Hann and Macfarlane, homo economicus would be that theoretical figure slowly emerging from the "social organism" to become the rational, sovereign self. Such a self becomes increasingly possible because assorted laws are also moving from an exchange of customary use rights over property toward the rights of marketplace exchange governed by the rules of abstract contract. Because these moves toward marketplace exchange occur gradually, it may be difficult to locate a causal entity occurring at a specific moment in history. What is happening resembles more a plethora of intersecting conditions and responses—in resonance with each other—that are shaping over time a rather loose but recognizable structure. Ultimately, the idea of the "social organism" cannot be killed, as evidenced in the work of Badiou and many, many others. Rather, it eventually takes up space within the emerging structure, which means that today it remains ever present within and in *ratio* to homo economicus. In my view, Foucault does not have a sufficiently robust view of the "social organism"—or what I will soon call "social ownership" or the "deep commons"—as foundational to and not erasable from homo economicus.

←↨→

Perhaps I have approached this chapter ass-backward. I have delayed providing an ethnographic account. Let us move away from theoretical speculation to a peopled world where contradictions abound. It is here along Paseo Boricua and Chicago's Humboldt Park where property, land, and things cease to be historical abstractions and have the clear power to renew. Claims of ownership and possession have a particular poignancy when people feel that they do not have much that is legitimately theirs. It is as if the self needs a not-self to draw into its orbit, a not-self that in some mysterious way will expand the self and make itself seem competent and worthy in its own eyes and in the eyes of others. For all the suggestive criticisms that I have offered regarding a politics of individuation as an egocentric, even anthrocentric, violent cutting up of the world—that is, forcing a human design upon the earth, squeezing the earth's beingness out of itself until it looks more and more like human being—I still return to the sheer poignancy, the human necessity that takes this profound (mis)step. The following ethnographic account, I hope, takes us to the heart of these complications, which ultimately seem so hard to judge via any facile moral theory.

In September 2001, I interviewed the young director of business development whose job was to steer Puerto Rican–owned businesses onto Paseo Boricua and then see to their well-being. What has always interested me about Paseo is the simultaneous absorption of and resistance to homo economicus. For instance, there is much talk about the need to cultivate Puerto Rican entrepreneurs, but at the same time Anglo-entrepreneurialism, in particular, is feared because, as we will see, it drives the forces of gentrification approaching from the east. There is something paradigmatic about this attraction and repulsion regarding entrepreneurialism, which speaks to the larger point that the political and economic confrontations occurring in large city neighborhoods such as Chicago's Humboldt Park are restricted to imaginative horizons largely constituted by homo economicus. As I discuss below, warring parties must play in the same game.

The young director of business development had no easy job. For one, the neighborhood had a long-standing reputation for gang activity. The gangs had diminished over the decades, but they were still present. As a result, attracting Puerto Rican entrepreneurs, home buyers, and tourists to the "old neighborhood" remained a difficult sell. Nevertheless, during the first decade of the 2000s he helped bring in a cluster of restaurants that eventually formed what many believe is the highest concentration of Puerto Rican restaurants (ten) in the country. Moreover, a number of affordable rental units were constructed both on Paseo and nearby streets. The larger intent behind these initiatives has been the creation of a kind of economic and cultural enclave that might boost not only the general wealth of Puerto Ricans in the city but also increase political clout at the levels of the city, state, and nation. In many ways, for the Latino activists and politicians on the north side of Chicago, maintaining political clout is the centerpiece of any antigentrification effort. As one of the Latino aldermen made clear during a meeting of housing activists[30] and as we have verified over the years through research, the demographics on the northwest side of Chicago are changing so rapidly that there might be in a few years a 75 percent shift from a Latino population to a white population.[31] Such a shift implies the end of any Puerto Rican enclave. The maintenance of such an enclave is not just about the possibility of growing the wealth of Latinos or securing affordable housing but is also about the concentration of political blocs that help to generate specific kinds of ordinances and laws. What happens to the undocumented in Chicago if the Latino caucus on the city council is no longer sufficiently strong to back with real commitment ordinances such as the one declaring the city a "sanctuary city"? As gentrification erodes the concentrations of poor minorities in specific neighborhoods, minority legislators lose their constituencies, indeed their wards. The dispersal of poor communities leads to a very different kind of city council, whose legislative initiatives may reflect another set of interests. That at least is the fear of ethnic activists and the larger political motivation behind antigentrification campaigns.

There is much at stake, then, in maintaining these sorts of enclaves. For several decades, the formula that the Puerto Rican activists and politicians have depended on is a fierce mobilization of the culture trope. But "culture" here acts a bit differently than one might expect. On Paseo, the culture trope enables the emergence of what the activists call a "critical space." Paseo, then, with its restaurants, affordable housing buildings, social service agencies, stores, studios, schools, and so on, is meant to be an economically viable "critical space," a staging ground for pulling others in, particularly youth, and for circulating a Puerto Rican critical analysis of Latin American history, politics, and social conditions.

This use of culture as a critical space is fraught with irony, of course. In what sense is "culture" ever "critical"? Imagine a similar space devoted to American analyses of the world and physically marked with the iconography of American "culture" functioning, in effect, as a kind of rhetorical sensorium representing all sorts of implicit and explicit arguments and narratives regarding American exceptionalism. Patriot groups might love its conservatism because "culture" is so readily appropriated by conservative ideologies. But Puerto Ricanness in the context of Paseo does not function in quite this way because it is manifested through the Puerto Rican independence movement. Historically, of the three main Puerto Rican political movements, independence has been the main source of oppositional or progressive politics because of ties, among other things, to socialism and Marxism. The commonwealth movement, in contrast, adjusted minimally Puerto Rico's historical, colonial relationship to the United States. Furthermore, the statehood movement has been typically thought of as the most conservative of all, having, for instance, deeper ties to the Republican Party of the United States and, most recently, instituting the privatization of public holdings. Hence the independence movement is the most distinctively "critical" of the three,[32] and, particularly in Chicago, it uses the trope of culture in order both to animate its criticism of the status quo and to concentrate Puerto Rican numbers in a particular location. If, for me, culture runs the risk of disabling the critical, my activist friends utterly disagree. They have a point, for the idea of culture is a flexible ideology and trope capable of mobilizing both a left-leaning politics and a right-leaning politics.

So there was much at stake for this young business development director-cum–community organizer and his successor. Both had to attract potential business owners, negotiate permits, and help with financing and advertising. This was not a spontaneous market—as described in a prior endnote—but a distinctively steered market functioning within the protective arches of giant, steel Puerto Rican flags spanning Division Street at Western as well as California. Indeed, the monumental arches, the renamed streets—Paseo Boricua, for instance, renames that section of Division Street between the flags—and even each business on the street function as land claims. That is, they are material manifestations of symbolic appropriation—a collective ownership by Puerto Ricans. The legal system may not permit this sort of collective ownership of land on the part of an ethnic group. However, as I have suggested at different times in this book, it is as if there is also an intuition within the law that the law itself is inadequate to satisfying human need. Thus the law allows groups to rename their streets and establish collective, symbolic possession. These are small actions to be sure, but they step into the vacuum. Interestingly, in late 2018 the alderman of these neighborhoods took an even bolder step. He was able to pass a city council resolution to name this area "Puerto Rican Town." This move was consistent with other moments in Chicago history, when other ethnicities named their neighborhoods and businesses China Town and Greek Town. Perhaps these forms of commercialization are a type of homo economicus working collectively and not individualistically. It is doubtful, however, that if one peered below the commercialization, one would see an equally intense political fight fending off majoritarian interests and their gentrifying capital. Thus "Puerto Rican Town" names commercial interests, to be sure, but it is also a cannon aimed against enemies.

At any rate, here is the business development director speaking in 2001:

CINTRON: So tell me about the flags—have they really worked?

DIRECTOR: Yeah, the reputation of Paseo Boricua as bordered by the flags. The eastern side of the flag has become known as kind of edgy urban. The people who live there may be artists and are at least semi-liberal. They're white and have proximity to the Blue Line.[33] It is the Blue Line that makes the area quite attractive to them. In contrast, the Humboldt Park area is thought of as dangerous. So the flags both kind of identify and protect the property values. Compare the property values outside the boundaries of the flag: $75 per square foot with a 20–30 percent increase per year. Within the flags, the values are at $35 per square foot with a 55–60 percent increase per year.

There is much to reflect on regarding the precision of a discourse of measurement[34] that can work dollar amounts to the "gnat's ass" of a square foot, all in the name of a kind of future's market available to entrepreneurs. The entrepreneurs can be of four types: homeowners, real estate speculators, real estate developers, and lenders. Indeed, all four are bound to each other insofar as they buy value with an eye toward future growth (20–30 percent increase per year during one moment in time) and are, therefore, dependent on each other's successes. Let us recall Foucault's analyses of homo oeconomicus. Any self-interested actor in the total economic system helps other actors, and what is necessary is the maximization of self-interestedness and not, for instance, central planning of the economy. Hence we can think of the real estate market on the north side of Chicago as part of a totality in which other market sectors are wedded to each other (construction, banking, building supplies and suppliers, the collection of property taxes and sales taxes on behalf of the city, etc.). We have, in effect, trillions of transactions occurring at any moment in a global economy that remains beyond our awareness and control. One's self-interest locates the self-interest of another and so on and so on, but no one has an idea of where the links start or stop. Any specific economic transaction is but a point in the firmament, and all that is required is the freeing of the system for prosperity to ensue. So goes the theory and narrative of homo economicus, but this narrative is altered as it enters the "critical/cultural space" between the flags, for here what is encouraged and planned for are Puerto Rican businesses. All other businesses are discouraged if they do not buy into the plan.

Thirteen years later, in 2014 and four blocks north of Division but still on Western, a new commercial district is trying to establish itself. The non–Puerto Rican entrepreneurs here call it WOW (West of Western), and they represent another set of agents who want to realize themselves economically. The flags indeed have prevented gentrification from fully jumping Western at Division, but there are no flags to stop gentrification from jumping Western at North Avenue, another major artery of the city that forms the northern boundary of Humboldt Park. Both North Avenue and Division—and the space in between, including Humboldt Park—have been thought of for several decades as mostly Puerto Rican, or at least Latin@, with a smattering of African Americans. From the perspective of the Puerto Rican activists, WOW is imagined in military terms as a kind of flanking move to the north. The flags may have protected Division, but they cannot help North Avenue—or so goes the thought. These new, hip entrepreneurs call the rebranding of the district a "renaissance." The following quotation comes from a small publication that typically focuses on "what's hot" in local neighborhoods in Chicago. After reading it, I interviewed the entrepreneur described below as the "goddess of WOW." She is African American and sensitive to charges of being a gentrifier. Still, she saw herself as more innovative and familiar with the forces of commerce than the Puerto Rican activists and businesses four blocks south of her. She thought of those businesses as stuck in politics and in the past. Here is how the article framed her:

> [She] was tired of hearing "West of Western" used as a warning by folks who knew little about a part of the neighborhood that houses her . . . shop.
>
> So she decided to go on a mission to rebrand a three-block strip of North Avenue from Western to Rockwell Street in Humboldt Park. Now, it's all about WOW.
>
> "I know this neighborhood very well and there was always that stigma of 'West of Western,'" she said. "Nobody wanted to go, they'd say, 'It's too scary'—then someone opened a coffee shop called Too Far West and it was on, baby."
>
> [She], who owns [The Furniture Store] with her husband, is now known as the "Goddess of WOW."

> The businesses backing WOW stretch from Western Avenue to Rockwell Street on North Avenue, but [she] said she'd eventually like to push the district farther west, to California Avenue and beyond.
>
> The label hasn't come without some protest from Humboldt Park residents who question whether the WOW District will raise property values and distance the strip from the neighborhood's identity as a Puerto Rican hub.
>
> The WOW District is "not a neighborhood, it's a district. It's not an exception, it's a feature," said [Joe], director of marketing and events at . . . a research and development consulting firm that recently opened shop on the block. "Twenty years ago, it was the ultimate warning, 'Don't go West of Western.'"[35]

So what is gentrification? As stated earlier, at one level gentrification is the capitalization of poor communities in which low-valued property functions as a kind of speculative futures market. One buys low in order to get good return ("$35 per square foot with 55–60 percent increase per year"). As low-valued property increases value, owners who have modest wealth stand to gain, though they may have to pay higher taxes, while renters more than likely are the biggest losers. The renting population disperses, and if they should represent a minority voting bloc, the ward (and possibly the state and federal district) undergo a population shift, leading possibly to a loss of legislative initiatives relevant to the dispersed population. When the aforementioned marketing director claims that WOW is a "feature," he seems unaware of how others, rightly or wrongly, have imagined this entire area as "their" neighborhood and, consequently, have controlled space and politics through their numbers.

But gentrification also needs to be understood from the perspective of homo economicus—in this case, the business owners of WOW. Through their eyes and those of their customers, gentrification is primarily a stylized aesthetic (youthful, hip, exposed brick, "edgy urban"); a celebration of creativity ("making it" because of one's skill and agility); the pleasure of extending oneself over a domain; an embodiment of freedom, autonomy, self-realization—in short, sovereignty over oneself and one's affairs.[36] All these elements add up to a branding of oneself and what one does, as when the "goddess of WOW's" distinctive flair becomes a synecdoche for the shopping district itself. But there is also a moral positioning—the risk-taking "goddess of WOW" makes it possible for others to realize their own well-being. (When I interviewed her about a month after the appearance of the article, she was quite proud of being known as a risk-taking, style-setter, a person moving honorably ahead of her own origins.) Indeed, for the shop owners in this little district she is the admired, energetic catalyst who is transforming the area on behalf of all other shop owners. Risk-takers of this sort are the heart and soul of the ownership society, representing, in effect, a totality: one self-interest spurring another, each atom jostling the next and so on and so forth until the potential of the whole is maximized. This maximization of potential is a long-standing philosophical concept that links, say, Aristotle and Agamben,[37] but it also appears as a cornerstone inside both democratic political theory and free market theory. Ultimately, this awakening and maximization of potential paints whatever it touches with broad ethical strokes, for the maximization of human potential—beingness coming into its fullness—would seem to make it deeply virtuous. If homo economicus in the minds of actors is associated with the maximization of potential as virtue, it cannot easily be dislodged from its privileged position. The "goddess of WOW," then, in good conscience can stand behind her actions and beliefs; meanwhile, gentrification rides in on her coattails.

For the Puerto Rican activists, then, the basic problem is how to answer this deeply internalized logic, its moral positioning, and the actions that it sanctions. WOW is simply the tip of an iceberg moving through the entire city. The goddess's actions and those of like mind can be stigmatized, of course, by saying that they lead to the emergence of "two cities—downtown Chicago and neighborhood Chicago." That is how Alderman Ricardo Muñoz, who represents a largely Mexican ward on Chicago's south side and heads up the progressive caucus in the city council, frames it.[38] The "two-cities" arguments, then, stigmatize by stating the obvious—not everyone is "maximized"; there are some who reap the benefits while others do not.

During an impassioned meeting of Puerto Rican activists and allies in the dead of winter 2014, the idea of "two cities" reappeared several times. A lawyer who directs an affordable housing agency said: "When people talk about finance, they talk about financing for Wall Street but not about communities. . . . I have seen the plans for the city. The plan is to gentrify the city. . . . The banks will not listen, so we need to do the work ourselves. We are only nibbling at the few things that are around us. We have to control the land." Still another voice framed it this way: "The city has always been a site of exclusion. St. Augustine's *City of God* excluded the Jews and Muslims. . . . [Today] the poor are being pushed to the suburbs . . . the black ghetto has moved to the suburbs. . . . We are splitting the rich from the poor." The same speaker had made this broader point earlier in the day:

> The Bloomingdale Trail is really the biggest obstacle facing us. We met with [Rahm] Emanuel [mayor of Chicago] about a month ago. For him the higher the real estate values the more tax revenue. The city slowly but surely is closing down to certain types of people. We are creating a Disneyesque city. With 60,000 students downtown you are predicting the future of the city. Puerto Ricans have been at the vanguard in shaping this city. We have been its nomads. We have had to fight to control the land, and everything depends on controlling land. I think it is time to lay claim to that legacy. This community has also been one of the most vocal about immigration and documentation. We have worked in solidarity with our Latino brothers and sisters. We need to keep the legacy of the Puerto Ricans alive. We need to be more intentional about what stabilizing means. We want to create a city for everyone. On Division on California [La Estancia]—we created that building. Division and Campbell [Teresa Roldan Apartments]—we created that one too. Both of those buildings are powerful statements. They control the land. We need to be intentional. We need to be careful and not lose this legacy. But we are close to losing it. What will happen to Clemente, to the vocational center? These are the places that we built. How long will they remain for us?[39]

In effect, "the tale of two cities" is a narrative that counters the narrative of homo economicus. If homo economicus says that individual potential can be maximized while simultaneously maximizing the potential of others, the "tale of two cities" speaks of class division, even exploitation, under the heel of homo economicus. At the root of both narratives is the ownership of land, for ownership, particularly for homo economicus, institutionalizes the maximization of potential, which at its most explicit is the felt experience of freedom, wherewithal. This point is important to repeat: under the presumptions of homo economicus, freedom is translated as the freedom to own and accumulate. According to these presumptions, freedom as a democratic value is simply too abstract and idealized. It must be translated into the freedom of the markets so that freedom can be genuinely experienced; hence the ownership and accumulation of things enable such an experience.[40] "A tale of two cities" as narrative, then, reverses homo economicus. It claims instead that if property values, for instance, are going up, then the well-off have a better chance of owning and accumulating and passing off some of that wealth to the next generation. Thus some experience the materialized freedoms of homo economicus while others feel distinctly not free. That is, if housing represents for the poor the single best source of wealth-making, the inability to enter the housing market represents entrapment, and therefore such folks are disposed to invent, as compensation, only transcendent or symbolic versions of freedom.

At a deeper level, this "tale of two cities" belongs to a resistance movement called "a right to the city." Coming out of the work of Henri Lefebvre, *Le Droit à la Ville*, and further elaborated in his *The Production of Space*,[41] the right to the city is today a general feature among cultural geographers and urban theorists. As Mitchell explains it, the right to the city makes a "normative argument that the city is an *ouvre*—a work in which all its citizens participate."[42] Or, as the Puerto Rican activist stated it at the February meeting in 2014: "We are splitting the rich from the poor" and "creating a Disneyesque city," whereas we ought to be creating a "city for everyone." In one sense, the right to the city is a tragic conception, for implicitly it admits that, in the game of owning and accumulating, those who have lost must compete on more symbolic, abstract grounds—namely, rights. Indeed, those who organize themselves under a right to the city would probably prefer owning parts of the city instead of claiming rights to it. Consider landlords who can raise rents on renters and thus seemingly expose renters to endless vulnerability. Renters can address their vulnerability with a right to the city claim and even win rent controls, but these fights require exceptional energy because they exist within a regime that prefers the freedoms and wealth-making capacities of homo economicus. For instance, rent controls cool the real estate market and attendant economic sectors. Thus strong believers in homo economicus claim, rather starkly (though implicitly), that those who have the means to own pieces of the city ought to do so, whereas those who can only claim a right to the city must struggle with the leftovers. Here, then, is how the right to the city movement is essentially tragic. As with all rights discourses, a right to the city mobilizes a cornerstone of liberalism (rights) to do combat against liberalism itself. The first is ensnared inside the webbing of the second and thus always compromised, always vulnerable to the shifting whims of ideology and governance. Why not distribute property itself instead of rights to property? Such a move would be a revolution against liberal democracy—that is, the use of the innate power of violence to establish a new foundational law—but to what extent is revolution another fetishization, a desire to perfect a social order until it overcomes the reigning limitations and replaces contradiction and instability with stability? So much rhetoric begins in the desire for escape as a first step toward a new perfection.

Nevertheless, a right to the city does speak to a public good, and there is some truth in its claim. In a city such as Chicago, for instance, if the working poor and marginal middle class are pushed to areas that have less access to public transportation, not only do workers and their families face extra costs but so do their employers and the environment. Consider the possibility, then, that inner-city affordable rentals represent a deep public good. (In the city of Chicago, one qualifies for affordable rents if one is at 80 percent of a city's medium income, or 60 percent, or 40 percent, and so on.) The solution may remain profoundly incomplete, but compared to rent controls it may be more practical and less controversial. At any rate, the Puerto Rican activists are determined defenders of affordable housing as one of the strategies in their right to the city claims.

←↨→

Atomized individuation is in ratio with collective interest. The theories of De Soto and Badiou seem to embody this ratio, but so do the ideas of homo economicus and a right to the city. Homo economicus seems to foreground the atomized individual whose success enables the collective, while the right to the city reverses that emphasis. What is further revealing is that the term *ownership*, which is so central to homo economicus, is also important when people collectively claim a right to the city. For instance, the Puerto Ricans in the Humboldt Park area claim to "own" the park. It is their slice of the city. Or as one of the more prominent activists said it in June 2017, "Humboldt Park is our house," and then someone to the side laughed and said, "And the whites [meaning gentrifiers] are wearing dirty shoes." Similarly, but from a different political orientation, the poster that opened this chapter showed a protestor claiming ownership of the nation and implied that migrants were trespassers on his property. Seemingly, then, both individual owners and collective owners claim possession of all sorts of entities and not just a right to the city. Both are equally invested in "myness discourse" as an answer to their existential conditions. In sum, an individualized "myness" and a collective "myness" cannot be eradicated from public discourse. This possibility compels me to look into the discursive and empirical structures of ownership—that is, possession.

Legal theorist Carol Rose has it absolutely right: "How do things get to be owned? This is a fundamental puzzle for anyone who thinks about property. One buys things from other owners, to be sure, but how did the other owners get those things? Back at the beginning, someone must have acquired the thing, whatever it is, without buying it from anyone else. That is, someone had to do something to anchor the very first link in the chain of ownership. The puzzle is, What was that action that anchored the chain and made an owned thing out of an unowned one?"[43]

Rose does an admirable job of showing how social theory and legal theory have devised many answers to this foundational question. There is, for instance, Locke's famous labor theory that became so important for Marx and Engels. Here Locke negotiates how the earth is a commons for the benefit of all men, but each man "has a property in his own person: this nobody has any right to but himself. The labour of his body, and the work of his hands . . . are properly his." From this premise, he makes the strong assertion that "whatsoever . . . he removes out of the state that nature hath provided, and left it in, he hath mixed his labour with, and joined to it something that is his own, and thereby makes it his property. It being by him removed from the common state nature hath placed it in, it hath by this labour something annexed to it that excludes the common right of other men." The passage concludes with a curious qualification—namely, that this right of possession depends on their being enough, "and as good, left in common for others."[44] What seems to be a strong justification is suddenly relativized—and probably wisely so—by the availability of resources. In qualifying his theory, is Locke admitting that his justification for property may not be as stable as first imagined? Locke may have been responding to the fact that Britain at the time still had a considerable amount of land set aside for "common use" by the inhabitants of villages. Rights of possession, then, did not just accrue to the strong individual removing stuff from nature. Something else might be at work with the potential to destabilize his justification. Hence how adequate is his argument? Rose does not work through this point, but she offers a series of other sharp critiques: "Without a prior theory of ownership, what makes it so clear that anyone owns the labor that he or she mixes with something else. . . . [And] even if one does own the labor that one performs, what is the scope of the right that one establishes by mixing the owned thing (one's labor) with something else?"[45] After all, despite the fact that legal theory has incorporated a considerable amount of Locke's theory of labor, police forces and legal systems routinely remove the shelters that squatters and the homeless build for themselves. Furthermore, what is a foreclosure if not the removal of a person, even a family, on the basis of the debt owed and not the labor that they have put into the property? In these instances, the holder of the debt can trump long-standing habitation and use but not always, for sometimes long-standing habitation and use can leverage a reduction of the debt. As an intuition regarding ownership, Locke's labor theory does not seem to cover the field.

Rose also points to consent theories of ownership, which were contemporaneous with Locke's, where the "original owner got title through the consent of the rest of humanity (who were, taken together, the first recipients from God, the genuine original owner)."[46] Any consent theory presumes all sorts of conundrums, as any rhetorical theorist well knows, but this version seems particularly dubious. The rest of humanity? Really? Because property, or whatever it might be called across the variability of humanity, is so fundamental for human provisioning, this particular consent theory seems to whitewash the contestable nature that must always haunt the concept of property.

Theories of first possession or occupancy are still another mode for justifying ownership, and they occupy a well-established place in American legal theory. But as Rose asks: "What counts as possession . . . and why does possession count as a claim to title?"[47] A series of court decisions have, over time, attempted to delineate coherent interpretations of first possession. Indeed, first possession, in and of itself, seems insufficient, and the courts have consistently required other sorts of attendant actions. For instance, if the property has been effectively abandoned over a long period of time and someone else has put it to "suitable use" also over a long period of time, the courts have often favored the trespasser, particularly if statutes of limitation are applicable. If, say, the trespasser builds a house and farms the land, and the original owner knowingly does nothing for twenty years, a statute of limitations may make the trespasser the new owner. As Rose tells it, these actions are called "adverse possession" and are linked to "suitable use" arguments. Taken together, they seem to echo a labor theory of ownership. In a similar vein, the courts have sometimes insisted that first-possession claims require a "clear act." In this sense, a clear act is a kind of statement that "I possess." It is a form of communication or public notice visible to or hearable by all parties, as when one establishes "suitable use" by building a house, laying a fence, or even paying taxes—anything that reveals the intentions and abilities of the claimant on the basis of first possession or occupancy.[48]

With these brief inquiries into "origin stories" regarding the birth of property, I am trying to make an important point. Legal rationality has had a historical interest in finding bedrock principles that might act as a basis for establishing mine versus thine or ours versus theirs. Given the importance of ownership and possession in releasing potentiality and producing sustenance and betterment, the stakes are high for finding such principles. But do such principles exist?

Let us consider briefly the notion of "clear act" as a basis for a first-possession claim.[49] Though belonging to ideologies of proof-making—because clarity is desired for the purpose of driving us to conviction and verifiability—a "clear act" in the context of the law can only be as clear as the filters of cultural and economic self-interestedness allow. In other words, one could say that a good chunk of colonialism's appropriation of land around the world was the result of not seeing clearly how natives' "first-possession" claims qualified as "suitable use." For the settlers, for instance, nomadic, seasonal routes did not qualify as "clear acts" of property ownership because barely altering the landscape was not evidence of "suitable use." For the European settlers, there was no presence, supposedly, of having put land under dominion, and so indigenous uses of land were insufficient to represent "public notice" communicating "this is mine and not yours."[50] The visible-invisible ratio, which constitutes how we regard materiality, may have constructed both colonial rule and the customary laws of the indigenous, but what was a "clear act" (visible) in one scenario was invisible in another. Or even if they were readable to each other, the idea of property as a way to maximize wealth-making; the transcendent values of civilization, progress, and freedom; and, ultimately, military might were sufficient for the Euro-Americans to impose the autonomous entities of individualism, private property, and the nation-state as global paradigms. Ultimately, then, "clear acts" are not self-evident. If determining justice in matters of property law depends on such suppositions, then justice as such is immersed in the thickets of cultural and economic self-interestedness, and therefore one party's justice may be deemed unjust by another party.

The more one digs into concepts of ownership and possession, the more interesting the concepts become. My claim is that ownership and possession are species of a very pervasive anthrocentric or anthropomorphic mode of reasoning. We can see this reasoning at work both among those who want to rationalize the idea of individual private property and those, as we have seen, who want to claim collective ownership. Locke, interestingly enough, allows us to see this anthrocentrism: "He hath mixed his labor with it, and joined to it something that is his own." What is this mixing of the laboring self with nature until nature becomes refashioned into property? One's labor gets "annexed" to nature, Locke says, and it is this action that removes that bit of nature from the commons. Private ownership thus comes into being.

In one sense, Locke's arguments seem to be almost a kind of universal common sense. For instance, some Cambodian tribal peoples acknowledge "rights of ownership" to those who labor and transform nature into objects for their own use.[51] Further, Tsing has documented how the Meratus Dayak, a people living in South Kalimantan, a province in the Indonesian territory of Borneo, have historically made ownership claims on parts of the forest. Their logic resembles Locke's analysis of "mixing" one's labor with nature. Customary rules, for instance, allow an individual to establish a kind of ownership by preparing, say, a tree that will then attract honeybees. "A man claims a tree by being the first to clean it, or if the tree has been abandoned by other claimants, by reviving its cleaning. He passes this claim to his children as long as they are active in maintaining the tree as a honey tree." Interestingly, sisters may also retain rights to the honey. These familial claims can extend across many generations.[52] The family in this sense seems to represent a kind of collective labor that grants collective ownership. But this very scaling up from the level of the individual to the level of the family and, further, to the village—which also maintains proprietary claims according to Meratus Dayak custom and, further still, to the scale of a "people" or nation—introduces, perhaps, a need to rethink Locke. That is, ownership, or whatever it might translate to in other languages, seems to be a kind of baggy metaphor applicable to many conditions beyond laboring individuals confronting nature. For instance, if the aforementioned sister does no labor to maintain the honey tree, what is it between brother and sister that can overcome the requirement of labor? Or, closer to home, if a parent invested one thousand dollars in a stock in the name of their newborn, and if the stock was utterly forgotten even as its worth doubled every year, what labor did the child, now eighty-five years of age, expend before receiving the surprising notice that they are fabulously wealthy? Here value is not determined by the labor spent. That is, legal ownership in these instances merely attaches a person to a thing, but the attachment is not determined by the amount of labor. Or, more trivially, if a person puts their hat and coat on a chair in a movie theater and then leaves for the bathroom, there is a general recognition—in certain cultures at least—that these objects are both extensions of a person and a sign of effort sufficient enough to make a claim on the chair. In all these instances, the labor claim is tenuous, and it becomes even more tenuous when millions, or even billions, of individuals make a collective claim over a patch of earth and say, "This is my (our) nation and I (we) are willing to fight for it!" In sum, "myness discourse" creates a tremendous amount of social ordering, but its basis for rationalizing ownership does not necessarily depend on much, if any, labor. Further, things acquire value not because of the labor we put into them but for reasons largely out of our control. Consider, for instance, runs on useless luxury items—where in all this is Locke's labor theory of value?

So Locke's ontological explanation regarding the origins of property as rooted in labor seems incomplete. Nevertheless, he is onto something. I wager that he is grasping how we anthrocentrically mix ourselves with the world. The aforementioned examples of ownership claims entail the mixing of objects and subjects. Sometimes this mixing is extensive but sometimes not. The point is that he has located an anthrocentric or anthropomorphic habit or propensity that links Cambodian tribespeople, Meratus Dayak, Euro-Americans, and many others. We do, indeed, mix ourselves with the world, meaning that the self has a propensity to leak into all imaginable phenomena. The self rubs itself into and across the world that it knows, and indeed "knowing the world" may be another sign of this anthrocentric propensity. In this sense, ownership and possession are metaphors that name, for the modern world, the human tendency to extend consciousness to stuff that is not us. Traditional communities that spiritualize their landscape and make it a sacred space are also mixing themselves with the stuff of their world, and they, too, claim it with their own metaphors. In this sense, the spiritualization of landscapes as ancient practice and ownership as modern practice are two variations of the same anthrocentric or anthropomorphic propensity. We label the mixing differently according to the reigning metaphysical and material imperatives. If in the process of mixing we give stuff a particular shape, then we have not only extended our consciousness into it but have also fashioned it into some semblance of ourselves. The stuff becomes difficult to part with because it has become so much a part of us. There is magical slippage, then, between self and phenomena by which we inhabit that which is around us. Why doesn't the self contain itself? Suggesting that it should is almost as nonsensical as saying that a lion need not mix the antelope inside itself. A self, any self, cannot afford to not extend itself into the world. Humans, interestingly, will rationalize what they take through, for instance, elaborate court decisions searching out "clear acts" of first possession that "clearly," as we saw, depend on all sorts of cultural suppositions that enable seeing and nonseeing. Locke's "mixing," then, is not so much an ontological inquiry into a labor theory of ownership as it is a rendering of the anthrocentric or anthropomorphic propensity through which human sentiment, reasoning, and imagining forcefully extend themselves into the world and claim it as its own.

Curiously, Locke's inquiries set the stage for translating his key terms of "mixing with Nature" into language that resembles contemporary, posthumanist thought. That is, Locke's property, ownership, and possession are terms by which human life invests itself into the life of the nonhuman—becomes entangled with it—and claims it as its own. Consider that if all ownership claims are essentially an extension of consciousness on the part of a self or group self toward a not-self, then we might understand all property law as dependent on a leaky mind that tells itself "this space, place, or thing is like us/me," or, deeper still, "this space is me/us." In other words, the leaky mind uses the mechanism of metaphor to establish identification that, in many instances, is both seemingly necessary for survival and sometimes deeply violent. Thus the not-self, the nonhuman, simply disappears. It loses its "thereness" and instead becomes consumed by the self or group self, which is a major theme in posthumanism.[53] But the larger point is that claims of ownership or possession start first as a motive, the anthrocentric urge; then, quickly, the motive or urge utilizes metaphor as mechanism to extend the self toward an object; and thus an identification is made. Property law, then, is a rationalization of this process. I do not think that law has any other choice but to proceed in exactly this way because it is built to serve the anthrocentric motive. Further, all ownership claims depend on hiding the mechanism and force of their origin in metaphor. I suspect that the public and particularly the courts want property relations to rely on something more substantive than anthrocentric or anthropomorphic metaphors. But technically speaking, the law cannot overcome its unprovable premises except by replacing what currently exists with another set of premises. It cannot unpremise its foundational premises. Recall De Soto's arguments on behalf of the informal ownership rights of squatters. Recall also adverse possession in American law. Both begin from premises that differ from standard ownership claims. Both have traction in the courts, and this suggests that the law chooses flexibility over consistency and certainty. Thus ownership and possession seem loosely metaphorical, but in acquiring legal form they allow humans, in all cases, to extend themselves toward the nonhuman. Or we can describe it this way: the law bundles a particular rationalization to the available material conditions, which means that any category of ownership should work well enough—if the material conditions permit. Given that the conditions will surely change, it is better for the law to rest upon unprovable premises and ungrounded metaphors. Thus the flexibility of metaphor triumphs over procedural certainty, meaning that the law at one moment can invent one rationalization only to replace it with another if the times demand it. But in all cases, the law, as it currently exists, wants the nonhuman to be consumed.

Last, I want to specify a bit more how anthrocentrism is also at play during collective ownership claims. Locke does not have an account of individuals imagining their labor in collective terms and "mixing" it with nature. Indeed, for him individual property claims are aimed against the commons so that the individual takes possession by ripping her part from the collective—as long as there is enough, "and as good, left in common for others." But the point is that collectivities do imagine ownership, and they do so instinctually and spontaneously without any prior theorization derived from, say, Marxism. Nicholas Blomley's account of inner-city Vancouver is a case in point. Early in the text, Blomley notes that the ownership model that pits private property ownership against state ownership depends on a grammar of spatial form. We find here, for instance, the spatial archetype of the "private, detached house" versus "the city park or street."[54] The seeing of bounded spaces in all their clarity becomes the foundational grammar for imagining private versus public or state ownership. Furthermore, the spatialization of ownership, as a grammar, facilitates hierarchies and economic relations that may ride roughshod over other ways of imagining ownership.[55] If ownership, indeed, is a manifestation of a kind of primitive anthrocentrism, it should equally underlie private ownership and state ownership, as well as—and in a more profound manner—an admittedly messy category that might be called "social ownership." At first glance, this social ownership would seem to be at most a kind of "metaphorical ownership" that cannot be as "real" as private ownership and state ownership, given the inclinations of legal thinking. But under the sort of anthrocentric and anthropomorphic view that I have been articulating here, all ownership claims have the same primitive origins, meaning that they are equally metaphorical and equally real. Power—who can muster it and how much of it on behalf of what position—plays an important role, but perhaps not the only role, in determining which position acquires the authority to be considered "real" versus metaphorical. At any rate, Blomley discusses social ownership claims circulating in his field site in Vancouver when poor communities confronted new owners. As might be expected, "use" and "habitation" claims on property have less force than monetary claims and thus seem less "real" and more "metaphorical." But as Blomley tells it, this is precisely the struggle in legal theory as social ownership vies to acquire the status of the "real" on a par with private and state ownership: "For local activists, the Downtown Eastside is locally owned . . . in at least two practical ways. First, collective 'investment' in the physical landscape has occurred through histories of copresent *use* and *habitation*. For example, to say that the Grand Union Hotel, a local residential hotel (single-room occupancy, or SRO), is owned by M & C Reserve Investments, Ltd., is from this perspective to deny the generations of people who have lived, died, suffered, loved, and survived there. Second the landscape has been locally *produced* through collective action and political struggle."[56]

To be sure, Blomley is not talking about anthrocentrism or anthropocentrism as a structure or baggy metaphor underlying ownership claims made by collectivities. But given its ancient pedigree, anthrocentrism offers some insights regarding both rights claims in general and, specifically, the "right to the city" claims that I discussed earlier. Here is Blomley again:

> Some legal scholars have claimed to identify a "reliance interest" within law that acknowledges and protects relations of mutual dependence between "private" enterprises and the communities in which they are located. Decisions on the part of private actors that destroy this relation—for example, a factory's decision to relocate—are thus seen as problematic. In response to the devastating closures in the steel industry in Youngstown, Ohio and Pittsburgh, Pennsylvania, residents began to articulate the idea that "some kind of community property right arises from the long-standing relation between a company and a community." . . . However, the power of the ownership model invites judges to search for a solitary "owner." Such an approach has been deemed misleading: "Property rights are more often shared than unitary, and rights to use and dispose of property are never absolute."[57]

←↨→

It would seem that Blomley's conception of social ownership splits into two kinds. The first quotation regarding the Downtown Eastside references a social ownership that echoes the claims made by Puerto Ricans in Humboldt Park. At first glance, these ownership claims seem rather informal, a kind of "group self" extending itself over space and place on the basis not of "real" ownership via the marketplace but, rather, a metaphorical ownership based on long-term use and habitation.

The second quotation describes a "reliance interest" in which a community has some sort of right to protect its livelihood if its source of income decides to move. A social ownership claim of the latter sort would be difficult to maintain on behalf of the Puerto Ricans in Humboldt Park. After all, there is no factory there threatening to close, leaving everyone high and dry. Nevertheless, arguments resembling a reliance interest are occasionally heard among Puerto Rican activists who are intent on protecting their critical, cultural space. Their arguments, as we have started to see, claim that an ethnic enclave encourages economic development. What is an ethnic enclave, they ask, if not also an economic entity providing jobs, housing, and goods bought, sold, and consumed—and, more importantly, what is such an enclave when broken apart and dispersed by "gentrification"? Do ethnic businesses lose their clientele, and do their clients lose access to the things they care about? Thus why can't an economic enclave represent a "reliance interest"? None of the activists believe that such an argument would gather traction in the courts given the current paradigm. The current paradigm, dominated by homo economicus, says, instead, something like the following: defending a right to self-preservation on behalf of an enclave economy are arguments that run directly counter to the free market and the values of dynamism and change, for enclave economies hope to resist changes to the enclave. But there are curious paradoxes on both sides of these argument machines: free markets seem to be, formally at least, progressive and dynamic, exposing us to ever-expanding worlds of difference, but conservative when they ghettoize the poor and place the rich into gated communities; in contrast, ethnic enclaves seem to be politically progressive when they try to empower the marginalized but conservative when they push hard for an ethnopolitics. But, to be sure, the Puerto Rican activists do not see paradoxes here: they assert boldly and clearly that their long history of first being colonized (Spanish and American colonization of Puerto Rico) and then gentrified in Chicago has not only eroded a kind of cultural substance that has left their youth groundless and vulnerable to a kind of lumpen self-hate but also has uprooted businesses and hindered wealth-making. Hence social ownership claims help activists create a community with purpose and coherence and to marry those elements to economic development.

Now the curious thing about social ownership claims is that they are available to any group. That is, as Blomley and I document, they are particularly appealing to marginalized groups fending off the interests of homo economicus or big capital, but Blomley does not seem to realize that social ownership claims are also available to those who would just as soon boot out the marginalized. Let's return to my fieldwork to illustrate how Humboldt Park and its neighboring streets are, essentially, a battleground where gentrifiers versus Puerto Ricans launch competing social ownership claims. Here's the upshot: democratic rhetorics offer little safe harbor. Instead, they represent weapons for our enemies.

I return to the former business development director-cum–community organizer, who wrote an email to me in the spring of 2014 when the activists were trying to formulate strategies for resisting WOW and other campaigns: "Events like Riot Fest, the Humboldt Park Earthday 5k, the music fest on California and Chicago, the establishment of read/write library, the Bloomingdale Trail, and the creation of the California Ave corridor . . . coupled with housing data . . . show the impact, growth, and spread of gentrification. This with real estate listings using the destinations as attractions . . . show . . . the perfect storm for gentrification."

He is pointing to gentrification wars waged at the level of symbolic culture. Each of the events listed, along with WOW, are not events sponsored by Puerto Ricans, who for decades have claimed their "ownership" over Humboldt Park via their own numerous parades and festivals in the park, such as the Annual Paseo Boricua Classic Car and Bike Show, Noche Jibara, Misa Jibara, Fiesta Boricua, Puerto Rican Jazz Festivals, the Annual Paseo Boricua Three Kings Winter Festival/Parade, and so on. In the eyes of the activists, one symbolic culture is pitched against the other's in a heated battle of identities. Controlling land and property values, of course, are the ultimate stakes of the game. So there are two competing symbolic cultures claiming "social ownership" over the same territory, and then there is actual currency that has the power to trump anybody's symbolic currency. If the symbolic culture of the newcomers can lay more and more claim to Humboldt Park through their own sponsored events, then the neighborhood will feel safer and more familiar to them, and more of them will come and buy property. But if these events replace the Puerto Rican sponsored events, then the Puerto Rican activists lose, Humboldt Park becomes known as a destination for new, hip buyers, and one class begins to replace the other, meaning that, once again, many Puerto Ricans, along with nonowning Mexicans and African Americans also in the area, become nomadic.

At any rate, the symbolic life of the newcomers versus that of the Puerto Ricans represents, roughly speaking, different aesthetics, spoken languages, ways of moving bodily through the world, educational levels, cultural capital (including connections and knowledge of how to navigate the lending markets), and so on. One *habitus*—to use Pierre Bourdieu's classic term—versus another. Of course, these two styles are hardly absolute and, indeed, overlap. For instance, the Puerto Ricans of a younger generation can usually slide between them. But if the youth should slide too far to the other side, then the Puerto Rican activists become worried. Consider that in May 2017, Oscar Lopez, the renowned *independentista* who had been incarcerated for thirty-five years for unproven terrorist acts, returned home to a hero's welcome in Chicago. He was ushered along several of the symbolic sites, some of which he had helped shape as a young activist before his incarceration: La Casita de Don Pedro y Doña Lolita, Paseo Boricua, the steel Puerto Rican flags at California and Division, and, finally, the boathouse pavilion in Humboldt Park, where he was honored by many and also where he spoke movingly. Keeping Oscar's legacy alive over decades among the younger generations has been critical for the older activists. If they had not succeeded to some degree, only the elderly would have greeted Oscar because the youth long ago would have drifted indifferently toward street gangs or menial labor or college degrees with not much remembrance of the island itself and Boricua politics. For the activists, preventing this drift from the invented center called "Puerto Ricanness" and its politics is the raison d'être for building and maintaining this critical, cultural space housed most intensely along Paseo. So the political theater of Oscar walking among the shrines of Paseo with a celebratory crowd and then addressing the sizeable gathering in the middle of the park was due to the constant stoking of a decades-long claim of Puerto Rican social ownership over this part of the city.

Now, there are moments when these opposing social ownership claims rise to a fever pitch. In these instances, "newish" homeowners, typically young "whites" and sometimes "right-wing Puerto Ricans," complain particularly against the Puerto Rican alderman of the ward as well as the Puerto Rican businesses and *independentista* Puerto Rican leaders, institutions, and businesses up and down Paseo. Invariably, the Puerto Rican leadership shoots back with charges of racism, as this comment in the early summer of 2013 indicates:

> During a heated debate that pitted several right-wing Puerto Ricans, in cahoots with racist newcomers to Humboldt Park, against progressive sectors of our community, the community overwhelmingly demonstrated support for the right of the Puerto Rican Parade to have a liquor license for its festival taking place June 12th to the 16th. This took place Thursday, May 16th at the Humboldt Park Fieldhouse during its monthly meeting

> of the Humboldt Park Advisory Committee. The racism was so blatant both in terms of words and deeds, when a year ago a predominately white grouping [*sic*] Riot Fest held a 3-day festival in Humboldt Park was allowed to have four beer gardens with the support of __________'s United West Humboldt Park. These same racist elements organized to deny the Puerto Rican Parade to a license for one beer garden.[58]

Ultimately, the goal is to control land, which leads to control over lifestyle and wealth-making.[59] In my experience, the Puerto Rican leadership is open to negotiation with the newcomers over many issues, but the area's Puerto Rican identity and institutional control over Humboldt Park and nearby neighborhoods is not negotiable. Here is a blog post from 2011 that I hastily copied even as I failed to jot down its source: "What's up with . . . [Humboldt Park]? No garbage cans, baseball fields in bad shape. Where and how is the park spending its funds? Especially with new events like Riot Fest that are providing additional funds. How is the Park manager [Rosario] and supervisor [Perez] taking care of issues and concerns? And if they are not going to do anything about it, how do we go about replacing them?" Years later, at a meeting of Puerto Rican activists in the spring of 2015, Rosario—mentioned previously and the manager of Humboldt Park for twelve years—described how the newcomers had been increasing their complaints regarding the management of the park but also exerting more and more control over the park's programming. She had never seen such intense appropriation before—as if they thought they "owned" the park, she said.

Who manages and controls public institutions (e.g., Humboldt Park), aldermanic offices, the Cook County Board of Commissioners, legislative districts, congressional offices, the City Colleges of Chicago, judgeships, and so on is of critical importance to the activists. The activists believe that if Puerto Ricans (or at least Latin@s) control land and space, then the voices of the activists will be heard, but if Puerto Ricans should be removed, particularly from the spaces that they feel belong to them (e.g., Humboldt Park), then they are being deprived of clout, jobs, and prosperity. For the Puerto Rican activists, each battle regarding ethnic control has implications for political and economic advancement. Here again is the urgency to keep expanding and maintaining ethnopolitics.

Hence the musicians who appear at Riot Fest are a threat, for they are decidedly not Puerto Rican, and neither are the shop owners along the California Corridor. These new stores are marked by an aesthetic and lifestyle that has cachet with the hip, young, blog-reading-and-writing internet crowd. Here is a posting from an internet source read widely by those who want to know what's cool in Humboldt Park and the environs close to it:

> The close-knit business owners behind California Nights will host a fifth installment of the neighborhood meet-and-greet Saturday.
>
> The first event kicked off on the night Vintage Quest opened on March 8, according to owner Keith Manners, and what began as five neighboring businesses has grown to include a rotating list of several others along California Avenue between Division Street and Augusta Boulevard. . . .
>
> That initial lineup included Space Oddities, Humboldt House, The Arborist, Meadowlark, and Vintage Quest. Recent California Nights have included music from a local jazz band and a food truck serving German food. This month, the Flying Saucer is set to join the party.[60]

The stores mentioned specialize in "cool" offbeat designs, furniture, and clothing. By most accounts, the owners of these stores see themselves as creative and committed to a kind of liberal politics, social justice, and so on. My interviews with similar owners from WOW suggest that they also see themselves as small-business owners whose activities will help other business owners in the area and, more importantly, help the "community" in general. In short, they see themselves as one type of homo economicus, though not the more atomized version that Foucault critiques. They acquire footholds here because the rents are cheaper than east of Western. In banding together, they brand themselves as a district with the clever titles WOW and the California Corridor, but in doing so they name themselves, knowingly or not, as rivals opposed to an older brand, Paseo Boricua. Not all of these owners, of course, are interpreted as rivals in the eyes of the Puerto Rican activists. The activists, in fact, are willing to work with anyone who supports their projects. But the new owners and their penchant for branding play into long-standing social ownership wars that touch a raw nerve among the Puerto Rican activists: "This is classic colonialism—people need to recognize what was already here before they arrived." Such comments play the ultimate trump card: gentrification equals colonialism. In this case, it was spoken during a meeting in July 2014 as the activists shaped a strategy for addressing WOW, but it is a common theme. It turns the Puerto Rican experience into a single narrative that counters a narrative that circulates among the new homeowners: "So you still have some crime and there are gangs, but they aren't hunting and killing white people for sport like . . . the HP of 10–15 years ago, not the HP of now, unless you go south and west."[61] From the perspectives of the Puerto Rican activists, this is hyperbolic, racist rhetoric that plays into larger interests that can justify the cleaning up of territory by gentrification in order to make it more habitable. In the eyes of the activists, such actions are forms of theft—in this case the "theft" of Puerto Rico and the "theft" of Chicago neighborhoods. Thus the activists feel compelled to claim the land back, if not through outright purchase, then through "use," "habitation," symbolic culture, and other forms of social ownership. Through these sorts of proprietary claims, the anthrocentric world of social ownership muscles its way toward a self-defense not only of Humboldt Park but of the island as well. In these moments, the politics and economics of gentrification become the politics and economics of colonialism.

I want to pause for a moment in this evolving argument and shift the tone a bit. I want to speak a few taboos with regard to my activist friends who eloquently encourage us "to understand the importance of critical space by seeing the community as an ecosystem where all things are constantly intersecting."[62] I do not speak against this language, much less my activist friends. Indeed, my activist friends speak sincerely. However, sincerity is not always free of self-deception; moreover, my own sense of "critical space" means that there is no "safe place." So this language of community, particularly the Puerto Rican community of Humboldt Park as ecosystem, touches larger themes regarding democratic politics.

Ecosystem is certainly an inviting term, a virtue term. Consequently, it is a slippery trope, which, I believe, betrays itself. It implies that any element in a larger system plays a necessary and valued role. The larger whole cannot be completed without the contributions of its many parts. An ecosystem, then, implies inclusivity without any apparent exclusivity. Thus it is a term imbued with democratic sentiment, for any popular, fetishized understanding of democracy claims that democracy is inclusive. So both terms, *democracy* and *ecosystem*, share the trope of inclusivity. Both terms share the belief that all beings are valued for their particular donation to the larger whole. Through the topos of ecosystem, then, my activist friends can certainly claim their commitments to a virtue term such as inclusivity and to the spirit of democracy. However, when a "community" perceives itself as under siege, its inclusivity can never be absolute.

Consider that when inclusivity is associated with ecosystems, it becomes something more than just a human idea. Inclusivity becomes part of how nature works, something already there in nature, a natural quality of any ecosystem. Democracy, in contrast, is a political order, a human artifact. Consequently, many believe that democracy is not perfect—the way nature seems to be—but it is at least adequate. But if we associate democracy with ecosystem—via the shared claim that both are inclusive—we "naturalize" the artifice of democracy and thus make it superior to other political orders. Put differently, if we pin ecosystem and democracy together—because our thinking on these matters is enthymematic and associative—ecosystems can take on the aura of democracies and vice versa. Through these associations, democracy becomes another "natural" ecosystem. Here is the slipperiness that I mentioned earlier: inclusivity as an underpinning virtue term allows democracy and ecosystem to slide through each other. Democracies start to look more "natural" than they are, and ecosystems can be read as something cooperative and not, as in the nineteenth century, "red in tooth and claw."

Now, many of the activists seem to find their unity and purpose through the threats mentioned earlier—colonialism, gentrification, the loss of control over institutional power, and so on. Even as they gather their purpose from the threats, they talk of community as ecosystem, but this ecosystem is only inclusive to the extent that the newcomer shares the strategies and visions of the activists. A radical Otherness, if there is such a thing, is like a toxic spill harming the ecosystem. Hence many of the activists must stand perpetually on the ramparts on the lookout. What is the cost of such political anxiety, as if the fruits of one's efforts are always about to erode? What is the burden of so much national pride, so much self-defense? What toll do people pay to harbor what they think is a righteous cause? Repeating the story of an unfair history—the colonization of the island, the repeated gentrification of one's neighborhoods—accomplishes what, exactly? So much labor devoted to creating a self-conscious ethnicity—sometimes it seems so exhausting and ultimately doomed, for the preservation of tradition requires a tremendous labor to fend off the array of forces that constitute the here and now. All this can only be worth it if the community is structurally marginalized—and the data does suggest this. Thus the activists are willing to bear the weight in the name of bettering the Puerto Rican "community." Still, has the reality of community already dissipated? Has the community already dispersed far and wide? Is it now too diluted after decades of living with others in Chicago? More profoundly, what internal differences does the term *community* always hide from view, and, further, what sentimentalities are necessary to prop up belief in the term? To a certain extent, the Puerto Rican activists are not overly worried about the disappearance of Puerto Ricanness, for they sense that it will morph creatively into something else. Perhaps some sort of class politics will emerge layered with something more Latin@ than Puerto Rican, they say. For now, however, it is clear that these activists are absolutely committed to their Puerto Ricanness, but it is not clear that other Puerto Ricans are. In a variety of focus group interviews, a repeated theme was that the young people are losing interest. In other words, even if the data says that the Puerto Ricans are structurally marginalized, it does not mean that that shapes them into a "community," much less an "ecosystem." Nor does wearing the *bandera* on a festival day. How, then, does one know if all the ideological labor and sacrifice waged by the activists will actually stick? But if it doesn't stick, then the social ownership claims will evaporate, and those who remain structurally marginalized will be on their own to make their way through, in effect, a private property regime. Social ownership may be a poor substitution for "real" ownership, but, as I have been arguing, it is also a political maneuver. In Humboldt Park, these maneuvers consist of the activists working with the aldermen to change the city's affordable housing policies by requiring developers to build more than 10 percent affordable housing on developments of ten units or more and forcing them to put their buyout monies into the ward as opposed to the city's general fund.[63] The vulnerability of a "community" has much to do with the fact that the Puerto Ricans have not accumulated multigenerational wealth.[64] Such wealth enables families to backstop their children, providing them with the leverage of an education and the ability to enter a whole range of markets. The activists and the cooperating aldermen respond to this lack of multigenerational wealth by offering social ownership claims and a sense of "Puerto Ricanness" that stimulate, supposedly, cultural capital and critical capital, which will, in time, they hope, leverage real capital. This hope is what underlies the entire project of Paseo: my activist friends ferociously defend this ethnic enclave because they believe it is married to economic development. The effort to keep this marriage intact requires, on occasion, a celebratory anniversary, and Oscar's return to its critical, cultural space after thirty-five years of incarceration was, for my activist friends, a kind of apotheosis of their entire project.

←↨→

Aside from various forms of private property, the common law of both Britain and America . . . recognized two distinguishable types of *public* property. One of these was

predictable from economic theory, namely, public property owned and actively managed by a governmental body. The other, however, was property collectively "owned" by society at large, with claims independent of and indeed superior to the claims of any purported governmental manager. . . . It appears that older public property doctrine vested some form of property rights in the *un*organized public. But what could it mean for the unorganized public to have "rights" in any property at all? How could its members possibly assert their rights except through a governmental body? . . . How could the unorganized public be thought the best property manager, or even a manager at all? Property in such a public would amount to an unlimited commons, which seems not to be property at all but at best only a mass of passive "things" awaiting reduction to private property through the rule of capture—and this, of course, is a situation that leads not to good management of resources but rather to their squandering, in the dreaded tragedy of the commons. Nevertheless, strange though it seems, precisely this unorganized version of the "public" is strongly suggested in some of the earlier public property doctrine—as it is in some modern law as well.
—Rose, *Property and Persuasion*

What is the law? The law names its objects of governance. Legal theorists sometimes call these objects "legal fictions," or something similar.[65] If there is sufficient power of enforcement, a specific world can come into being. Rose is pointing to the creative power of the law when she names private property, public property, and something loosely called "unorganized public" property. The latter category resembles the social ownership practiced by the Puerto Ricans, but it also resembles some of the collective practices of the Meratus Dayak discussed earlier. Thus both contemporary law and customary law invent their objects of governance, but if the laws are to be considered legitimate, they must stay inside the boundaries of the reigning ideology. That is, they must be considered necessary, fair, and rational by a majority of those subject to the law. Consequently, laws can only bring parts of their intended worlds into being.

But Rose also points to something else, something extraordinary: the *unlimited commons*. I prefer the term *deep commons* because I am unsure that anything is genuinely "unlimited." At any rate, this idea of the commons underpins all discussions of land and ownership occurring in Humboldt Park, such as gentrification and colonialism, but it also underpins all discussions of property whether private, public, or unorganized public. But the activists do not discuss the commons. Indeed, no one does because the deep commons is largely unthinkable. What we can think about are lesser terms such as gentrification, colonialism, homo economicus, the different types of property, ownership, possession, and so on. These terms name different types of relationships between people in relation to the things of the world, but behind these names is the deep commons. The deep commons is what these other names prey upon in order to initiate someone's advantage at the expense of someone else. In some ways, the very intention behind these names and the legal fictions associated with them is rather pernicious. That is, they hide the deep commons until it disappears from everyone's view. I talk more about the deep commons later in the text.

Another term discussed by Rose and used by most economists and legal theorists is *resource commons*. I consider the term a distinctly "thin" version of the deep commons. As long as the resource commons remains the governing legal fiction, we will not properly witness the deep commons. Now, the term *commons* is an ancient concept referring to various forms of ownership of a resource such as common pastures, ocean fisheries, and tidal lands and all the life-forms that grow there. The "tragedy of the commons"[66] in Rose's quotation refers to the depletion of these resources, as in overgrazing, when everyone is allowed unrestricted use. Thus most economists today consider the tragedy of the commons the best justification for founding a private property regime. For all practical purposes, it has replaced Locke's origin story for private property. That is, to understand property rights we do not need Locke's labor theory of value, much less his metaphysical analyses of "man in a state of nature." Instead, there is general agreement today among economists and legal theorists that property rights emerge as a pragmatic solution to waste insofar as the ownership of property guarantees, they say, better stewardship. In this sense, they argue, private property is superior to public or state-owned property because "when things are left open to the public . . . they are wasted, either by overuse or underinvestment."[67] Hence the tragedy of the commons refers to the abuse that emerges when a resource commons is open and free to all. By understanding this notion of "tragedy," one can grasp the nearly shocking libertarian argument that public parks and beaches ought to be privatized if we are serious about preserving them.

What is at stake in the notion of "the tragedy of the commons"? When strong private property advocates express disdain for almost all forms of public ownership, they are expressing a variant of the tragedy of the commons. In Humboldt Park, the complaint regarding the presence of litter and trash can be, at one instance, a racialized complaint against the "habits" of Puerto Ricans but, at another instance, a complaint about the inferiority of public resources and management when compared to the private sector. The economist Harold Demsetz provides a particularly forceful rationalization to ground these latter expressions of disdain.[68] He asserts that private property puts land use under individual rational controls. It creates a type of enclosure that enhances productivity and stewardship because individuals are incentivized to manage well the sources of their livelihood. In contrast, common uses of resources—such as the harvesting of ocean fish or traditional villagers allowing their pigs to forage in nearby forests where the villagers also harvest lumber—represent no cost to the users, who are therefore tempted to take all that they can. Here, then, is the "tragedy of the commons," and for Demsetz, at least, the historical rise of private property functions as a nearly inevitable process that might stem the tragedy and salvage the sustainability of resources. (This battle between private property and the commons reappears in the current controversies over the internet, a kind of commons that is being challenged by rent-seeking enclosures.)[69]

Framing it in economic language, the tension is between "externalities" and "internalities." Externalities (consider air pollution) are not priceable within the marketplace and therefore not controllable. But if an externality can be internalized—that is, if it can be given a price and therefore provide information to help determine a possible gain over and above its cost—then that very action has created a new kind of property functioning within a specific market. For instance, if excess carbon emissions (pollution) can be turned into a commodity that can be bought and sold at steep prices, a new market selling new properties has been invented with the hope of curbing otherwise "free" emissions. At one moment, the air is a commons—it is, therefore, free, open, and waiting to be used up or polluted by anyone—but at another moment carbon-filled air is priced at each metric ton of carbon emission. An externality has been converted into an internality. In the eyes of homo economicus, this constant creation of new markets by converting externalities into internalities is one of the dynamic features of capitalism and thus far superior to protective, regulatory regimes that depend on the strong arm of government. But notice how the making of internalities by giving externalities a price might resemble a kind of frenzy in which the opportunity to create a market can be aimed at waste and many other things.[70] The maddening suggestion that Demsetz and others present is whether *any* externality ought to exist. Should all externalities be priced and thus become an internality, that is, become internal to some market or another?

Ultimately, buried at the very core of the tragedy of the commons is the myth-building, seventeenth-century state-of-nature parable, a trope that has served many uses in the invention of Euro-American modernity. Elinor Ostrom links the state of nature to the tragedy of the commons: "Hobbes's parable of man in a state of nature is a prototype of the tragedy of the commons: Men seek their own good and end up fighting one another."[71] This is the infamous Hobbesian claim of the war against all, where we have the "natural right" to take what we can and to kill in order to protect what we have. Because of fear we are motivated to sacrifice our "natural" freedoms to the Leviathan, the supreme sovereign, who will now guarantee a social order of limited freedoms in exchange for guaranteeing and protecting contracts and property. But for Ostrom, Hobbes's state of nature and its later incarnation in the tragedy of the commons are not inevitable, meaning that a resource commons is not necessarily depleted, nor does it demand a private property regime to stop overgrazing.

Let me pull together quickly some of the major lines of thinking in the resource commons literature. Demsetz, Hardin, Ostrom, and, looming behind all of them, Hobbes frame, with notable differences, the ideas of property and freedom as conditions bound to abundance and scarcity. Hardin, for instance, frames the "tragedy of the commons" as a kind of apocalyptic collapse of enlightenment freedoms and a dangerous return to the state of nature: "The only way we can preserve and nurture other and more precious freedoms is by relinquishing the freedom to breed, and that very soon. . . . Only so, can we put an end to this aspect of the tragedy of the commons."[72] Hardin's arguments are particularly disturbing, for his target is overpopulation as the world's peoples consume the largest resource commons of all, the planet. The impending future of environmental degradation cannot be technically solved, he believes, and in this sense he argues for coercion and the end of our "freedom to breed." If for Hardin not even the private property regime can save us, for Demsetz—and for Locke as well—freedom is achieved through the private property regime itself, and thus they echo the libertarian faith in marketplaces and homo economicus. For Ostrom, who empirically studied small communities that had implemented rational management of their various commons (e.g., ocean fisheries), freedom and abundance, as opposed to scarcity, could be had through the efforts of local, deliberative communities. Ostrom, whose work won a Nobel Prize, regards a resource commons as something that does not necessitate central planning, nor is it abused by "overgrazing" on the part of selfish individuals. That is, those who make use of a commons freely find their own management solutions, and thus a private property regime is not inevitable and in some cases might not be preferred. For all these theorists, however, the paradigm is rather similar: the potentiality of humans is derived from the stored potentiality within nature, and thus forms of stewardship, whether through a private property regime or a self-regulated commons, are necessary if scarcity is to be avoided.

This paradigm, I want to argue, underlies all current ownership claims—private, state, social, and unorganized public. Ownership makes the world work in particular kinds of ways. To utter the term *ownership* pitches us into a discursive network containing other terms such as *freedom, abundance, scarcity, potentiality,* and so on. For instance, many homeowners in Humboldt Park believe they have the right to a certain abundance that is available to them that does not exist for their neighbors in affordable housing. They would call that abundance rising property values. If they buy low and sell high, which they would say is their right, they will have actualized the potential stored in their homes. Hence they hope to increase their abundance by encouraging even more abundance around them, and so they sometimes resent those in affordable housing and would prefer that they leave. Affordable housing deflates property values, they argue.[73] Further, these homeowners regard their property as representing a kind of freedom, a freedom to buy and sell (Hobbes's bourgeois state)[74] wherever they please. Meanwhile, the activists who defend right to the city claims or social ownership are attempting to create a possible and different kind of abundance—cultural capital if not outright capital—for those who are distinctly unfree because their choices in the marketplace are restricted. The activists believe that cultural capital is another kind of potentiality, a potentiality based on knowing who one is as a counter to self-denigration as a consequence of class marginalization.

←↨→

Rose described earlier the "unlimited commons" as being a "mass of passive 'things'" that had not yet become productive because they had not yet been subjected to a private property regime. I shy away from Rose's term *unlimited* despite the fact that I adore *limitlessness* as a core principle for rhetorical theory. Hence I substitute *deep commons* for Rose's *unlimited commons*. But the referent remains the same: the deep commons might be likened to pure potential, but in becoming property it starts to become actualized for someone like Locke—or ripe for overgrazing and abuse for folks like Demsetz and Hardin. The point is that the deep commons seems to be a profound condition always lying in wait, for it constitutes whatever exists prior to becoming refashioned into property. It is prior to any anthrocentric or anthropomorphic capture via ownership—individual, state, or unorganized public. If property, then, is a kind of "thingness," what is the commons? Perhaps it represents a totality, or original abundance, that has yet to be individuated into prices and markets because it is the source of both. But if it can't be priced, it will remain largely invisible (an "externality" perhaps?), even if it extends across the entire economic horizon. As a result, it is hard to estimate the deep commons or take an accounting of it, say, in GDP terms, because nothing is produced and yet it is the source of production; hence we simply do not know of it, and it becomes economically irrelevant. As long as private property and ownership remain materially and ideologically dominant, they control the economy, and we are unable to theorize the deep commons much less realize it and establish it as an ethical foundation.

Let us provide some examples of a deep commons. Notice in each case the problem of pricing. Notice also that each example does not seem to be a resource commons that can be overgrazed. It seems to be something more implacable, a kind of ever-present "thereness" that precedes the coming into being of property and its pricing.

The commons comes in many packages. Consider the very notion of private property: "[the] entire private property regime—whether governmental or customary—may be understood as a managed commons: a private property *regime* is itself a metaproperty, held in common by those who understand and follow its precepts. In a sense, when we decide to divide up the commons into private property, we are only moving from a commons in a physical resource to a commons in the social structure that safeguards individualized resource management."[75]

Rose, here, distinguishes between a "commons in a physical resource," which in effect is what the "dreaded tragedy of the commons" is all about, and a "commons in the social structure." Social ownership of land via one's cultural capital, I argue, resembles this "commons in the social structure," or, better, the deep commons. This sort of commons represents a kind of enormity beyond a resource commons, and thus it is difficult for current economic theory to take account of it. Hence the arguments by Demsetz, Hardin, and even Ostrom, which only theorize the idea of a resource commons, seem to have no intuitions at all regarding the deep commons that seems vaster and far more mysterious in its makeup.

According to Rose, there is a metaproperty that sanctions any private property regime. That metaproperty, as vague as it might seem, would have to precede every private property transaction, for it constitutes the common agreement, the common sense, that encourages the newcomers around Humboldt Park, for instance, to first imagine and then actualize what they think is the potential stored in their homes. At the same time, it also precedes and, therefore, allows the activists to invent a counterstrategy—namely, a social ownership claim that has less traction in the courts but is nevertheless symbolically powerful. The steel flags on either side of Paseo and the No Se Vende campaign—which for a few years placed signs up and down the windows of Paseo and meant "Not For Sale," and more broadly "Humboldt Park is not for sale to 'outsiders'"—are examples of a cultural capital whose material presence replies to the newcomers that this is ours, not yours. In these types of wars, of course, social ownership seems inferior to actual ownership, but clearly symbols also have impact. At any rate, the deep commons functions in this case at the metalevel, for it includes all the implicit and explicit agreements that allow a people devoted to commerce to make "commonsensical" decisions within their private property regime—even decisions that resist the regime. This metalevel has a variety of instantiations in the United States Constitution and in each Supreme Court decision that has wrestled with possession and ownership, private property, eminent domain, public trust law, customary rights, and so on. So every private property transaction can only come into being when people already believe that individuated selves ought to be free to buy and sell individuated land and other entities. In other words, these beliefs exist in a commons called the Constitution. The Constitution holds these beliefs in potential but actualizes them in specific laws passed, again, by common agreement. Recall that for Mohammed Bouazizi another sort of metaproperty—one that he resents—is in charge of his economic life.

At any rate, many elements represent the total volume of abundance held in the commons called the "private property regime," which, as Rose notes, is a matter of "social structure" in contrast to a resource type of commons such as fisheries or waterways. It seems difficult, if not impossible, to rationalize and price a social structure type of commons—and the Constitution is, in essence, a commons. That is to say, its value is its abundance flowing through the capillaries of social life and providing the foundation for the invention of property, ownership, and price—and yet, and this is of the highest importance, it itself has no price. It is astonishing that that which enables the creation of price has no price—and yet it must exist somewhere inside every price. Can we render its value as a portion of the price? Would this hidden price be an extraordinary amount or a miniscule amount? One would think that its foundational and enabling power would be extraordinary—75¢ on the dollar or even 98¢ on the dollar—or maybe it is miniscule: only 2¢ on the dollar. The first set of calculations (and I do not know if this commons is indeed measurable) suggests that social ownership is the major player. It raises the ultimate question: On what basis does the individual own anything? Mustn't ownership as a paradigmatic and institutionalized way of being precede any individual act of owning? In contrast, the last calculation, 2¢ on the dollar, establishes the legitimacy of the private owner, for the bulk of the price would not be socially constituted but a consequence of individual effort. Liberalism as an economic and political philosophy synonymous with homo economicus rests on ethical premises that rely on the last calculation being a kind of truth claim. But the deep commons rests on another truth claim with its own ethical premises that state, in effect, that individual effort accomplishes little because it is wholly dependent on the specific commons to provide its ideology and rationalization, and, finally, to provide the social institutions through which individual effort realizes itself.

We also might turn to money because it, too, functions as a "socially structured commons" and is not a resource commons. Money is a technology that enables the pricing system. Hence money enables an economy to transform invisible externalities into visible internalities through the power of pricing. Pricing, as stated earlier, allows markets to come into being, for market participants are able to calculate costs and benefits more exactly through pricing than through, for instance, trade by barter. That is, money, which we hold dear, is an exacting technology that reduces the contingencies and ambiguities of what is valued into something more manageable and visible—namely, a price.[76] In other words, people may dicker forever over the value of something, but once the something acquires a price, the contingency has been reduced. Now, the strange irony is that Demsetz argues that both private property and pricing ought to replace a resource commons if we are to properly manage and preserve the resource itself, but he does not realize, apparently, that the ideas of private property and money, upon which pricing depends, are two articulations of a broader, deeper commons. Again, it seems that economists ignore, for the most part, the idea of a deep commons, and therefore it is not theorized. But the deep commons ought to be a subject of ontological inquiry, and that is what the social theorist Ole Bjerg attempts to do in his inquiries into money. For Bjerg, money surpasses its utility as a technology that enables pricing:

> Money is a system for keeping track of the purchasing power that each individual in the system is entitled to command. . . . It is at the same time also a collective system that is common and shared by every member of the collective. . . . The beggar and billionaire contribute equally to the system insofar as both act as if the token circulating as money in the community is in fact money. The beggar and billionaire may differ in the amount of money they own as individuals, but they have an equal share in money as the system which structures their economic interaction. . . . The money of rich people has value only insofar as even poor people accept this money as money.[77]

Money, as a commons, is more unusual than the Constitution and the private property regime contained therein. On the one hand, money is mass produced, a kind of widget rolling off an assembly line. Indeed, it has fixed costs such as the machinery that makes it, paper and ink (indeed, production costs constitute about 93 percent of the 726.6 million of the 2017 currency budget), transport services that deliver it, quality assurance, counterfeit deterrence, and so on.[78] On the other hand, unlike a widget, these costs do not raise the price of a dollar bill. For instance, in 2018 every dollar contains about 5.5¢ per note, every fifty dollar bill about 11.5¢ per note, and every one-hundred-dollar bill contains about 14.2¢ per note. (Interestingly, in 2014 a penny and a nickel cost more than they were worth.)[79] But these costs are not added to any piece of currency. Indeed, they are absorbed by the government, or Rose's organized public, and wisely so because of the enormous value that currency represents. Money has special properties that make it invaluable. It has the capacity to be stored or to freely circulate, but surely its most significant property is as a medium that can be applied to every object and social relation. As a universal index, it has the ultimate power to determine meaningfulness. But these peculiar properties are not monetarily represented at the moment of exchange. Moreover, as Bjerg suggests, the more significant collective agreement of rich and poor regarding the meaningfulness of money is also not represented. That is, we do not pay for these properties when we put money to use. They are free or unpaid for. If we were to calculate the portion of the wealth that is due to the commons called "money," how much wealth would be left over that either the rich or the poor could call their "own"?

We can calculate production costs on, say, every hundred dollar bill (14.2¢) that we, in effect, do not pay for. But all other social properties are an additional portion. The point is that whatever the amount of the social sum, wealth is only partially attributable to the efforts of an individual and significantly attributable to the commons itself. For how could the wealthy have accumulated so much without the technology of money functioning at the deepest levels of their money-making? Moreover, what percentage of their wealth is due to the social presumptions that value wealth itself and, finally, all the institutions, which are also not the result of their effort but enable their wealth to come into being?

We might call the deep commons by another name. Certainly, the *general intellect* might be a candidate. Paolo Virno runs through some of its historical legacy and emphasizes Marx, but I find Virno's understanding of the term superior to anyone else's: "Mass intellectuality is the prominent form in which the general intellect is manifest today. The scientific erudition of the individual labourer is not under question here. Rather, all the more generic attitudes of the mind gain primary status as productive resources; these are the faculty of language, the disposition to learn, memory, the power of abstraction and relation and the tendency toward self-reflexivity. General intellect needs to be understood literally as intellect in general: the faculty and power to think, rather than the words produced by thought—a book, an algebra formula, etc."[80]

The deep commons, then, as also including the general intellect, would point to education, language, weights and measures—indeed everything that might be understood as the store of knowledge that enables any innovation, small or large, a turn of phrase, any creative act, any technological solution. One might just as soon include rhetorical knowledge itself and pay particular attention to Aristotle's "available means of persuasion" as, for instance, a fund of shared topoi, for what would the English translation "available" mean if not something that precedes any participant because it is what is summoned at any given moment by those who must show themselves to each other? The vast values of all this are never calculated into prices or costs. They represent the common wealth upon which all wealth-making depends. In sum, the wealth that both the wealthy and the poor call their "own" is, to a significant degree, a borrowing from the common wealth. But the loan is never paid back. Rather, strangely, the individual (or individual corporation) claims it as their own. Liberalism and homo economicus depend on these sorts of magical acts.

One final example will help pull together some of the notions that I have been pursuing—namely, the idea of a self extending itself, via metaphor, toward a not-self and claiming it as its own, and the idea of a deep commons as the basis of a huge percentage of everyone's wealth so that it becomes extraordinarily difficult to claim that one's wealth is due to one's initiative or effort. In a sense, the second idea cancels the convictions that people create when they believe the first idea. My argument builds from anthropologist Anna Tsing's claims in a recent book titled *The Mushroom at the End of the World.*[81] She talks eloquently about "salvage accumulation." Salvage accumulation seems to be at the heart of all forms of wealth extraction. It represents the stuff that is largely outside markets—such as the primordial fertility of the earth and the eons it took to create fertility that could be powered by sunlight. All this is largely unpriced, and yet it must exist as part of the price that the agriculturalist receives for her vegetables, and the primordial changes in DNA, including nonhuman DNA, that have made humans very innovative but remain largely unpriced in the prices of every innovation. This primordial, deep commons exists prior to any individual's wealth-making. Individuals are lying when they claim that the wealth they made is utterly theirs. That is, every ownership claim scissors the world into mine and thine, which, in effect, rationalizes away our social dependencies, the deep commons upon which our lives depend. Consider a high rise at the edge of Lake Michigan. A condo of a certain square footage that faces the lake will be more expensive than another condo of the same square footage and vintage a half mile inland. The reason why, of course, is that the lake condo is directly exposed to the spectacle of nature. An approaching storm, for instance, swirls around the building, but the owners are safely tucked away behind floor-to-ceiling glass. By paying extra money for their condo, they are both protected from and immersed within the vicissitudes of nature. At one time, storms were outside insurance and real estate markets. They were a kind of externality, but then they became domesticated by these markets when, for instance, technological innovations appeared that allowed people to live safely high in the air, almost in the middle of storms, so to speak. At that moment, the externality called "storms" became an internality, for they were brought into the housing market and given a price. Indeed, one could technically calculate with some exactness the "added value" of storms and beachfront by comparing condo prices at the lakefront to equivalent condos a few blocks inland. Real estate agents and sellers pocket that added value not because of their individual effort. The added value is due to the beachfront, which is publicly maintained; building materials that were invented rather recently; insurance institutions and their databases; and, ultimately, the storms themselves. Thus when the condos are sold, a percentage of the selling price will be due precisely to the general intellect and spectacles of nature that cannot be owned. To repeat: do the owners of their condos own the history of engineering innovations, or the spectacle of nature outside the building, much less the storms that swirl around them? No. Have they mixed their labor with nature and therefore acquired rightful ownership over the spectacle? No. Are they "overgrazing" a common resource? Possibly. One could imagine a building boom of shoddy housing up and down the lakefront—in this sense, higher prices on the lakefront have prevented that boom, as Demsetz might argue. But the larger point has to do with the deep commons, how it functions as the source of a potentiality, which when tapped becomes a cornerstone of economic development that ultimately cannot be owned or possessed through the current paradigms of wealth-making.

It is probably best to say that the deep commons is not "ownable," even though salvage accumulation attempts exactly that. But we seem to be trapped inside the metaphor of ownership. I keep saying, for instance, that common ownership is always invisible inside the accumulation of any individual ownership. Common ownership, as a result, disappears into the ether. Or I say that the individual property owner takes her price and subtracts her cost and never takes an accounting of the socially owned part. No compensation or dividend is made to social owners despite the fact that without its vast labor, or at least presence, the price itself might not exist. Figuratively speaking, the commonwealth hands its wealth over to the individual, and the individual never takes notice. It is tempting to call individual wealth a form of unconscious theft against the commonwealth insofar as the individual or corporation claims as part of her wealth that which is attributable to the commonwealth. Such unconscious theft is aided, even sanctioned, by law; it disappears beneath a consciousness of right—that is, a property right that has become fully naturalized. But I ask the reader to take note: this language of "theft" tells us how deeply saturated we are with the metaphors of ownership and property. Each metaphor names a small slice of the deep commons and over time takes on the appearance of a "reality" beyond metaphor; meanwhile, the deep commons—reality as such, or so it seems to me—becomes unwitnessed and unthinkable.

In the name of fairness, should we instrumentalize the deep commons by distributing to the broader commonwealth some "social dividend" to those who enable wealth-making but do not capitalize on their contribution? Actually, a variety of instruments such as a progressive tax and universal basic income do this sort of work without any of my fancy philosophizing.[82] As Rose might say, such instruments convert the unorganized public into an organized public, meaning that such instruments are established and maintained by the state. Such instruments, of course, are part of the technocracy of socialism, and it is not at all clear if one can still envision the deep reservoir of the commons underneath socialism's version of managerial modernity. The deep commons may seem palpably real when articulated in this text, but its undifferentiated qualities make it unreal and invisible. To become visible, the state would have to submit it to individuation and social engineering, and couple it with a fetishization of fairness. So if we did submit it to a kind of absolute rationality by tabulating all human and nonhuman contributions and strictly observing a morality of fairness, would we, in effect, slaughter the deep commons by transforming its totality of externalities into internalities? The commons as potentiality would become reduced to actualities. All aspects of the deep commons would have a price. The dream of Demsetz?

I suspect that the deep commons and social ownership claims cannot be fully included in our current economic and legal regimes. They belong to a kind of Otherness that inevitably escapes instrumentalization. This Otherness relegates them to a kind of nebulousness. Nevertheless, at the same time, the deep commons and social ownership claims continue to exist irrepressibly in our intuitions. They cannot be undone, and therefore they contain a chaotic potential that, at times, wants to undo liberalism's bifurcation of property into either private or state ownership. Hence the courts allow the deep commons and social ownership claims to remain mostly dormant, except in limited cases.[83] Granted, Rose, ever the legal theorist, does not approach the deep commons or social ownership claims as having this sort of chaotic potential, but Blomley is so inclined. Occupy movements, for instance, let loose this potential that is eventually reined in by the police. If it were not suppressed, it would probably grow into Hobbesian-like civil war. People feel dispossessed, abandoned, and bitter at the moment of foreclosure when they realize that the self is about to be separated from its not-self, even if they rationally understand debt default. Extend this to group claims over indigenous lands and the removal power of states serving the interests of mining and lumber companies. In all these instances, it is the job of the state to keep these social ownership claims in perpetual Otherness, to give them the status of "mere" metaphor—even if some sort of palpable reality lies underneath. If claims about long-standing use and habitation were allowed to rise up as foundational claims—the way that Puerto Rican activists seem to regard Humboldt Park—the claims would enter the courts and forcefully expose the fragility of the private property regime as also resting on the same metaphorical apparatus. What then?

At times, however, these claims of the deep commons and social ownership are articulated in very mundane, everyday terms. That is, the fact that these claims can have both a disruptive Otherness and chaotic potential, as well as an absolutely mundane existence, seems to locate the claims themselves as a deep reality that cannot be undone and as an expression of our beingness with others. Consider the difference between a bank and a credit union. Individuals deposit their small sums into a bank and the bank aggregates those sums when it invests in financial instruments or provides large loans to, say, a developer. That is, "individual monies" become aggregated into a commons that is now "owned" by a bank. Individuals may withdraw their monies and collect a modest amount of interest, but they have no claim regarding the use of their monies and no claim over the profits (or losses) of the bank's investment decisions. In effect, each depositor at the moment of depositing signs a quit claim regarding any future profits that that small amount of money may enable. Thus individual monies disappear into a "common pot" that becomes the property of the bank to be put to further use. In sum, if a bank makes 7¢ of profit from the dollar that you put in, the bank may pay you 1¢ worth of interest, but because you signed, in effect, a quit claim on their use of your dollar, that 6¢ is theirs, even though the bank would not have made that extra money without your dollar. Why is the 6¢ utterly theirs? In contrast, credit unions recognize a continuing "social ownership" claim insofar as depositors receive a "social dividend" for the use of their money in the form of higher interest rates and lower loan rates. Technically, it is a nonprofit cooperative, but we can see how it implies the ideas of a deep commons and social ownership. Both credit unions and banks bring a commons into being, and they do so with the authority and oversight of the state. If the credit union commons acknowledges the authority of social ownership by paying a "social dividend," the bank commons does not. If banks were not profit-making institutions but utilities—that is, conduits for aggregating the commons of money and channeling it to broader uses—they would be on their way to serving a more significant social ownership function. But they do not. The larger point, however, is that the commons in its original form as a socially unorganized public, a deep commons, is still not representable in the commons of credit unions or in the commons of banks. Nevertheless—and this is what is remarkable—the deep commons is there, though not fully expressed. Its fuller expression seems to be outside the state's ability. It remains a vast Otherness and a potentiality that cannot be depleted by any particular actualization. Still, only when it is harnessed or institutionalized by taking, for instance, the shape of a credit union can the commons mobilize its social ownership claim and make it materially useful. We face, then, a conundrum: If the deep commons, indeed, is a kind of palpable reality beneath private property ownership, should we not try to realize it? Even if it is only sporadically realized in state ownership, should we not find ways to do so? Shouldn't a social dividend be paid off somehow?

In sum, the idea of social ownership suggests that there is a vast equality of contribution that underlies the general wealth. Because of property rights, this vast equality of contribution legally flows into the coffers of private ownership. Social ownership thus disappears, as if by magic, when private property owners legally claim the contributions of others as their own. Underneath this system are profound questions: Who owns? Who owns what? How so? But no matter how these questions get answered, we seem to be possessed by possession. Obviously, social ownership is not outside the ideological box of possession. For instance, the discursive grip of liberalism structures the disputes between property owners, as well as the disputes between property owners and state ownership. This same discursive grip has not allowed social ownership to carve out much space within these disputes, and yet, intuitively, it makes sense to do so. Tragically (or not), the only way to carve out such space would be to make a rival claim to "rightful" possession—and in doing so the commons enters the fray as something to be rationalized. Will the swelling of managerial modernity never cease?

5

Closings/Openings

Writing from Moscow during the collapse of the Soviet Union, Susan Buck-Morss in her book *Dreamworld and Catastrophe* argues that the "ideological divide" of the Cold War masked a problem shared by both communism and liberalism. As she states in her preface: "[This book] interprets cultural developments of the twentieth century within opposed political regimes as variations of a common theme, the utopian dream that industrial modernity could and would provide happiness for the masses."[1] This dream, or "dreamworld," as she puts it, can be traced to the revolutionary moments of the eighteenth century, particularly the French Revolution:

> The end of the old regime was perceived in 1789 as the *return* of power to society, a reappropriation by the people of their sovereignty, a recovery of their *natural* rights. Of course, just this notion of power residing equally in all the people rather than in the monarch, just this secular conception of legitimate power in opposition to the idea of divine right, *was* utterly new, and it marked a decisive rupture from the political imaginary that had existed until then. To found legitimate power on a popular basis, without recourse to divine explanation or unquestioned obedience to authority—this became the political project of modernity. It is a project that we have yet to realize.[2]

Thus modern mass societies, at heart, represent a management problem. The attempts to realize any utopia will face the problem of constantly fueling conviction in the utopia, even as it dampens the inevitable emergence of disappointments and disaffections. In other words, utopian dreamworlds are fetishizations, and they require exquisite management. They must have the ability to name the specific limitations that the people feel and then provide solutions that point to "limitlessness," a "release of potentiality" that the people consider their birthright as faithful citizens of the utopia. In sum, the differences between these Cold War rivals were superficial. Underneath the surface were shared structures having to do with modernity's fascination with utopianism. As a result, Soviet communism and American liberalism, as expressions of modernity, faced similar challenges: Who is the ultimate sovereign—the state or the utopian concept of the "people"? How does one institutionalize the utopian concept of equality? How does one establish governance—through the efficiencies of fiat or the inefficiencies and impossibilities of representation? These questions, as I've argued throughout this book, point to the larger issue: managing the utopianism and messianism of modernist political life finds its locus in the problem of territorializing deterritorialized dreamworlds.

This problem means that managerial modernity contains an internal war when, for instance, utopian sentiments of nativist belonging clash with utopian sentiments that all belong, whether citizen or not, simply because of a shared humanity—how does the state territorialize both? This internal war becomes visible (presences itself) when we claim "rights."[3] For instance, the Wittgensteinian philosopher Elizabeth Wolgast describes rights as furthering an atomistic society because rights function as moral possessions securing the singularity of an individual or group against other individuals or groups. Making matters worse is the notion that rights are sanctified as transcendental birthrights.[4] In sum, deterritorialized rights become territorialized in constitutions and particularly in the courts, and the utopianisms of equality or a universal "freedom of movement" become territorialized, even erased, by the nation-state's sovereign right to determine its rules of belonging. The rhetorical principle of limitation → limitlessness, which tries to depict the rhetorical movement from one to the other, correlates with or is based on the material problems of territorializing concepts that are deterritorialized. Or, phrasing it a little differently: the internal wars of managerial modernity are visible in many of our rhetorical moves.

In sum, Buck-Morss points us rightly, I believe, toward modernity as a release of utopian dreamworlds, or, as I call it, "the release of potentiality." For the nation-state, this leads to a problem of managing the ensuing material and rhetorical forces. Indeed, consider that the state as territorialized entity is part of the problem, for many of our utopian philosophies do not wish to be territorialized by nation-states. Thus the constitutions of states, and perhaps the United States Constitution in particular, are ideal documents for examining the push and pull of territorializing the deterritorialized. I argued in chapter 3, for instance, that the Fourteenth Amendment contains these tensions in the shifts between "citizen" and "person," suggesting that citizenship always territorializes personhood and personhood deterritorializes citizenship. In a similar vein, I argued that, though the Constitution as an economic document sacralizes property, it cannot guarantee horizontal distribution; rather, it presumes that the horizontal problem will get resolved if everyone has the right to vertical accumulation, an accumulation that cannot be "rightfully" capped. Hence does the Constitution inscribe, honor, and protect enlightenment freedoms and liberties, including the liberating potentiality of property, or is it a kind of operating manual for managerial modernity? The answer could be that the two possibilities are in ratio, but since we rarely hear the second possibility, let me be clear about my suspicions: deterritorialized freedoms and liberties provide a sense of limitlessness that helps states manage mass populations who, in liberal democracy and elsewhere, are in perpetual need of limitlessness in order to endure their burdens.

←↕→

So I agree with Buck-Morss that our modernist mass societies have been built on utopian dreamworlds. Soviet communism and America's liberal democracy represented in their respective ways a difficult burden—namely, the need to plant utopian principles into a political regime. But underneath any utopian image of coherence lies fault lines of incoherence. These incoherencies tend to endure underneath long histories that try to rationalize them away. I have been concerned in this book with delineating a few of these incoherencies, these ruses, of managerial modernity as they are lived out in democracy, particularly liberal democracy.

When I was in Kosova, I witnessed the residual presence of the former Yugoslavian dreamworld, which was itself a species of Communist utopianism. The dreamworld was built into the physical landscape in the form of monumental architecture such as ugly public housing or the dullness of the Grand Hotel Prishtina. The collapse of that dreamworld was evident in the city parks that had long ago run out of resources for their maintenance. Furthermore, there had been an active resistance to that dreamworld in the form of family compounds that constructed private life behind traditional high walls. Kosovars often spoke of the sharp divide between public life, Communist life, which started outside the walls and remained financially neglected, and private life, which began inside the walls and was immaculately well kept, whether poor or not, in keeping with Kosovar traditions of personal and familial dignity. There were two domains, however, in which the Communist dreamworld achieved some success, the pension system and public health care. Retirees, doctors, and former patients typically mentioned these, but beyond that the dreamworld mostly failed to be realized.

I also witnessed in the early 2000s the dismantling of collective property, or socially owned enterprises (SOEs), as they were called. SOEs had been one of the pillars of that older dreamworld. The privatization of the SOEs—according to the international experts (managers) who led the way until at least Kosova's independence in 2008—was to be the material foundation for the new market economy that would enable entry into the new dreamworld of the global free market. Privatization was the new game in town. Those who had the wherewithal, including an emerging class of politically connected oligarchs, were in a rush to acquire land; those without wherewithal were losing ground. However, Kosova remained significantly rural, and because all rural families still lived in large compounds with significant land holdings that had not been collectivized, things could have been much worse. Because of my personal interests in agriculture, I talked to many farmers, and their consistent story was not about the loss of land but the new costs of production, such as fertilizer, new machinery, livestock, and most importantly lending rates that discouraged farmers from planting. They also complained of the new oligarchs maneuvering political patronage to favor some farming areas and not others. If the vagaries and costs of entering the market seemed to expose the ruses of the new dreamworld, these same farmers a few years earlier had experienced the ruses of communism. Nevertheless, they remained relatively confident that somehow, someday the fact that they owned land would lead them to success.

This sense of wherewithal, or potential, that might be realized at some point in the future has been just as important in the liberal democratic imaginary of the United States since at least the country's founding. For instance, according to the legal theorist Stanley Katz, the American system of property, land, and ownership was the result of a fusion of Jeffersonian and Lockean ideals. "For Jefferson, America was the perfect environment for the operation of the Lockean theory of property shorn of its limitations, for in America the endless abundance of land in the inexhaustible continent rendered it unthinkable that either mere accumulation or unavailability could deprive each man of his due share of the natural stock of plenty."[5]

"Endless abundance of land" in an "inexhaustible continent" would allow everyone to own property, and thus individual liberty would flourish. The Northwest Ordinance of 1787, the Louisiana Purchase of 1803, and the Homestead Act of 1862 were about, among other things, the domestication of land, that is, the transformation of something raw into something owned. These acts of managerial modernity presumed that individual land ownership could foil the emergence of wealth-based aristocracies or oligarchies.[6] Furthermore, the sheer abundance of resources in the Americas meant its inexhaustibility, meaning that concentrated accumulation, as had occurred under the aristocrats of Europe, could not occur in the United States because there would always be enough to go around. In sum, the very idea of private property in the American, liberal democratic incarnation grounded different forms of limitless potential, which managerial modernity was burdened to release.

In sum, managerial modernity has imagined potentiality as inhabiting three domains. It has imagined (1) the human as pregnant with potential and imagined (2) property, particularly the ownership of land, as a vehicle for the realization of that potential. Collective ownership and individual ownership may look, at first glance, diametrically opposed. For instance, the democratic rhetorics of rights, freedom, and liberty provided a legal basis for private ownership and unfettered acquisition, while collective ownership favored the distribution of acquisition, but the larger point is that both socialist and liberal legal systems were variations of each other tasked with the management of property. Both legal systems ordered the things of the world and made them manageable so as to release their potentiality on behalf of the human. (3) Last, innovation and technology, through the power of engineering, functioned with a kind of telos—namely, the transformation of human limitation into limitlessness. That is, enlightenment beliefs regarding the potentiality of the human functioned as a kind of moral obligation, and so the state had to instrumentalize both nature and technical capacity, as Buck-Morss documents well. Democracies of all sorts, socialisms, communisms, and even fascisms and anarchisms grounded their legitimacy in the release of these potentialities. They produced ideological competition: the limitlessness of the individual versus the limitlessness of the collective versus the limitless spirit of the nation. Each ideological system named one of the others as tyranny, as its rhetorical opposite, in order to establish itself as the one and only *true* expression of modernity: that is, the only genuine utopia embodying the release of potentiality. However, because each system was but one expression of managerial modernity, it was inevitable that each existed in ratio with the others.

←↨→

The most remarkable analysis of property as the release of potentiality is, I believe, Hegel's *Philosophy of Right*. Hegel's text, published in 1821, tries to combine the subjectivism and selfhood embedded in Kant, Lutheranism, and the French Revolution's idea of the "people" with the ontotheological traditions of the classical Greek philosophers and medievalists. More particularly, Hegel applies his speculative philosophy as it appears in his *Phenomenology of Spirit*[7] to the formation of the state and its laws and, more generally, ethical life. In sum, he is trying to pull down universal principles and actualize them in the particularities of everyday living. He is trying to shape the modern world, and one can see in his thought the utopian rationalizations of socialism and liberalism, as described by Buck-Morss, taking shape. (Marx's socialist reading of Hegel, of course, was about to step forth onto the world stage, and both authors had absorbed Locke's liberalism as a release of human potentiality releasing, in turn, nature's potentiality.) But what interests me the most is how Hegel's metaphysics of freedom transforms the idea of property (property as the ultimate territorialization) into a vehicle for the deterritorialization (perhaps "spiritualization" is a more accurate word in Hegel's case) of the human. I will try to explain this double move as belonging in some form or another to all property relations. Here's a passage from Hegel's text that helps me to expand what is at stake:

> A person has as his substantive end the right of putting his will into any and every thing and thereby making it his. . . . This is the absolute right of appropriation which man has over all 'things.' . . . To have power over a thing *ab extra* constitutes possession. The particular aspect of the matter, the fact that I make something my own as a result of my natural need, impulse, and caprice, is the particular interest satisfied by possession. But I as free will am an object to myself in what I possess and thereby also for the first time am an actual will, and this is the aspect which constitutes the category of property, the true and right factor in possession.
>
> If emphasis is placed on my needs, then the possession of property appears as a means to their satisfaction, but the true position is that, from

> the standpoint of freedom, property is the first embodiment of freedom and so is in itself a substantive end.[8]

This short passage seems to capture so much regarding the role of property in the liberal democratic imaginary. I am not saying that Hegel is a liberal democrat. Indeed, he cannot be reduced to that, much less a socialist, and one can see some of that refusal in this very passage, for his take on the matter of property is more complex than Locke's or Jefferson's. For Hegel, property not only satisfies physical needs, but, more profoundly, humans complete their purposefulness through property. Property, then, is a kind of potentiality fulfilling the potentiality of the human, who will now have, because of property, the power to actualize themselves. This is as clear as it gets if we want to understand what is secreted away inside the humdrum of property rights, including patent laws and so on. That is, Hegel's "property" is vibrating with metaphysics, and for Hegel metaphysics is both something more than and other than politics.

One way to understand this notion of property as being a physical object with metaphysical overtones is to examine Hegel's understanding of freedom. The freedom that Hegel describes is not just the political freedoms of liberal democracy, or any other political order. Freedom for Hegel is foundational for establishing self-awareness, and it is only through self-awareness that we establish meaningful being. So in order to become truly self-aware or to arrive at genuine self-consciousness, we must be free. Otherwise, we live inside a truncated awareness. Hence this alignment of freedom to self-awareness and self-consciousness suggests that freedom here is also a metaphysical or spiritual condition, which is something more than any political condition.

His understanding of freedom is related to his understanding of property as a stand-in for all external objects. For Hegel, objects are important because they are in dialectical relation with subjects and their subjectivity. That is, subjects move toward consciousness and awareness through their engagements with the objects of the world. The empirical sciences are a model for understanding how these engagements seem to work. The point is that "freedom" seems to emerge during this move toward greater awareness. That is, the dialectical relation between object and subject contains the potentiality of releasing ever more freedom. The subject is in a kind of constant renewal, gathering ever more freedom as it passes from one dialectical engagement to the next.

Let's be clear: what seems to separate Hegel's view of property from that of liberal democracy's views (as embodied in, say, Thomas Jefferson) or in economists' views (say those of Demsetz or De Soto) is that freedom is more than political freedoms or "free" market values. In other words, this inaugural discussion by Hegel is rather free of the groundings of those who would locate freedom only in politics or the market; still, it ironically inaugurates the fetishization of the individual, a cornerstone of humanist philosophies. Thus, on the one hand, Hegel's view of property means that property cannot be framed just through utilitarian self-interest or even as a matter of something to be exchanged. There seems to be something much more: the beingness of property or the beingness of objects allows the beingness of the subject to come into being. On the other hand, we should be simultaneously interested precisely in those liberal democratic and economistic reductions. The implication is that secreted away inside these reductions is a residual metaphysics. Consider that if I purchase an object that is vitally important to me (e.g., a home), perhaps I hope that it will enlarge me not just for the sake of personal ostentation but also because it will enhance my knowledge of self—that is, objectify my consciousness to myself. What if we approached economic exchanges as having these sorts of meanings—that is, as being something more than matters of consumption or self-display? I suspect that this experience of meaningfulness informs Marx's appropriations of Hegel insofar as meaningfulness ought to replace the condition of the worker reduced to an automaton producing and consuming dead objects. After all, the economy that Marx wants is one that replaces exploitation, which we need not frame as strictly the consequence of capitalism. Exploitation occurs in any scene in which, figuratively speaking, dead subjects produce dead objects—or, phrasing it a bit differently, in which subjects have been reduced to a condition where they cannot extend their living being into objects and objects cannot do the same for subjects. Thus exploitation kills our sense of being free, while the experience of meaningfulness enables us to feel free and expand our sense of wherewithal. In sum, what both Hegel and Marx want is a kind of ceaseless interanimation in which objects filled with human purpose remake subjects and their subjectivity, which in turn cycles back on behalf of objects. This movement of interanimation, I take it, is dialectical. Its end is a metaphysical freedom that remains locked, but there nevertheless, inside political and economic freedoms whose natures are unable to release their secreted potential.

I would be remiss if I did not consider again the opposite and more tragic reading of this same passage in Hegel's text. "The absolute right of appropriation which man has over all 'things'"; "the fact that I make something my own . . . is the particular interest satisfied by possession." Hegel may be criticizing these more utilitarian interests, but the fact of the matter is that we continue to hear these sentiments every day. Indeed, they are wedded to everyday discussions of freedom. These discussions are hallmarks of liberal democracy. They help shape a self and selfhood hyperfocused on the freedom of appropriation. Liberal democracy encourages such a self and secures it through the law. Liberal democracy, of course, does not "produce" just one kind of "self," but this sort of amplified self is one of its proclivities. I have made in this book a counterclaim: these rights of appropriation that the self wields on its behalf are the foundations of a politics of individuation (or atomization as Wolgast might call it), and this sort of individuation is illusory, a fetish. Underneath the politics of individuation is a primordial commons that, in my view, is unnamable and hard to recognize. This commons tells us one thing: the self has no shape in and of itself, and being mostly for oneself is a profound act of forgetfulness, not an act of freedom.

Now Hegel (and, of course, Marx) would agree. They, too, would denounce a politics of individuated selves who call on "mere" liberal democratic freedoms to substantiate their moral positioning. This sort of freezing oneself into a self-interested self simply stops dialectical movement. Such a self—self-assured but stunted—cannot move forward. There is no dialectical momentum. In contrast, the dialectic restarts when subjects encounter other subjects and objects, for this leads to a likely self-critique and, more deeply, the self-awareness that dawns from critique. Such critique upends. Ultimately, the freedom that Hegel favors—and Marx, too, I suspect—starts as an upending. In contrast, the freedom of liberal democracy seems to encourage a subject to separate from other subjects—hence a politics of individuation—versus encouraging a subject to encounter other subjects as a source of enlightenment. Here is the irony, then: both envisionings have their arguments in the same passage by Hegel. I think of the gated communities of our own era as a type of property that does not encourage subjects to encounter opposite subjects as part of their "enlightenment," and that this kind of "property" can also exist paradoxically in Hegel's words. Thus Hegel seems to contain in himself the values of liberal democracy—Marx critiqued these as belonging to the bourgeoisie—even as Hegel also upends such values.

←↕→

Was Hegel's vision of property antinomic? Perhaps. Now, I am convinced that the topoi of democratic rhetorics, which I have described as storehouses of social energy, are antinomic. They have their beginnings, I believe, in the experiences of abandonment. Thus they are available to all no matter a person's political commitments. From that experience, we invent escape routes, from both hard realities and confining others, that hold a glorious promise. We name the escape routes "freedom," "liberty," "justice," "rights," "transparency," and so on. The broad promise is that we can institutionalize these wonders and thus move ourselves toward some other place that seems more just or more free or more equal. We rev up the gears of managerial modernity in order to realize the promise. But the promise is so abstract, so deterritorialized, that we can never fully inhabit the sort of relief that is promised. What begins to take shape instead is a gray territorialization of the promise.

Let me find another set of words to say all this: what I know, what I experience or think I experience, is the lash of inequality, the lack of freedom, the lack of justice—and what I invent, rhetorically as it were, from these compelling conditions are their opposites. That is, I move along the rhetorical architectonic of limitation → limitlessness. Rights, equality, freedom, and justice are, in effect, Burkian god terms or principles of perfection by which we move away from the grip of some highly specific experience of tragedy toward some resting place. We perfect ourselves out of our desperate conditions. We used to ask religious ideology to be that resting place, but now we ask the democratic rhetorics to do that work. Because politics cannot bring salvation into being but instead territorializes it into something less, the tragedy only deepens. Hence what structures political campaigns is the sheer presence and comic absurdity of the lie.

In sum, I doubt the realities that the democratic rhetorics supposedly name. I prefer to not rally behind them with naive political enthusiasm. Rather, I see them as quintessential storehouses of social energy, compressing inside themselves tragedy alongside the powerful desire to be elsewhere. But what is most interesting about them is that they do not seem to be equipped with any shutoff valve. And so the fetishization that they engender on the part of both the left and right never seems to cease, as if we inhabited an opening without any conclusion, which is simultaneously a shut door that never opens. It seems like a wondrous paradox that touches me to the core of my being.

←↕→

Imagine the sudden appearance of a political movement in Chicago, say, of busboys and cooks linked to other undocumented. Out of the blue, they start to walk out of the restaurants of Chicago and other businesses. They step onto Michigan Avenue. Suddenly, they are joined by many, many more. They have not asked for any permission from the state to do a march. Indeed, they are not marching. They transcend the idea of the march. They are revealing their presence. They demand not the rights of inclusion according to the nation-state. Indeed, they are not demanding anything. Rather, they are starting to write a new Constitution, and they are doing it on the street! The police cannot do anything about it because millions are now occupying the lakefront. And now even the citizens—the born intos and ritualized intos—are starting to wander in. They heard the buzz. People are using their cell phones to call home, and back home is everywhere around the world. An agreement is starting to emerge. The fiber networks and satellites are approaching overload. Everyone is starting to write a planetary Constitution that does not belong to any group. The Constitution is starting to record—as if the present were writing it—a new set of planetary social relations as well as the social relation between all humans and the planet itself. Even the oceans and deserts are writing themselves into the Constitution. Governments are starting to fall on their own. People are too busy to lift a finger against them, much less for them. Even the past, present, and future have decided to pitch in and remove their differences. Cosmology, sociology, economics, chemistry, physics, geology, rhetoric, and more are starting to deteriorate as they become a more foundational knowledge. "We are present where we are and where we are not. All are present with us, and the planet is present with us. There is nothing except this presence"—and thus the preamble begins.

But suddenly, out of nowhere, a singular Other appears. Everyone is hushed by the sight. The man is headless—or rather his head is tucked between his right arm and ribs. He seems indifferent to that fact. He is dripping wet as if he had walked through oceans and then the Great Lakes. Someone from the masses cries out: "Who are you? Where are you from?" He answers in French: "Je suis Gracchus Babeuf." But those who only understand English hear only the English that he is speaking, those who only understand Spanish hear only the Spanish that he is speaking, and so on for all the languages of the world. The babble is no longer a babble. He speaks, "The past has released me from its clutches. Now I speak to all in the utter present. That was my intention from the beginning. Let us dissolve the self and thus dissolve our need of the law. Let us dissolve ownership, possession, property, citizenship, for if there is no need for need, no(thing) will be mine or yours. Objects and concepts too are now free to be themselves. They have no need of us, we no need of them." In the old days, this sort of ancient, stentorian figure would be laughed at, but in this moment of dissolution and emergence, of closings and openings, it seems as if the truth has arrived, which is more than the presence of the truth.

As the masses gaze about them and gaze at the words that are writing themselves onto the planetary Constitution, it is becoming increasingly evident that a certain self-evidence is replacing the words themselves. Someone yells in a high-pitched voice: "We are no longer living according to words and meanings." The Constitution, which at first was being furiously written and then suddenly began to write itself, has decided to take a different shape. It is becoming the new world itself in four dimensions. People are beginning to walk into the Constitution and onto its boulevards. As they take their first step, they turn around and toss all their properties behind them, which makes a great rattling sound along Michigan Avenue. As they step further, the vistas in front of them spread far and wide. And the deeper they go, knowing starts to replace not knowing and hunger for anything disappears. Wherewithal, not the cheap kind, inhabits them. They sway in the glory of it all. Suddenly, there is a collective self-realization: they have answered the isness of the what-is-question! There is nothing left, and so they start to disappear equally into the nothingness of each other. They will never rise again, and there is no regret.

Notes

Chapter 1

1. The key term might be his notion of *flesh* as something shared by both object and subject. "The thickness of flesh between the seer and the thing is constitutive for the thing of its visibility as for the seer of his corporeity; it is not an obstacle between them, it is their means of communication. It is for the same reason that I am at the heart of the visible and that I am far from it: because it has thickness and is naturally destined to be seen by a body." Maurice Merleau-Ponty, "The Intertwining—The Chiasm," in *The Visible and the Invisible*, ed. Claude Lefort, trans. Alphonso Lingis (Evanston: Northwestern University Press, 1968), 135.

2. In *Capital*, Marx calls money the "universal equivalent" (162–63). In noting that money "begets money," that is, grows it (256), as if money itself were living tissue, Marx is animating the inanimate. The "universal equivalent" provides a measure to determine the value—hence the meaning—of all things. Further, the relation of use value to surplus value becomes the relationship of God to Son in which both become One (256). Clearly, for Marx the metaphysics of religion often analogizes a metaphysics hiding in and animating economic relations. Karl Marx, *Capital: A Critique of Political Economy*, vol. 1, trans. Ben Fowkes (London: Penguin Books, 1990). Kenneth Burke is even more explicit in making the analogy. In his comic drama "Epilogue: Prologue in Heaven," the Lord says: "Once they [humans] arrive at money, they will have arrived at desire in the absolute. Their love of money is the nearest they will ever come to symbolistically transcending their animal nature" (291–92). And later in the play Satan remarks: "I see how perfectly it [money] burlesques the godhead. Out of its simplicity there emerges a great complexity" (293). Kenneth Burke, "Epilogue: Prologue in Heaven," in *The Rhetoric of Religion: Studies in Logology* (Berkeley: University of California Press, 1970).

3. Mark Leibovich, "Donald Trump Is Not Going Anywhere," *New York Time Magazine*, October 4, 2015, 32.

4. Ibid. See also Jeff Sharlet, "Donald Trump, American Preacher," *New York Times Magazine*, April 12, 2016.

5. Those who know the work of Nietzsche know that I am cherry-picking and cobbling his words for my own rude purposes: "True enough, when a nation is on the downward path, when it feels its belief in its own future, its hope of freedom slipping from it . . . then it *must* overhaul its god" (emphasis original). Friedrich Nietzsche, *The Antichrist*, https://ebooks.adelaide.edu.au/n/nietzsche/friedrich/antichrist/chapter1.html.

6. Rachel Weber, *From Boom to Bubble: How Finance Built the New Chicago* (Chicago: University of Chicago Press, 2015).

7. Regarding fieldwork: the specific methods that I rely on are participant observation and unstructured interviewing. Because of the length of time that I have been working alongside the Puerto Rican activists (PRA), everyone in this group regards me not as someone doing research in the community but as simply another contributing Puerto Rican. For instance, along with the rest of the membership, I help make policy. Typically, we meet once a month. I take copious notes during these meetings as well as at other events involving the PRA.

Perhaps the most interesting project that has emerged from my involvement on the north side of Chicago, aside from my work with immigration restrictionists, began in March 2014, when I was elected to the Board of Directors of LUCHA, a nonprofit, social service agency that builds and manages affordable housing. I am currently the president of the board, and I am particularly involved in the Strategic Growth Committee, where, among other things, we have been constructing alternative modes for financing our housing projects. I do not know exactly when, but at some point during the seventeen years of doing this work with the PRA my fieldwork became a kind of deep immersion, far more profound than doing "urban research." Those of us at LUCHA, for instance, are imagining this nonprofit as a platform for launching social experiments that directly address urban poverty, the needs of the working poor, and even how social service agencies understand and finance themselves. Deep immersion, then, implies that I speak from something more than fieldnotes and interviews.

The fieldwork in Kosova was of a different nature. There, I was always a foreigner with a very incomplete understanding of Albanian. The first few years consisted of sporadic visits that would last about a week. During that time, I examined the fieldnotes and interviews of the ethnographer-students that we were training so as to build knowledge about mental health in its social context. In 2007–8, however, I lived one year in Kosova teaching political science and conducting fieldwork. I conducted approximately 160 formal interviews with Kosovars and internationals. Many of the interviews were multiple interviews with the same persons. There were many more informal conversations. I also advised the projects and theses of the graduate students, all of whom were writing about the political scene in Kosova. In sum, fieldwork both in Chicago and Kosova emphasizes detailed note-taking over tape-recorded interviews. In Kosova, because I had more time, I also wrote "elaborated fieldnotes" and "theoretical memos" within twenty-four hours after each fieldwork session. As of this writing, I have written approximately seven hundred pages of fieldnotes, and this book incorporates only a portion of the information and knowledge gathered in those pages.

8. I use the English spelling of the Albanian Kosovë (Kosova) instead of "Kosovo," which is the Serbian pronunciation and standard international spelling. Different spellings, such as these, are no small matter, as Navaro-Yashin makes clear. These spellings are the surface indicators of fiercely competing sovereignties that date at least to the nation-building projects of nineteenth-century Europe. See Yael Navaro-Yashin, *The Make-Believe Space: Affective Geography in a Postwar Polity* (Durham: Duke University Press, 2012).

9. See David Bleeden, Caroline Gottschalk-Druschke, and Ralph Cintrón, "Minutemen and the Subject of Democracy," in *!Marcha!: Latino Chicago and the Immigrant Rights Movement*, ed. Amalia Pallares and Nilda Flores-Gonzalez (Champaign: University of Illinois Press, 2010), 179–97.

10. I provide considerable detail regarding the socioeconomic scene between 2000 and 2017 in "Bus Trip Named Desire: Doing Fieldwork in the Balkans," in *Field Rhetoric: Ethnography, Ecology, and Engagement in the Places of Persuasion*, ed. Candice Rai and Caroline Gottschalk Druschke (Tuscaloosa: University of Alabama Press, 2018), 120–47.

11. Here are other texts that make similar observations: "The [Albanian case] study provided an answer to two questions relating to the study of democratic consolidation. First, given that the outcomes of the political game in Albania are often undemocratic, why does the democratic order prevail when its practical implementation falls far short of expectations? Second, since the democratic order seems to be durable, why is there no tangible progress towards its consolidation?" Eno Trimçev, *Democracy, Intellectuals and the State: The Case of Albania* (Tirana, Albania: Albanian Institute for International Studies, 2005), 159. For Kosovar commentators, see Nexhmedin Spahiu, *Serbian Tendencies for Partitioning of Kosova* (Budapest, Hungary: Central European University, 1999); Naser Miftari, "The

In-Between States: Enduring Catastrophes as Sources of Democracy's Deadlocks in Kosovo," in *Culture, Catastrophe, and Rhetoric: The Texture of Political Action*, ed. Robert Hariman and Ralph Cintron (New York: Berghan Books, 2015), 68–86. Other relevant texts are Andrew Grann, "Chronotopes of the Political: Public Discourse, News Media, and Mass Action in Postconflict Macedonia," in Hariman and Cintron, *Culture, Catastrophe, and Rhetoric*, 47–67, and Dušan I. Bjelić and Obrad Savić, eds., *Balkan as Metaphor: Between Globalization and Fragmentation* (Cambridge, Mass.: MIT Press, 2002).

12. Trimçev, *Democracy, Intellectuals, and the State*; Miftari, "In-Between States"; Anika Bishka, "At the Margins of Sovereignty: Politics, Policies, and Actors in Post-Conflict Kosovo" (Ph.D. diss., University of Illinois at Chicago, 2014).

13. For historical accounts of "head-man politics" in the region, see Noel Malcolm, *Kosovo: A Short History* (New York: HarperCollins, 1999), and Edith Durham, *High Albania: A Victorian Traveller's Balkan Odyssey* (1909; London: Phoenix Press, 2000).

14. Writing from the perspective of international law, Bernhard Knoll articulates well the paradoxical meaning of sovereignty when a postconflict territory is administered by international organizations as opposed to an indigenous population. International organizations are not necessarily obeyed. "This study strikes at the heart of the current debate over the powers that the UN exercise [*sic*] both within an internationalized territory and from outside. Its supreme organ, the Security Council, is increasingly called upon to balance the sovereign's weight of the inviolable and static borders against indigenous bids at determining the dynamic 'self' in a people." Bernhard Knoll, *The Legal Status of Territories Subject to Administration by International Organizations* (Cambridge: Cambridge University Press, 2008), 10.

15. Trimçev establishes a difference between mature, strong states and weak, emerging states that is fairly standard among political scientists: "First of all, differently than a weak state, the strong state has full control of the territory of a political unit and is capable of curbing local power centers whose existence is inimical to the state. This control is a necessary precondition for the exercising of democratic citizenship by the *demos*. Second, the strong state . . . has, by definition, the institutions necessary to prevent individuals from curbing the rules in such a way as to benefit their narrow interests at the expense of democratic procedure." Trimçev, *Democracy, Intellectuals, and the State*, 21. "In weak states, individual ambitions are very poorly constrained by formal institutions. Democratization has been particularly difficult to achieve in countries where structure, authority, and the rule of law have fallen apart or were never an integral part of the fabric of the *polis*. Democratization of a collapsing state may very well hasten state collapse, which puts pressure on the political system favouring the termination of the democratic experiment" (26).

16. Francis Fukuyama, "The End of History?," *National Interest* (Summer 1989), http://www.wesjones.com/eoh.htm.

17. Julia Paley, "Toward an Anthropology of Democracy," *Annual Review of Anthropology* 31 (2002): 469–96; quotation on 471.

18. Hannah Arendt, *The Origins of Totalitarianism* (New York: Harcourt, 1976).

19. That the undocumented might become lawyers represents a fascinating sociolegal experiment. At such moments, the law reveals itself as built on arbitrary rather than primordial principles. The former dean quoted below is wrong: there is no "real" problem. Rather, there are conflicting impulses within democracy—namely, the desire to make democracy deterritorialized versus the need to make it territorialized. "In 2014, California became the only state in the country to allow undocumented immigrants to practice law. The next year, New York courts reached a similar conclusion. There is no official count of how many undocumented immigrants are now working as lawyers, but Mr. Reyes Savalaza can name about a dozen." "You're taking the oath to uphold the Constitution of the United States, while

you are simultaneously breaking those laws," said John C. Eastman, a constitutional law expert and former dean of the law school at Chapman University in Orange, California. "You're violating the oath of office from the moment you take it—that's a real problem." Jennifer Medina, "Undocumented Lawyer, but No Less Defiant," *New York Times*, July 18, 2017, A8.

20. Thomas Paine, *Rights of Man* (1894; New York: Barnes and Noble, 2004), 82.

21. For a sobering analysis of how a monied class interested in protecting "free markets" from "big government regulation" has grown, since at least the 1950s, into a war machine capturing governance on behalf of conservative politics, read Nancy MacLean's *Democracy in Chains: The Deep History of the Radical Right's Stealth Plan for America* (New York: Viking, 2017). To be sure, I believe her term *democracy in chains* is fetishization from the left because democracy has always been synonymous with economic interestedness that can quickly spill over into oligarchy. Nevertheless, "what becomes clear as the story moves forward decade by decade is that a quest that began as a quiet attempt to prevent the state of Virginia from having to meet national democratic standards of fair treatment and equal protection under the law would, some sixty years later, become the veritable opposite of itself: a stealth bid to reverse-engineer all of America, at both the state and the national levels, back to the political economy and oligarchic governance of midcentury Virginia, minus the segregation" (xv).

22. Long before Kant's celebrated analysis, the idea of antinomy as embedded inside the body politic was already anticipated in the classical era: "And illness is bad for the sick but good for the doctors. And death is bad for those who die, but good for the undertakers and the grave-diggers. . . . And it is bad for the ship-owner if his merchant-ships are involved in a collision or get smashed up, but good for the shipbuilders" (48). Anonymous, "Dissoi Logoi," in *The Rhetorical Tradition from Classical Times to the Present*, ed. Patricia Bizzell and Bruce Herzberg (Boston: Bedford / St. Martin's, 2001), 47–55.

23. Thomas Hobbes, *Leviathan*, ed. C. B. Macpherson (1651; London: Penguin, 1985); Carl Schmitt, *The Leviathan in the State Theory of Thomas Hobbes*, trans. George Schwab and Erna Hilfstein (Chicago: University of Chicago Press, 2008); Walter Benjamin, "Critique of Violence," in *Reflections: Essays, Aphorisms, Autobiographical Writings*, trans. Edmund Jephcott (New York: Schocken Books, 1986).

24. Hobbes, *Leviathan*, 196:

> If a Covenant be made, wherein neither of the parties performe presently, but trust one another; in the condition of meer Nature, (which is a condition of Warre of every man against every man,) upon any reasonable suspition, it is Voyd: But if there be a common Power set over them both with right and force sufficient to compell performance; it is not Voyd. For he that performeth first, has no assurance the other will performe after; because the bonds of words are too weak to bridle mens ambition, avarice, anger, and other Passions, without the feare of some coerceive Power.

25. "Liberalism [establishes] neutrality toward final claims. . . . Here one thinks of the work of John Rawls, who explicitly denies that his theory of justice requires a notion of truth and is composed only of that to which reasonable beings with a similar history will rationally consent. This perhaps seems safe but it may also make people yearn for something more and runs the risk that the satisfaction of that yearning [for final claims] will be disastrous." Tracy B. Strong, foreword to Schmitt, *Leviathan in the State Theory*, xxviii.

26. "Before the names of Just, and Unjust can have place, there must be some coercive power, to compel men equally to the performance of the Covenants, by the terrour of some

punishment, greater than the benefit they expect by the breach of their Covenant . . . and such power there is none before the erection of a Commonwealth." Hobbes, *Leviathan*, 202.

27. St. Aurelius Augustine, *Concerning the Teacher (De magistro) and On the Immortality of the Soul (De immortalite animae)*, trans. George G. Leckie (New York: Appleton-Century-Crofts, 1938).

28. Compare Augustine's law of speaking to the contemporary rhetorical theorist Edward Schiappa talking about entitling, a central conception in the oeuvre of the twentieth-century rhetorical theorist Kenneth Burke: "One rhetorical effect of entitling a new 'thing' is that it creates the impression that the 'thing' has been 'out there' all along, waiting to be discovered and described. Nouns, in particular, suggest things-that-already-exist: 'And that no doubt accounts for the feeling that when one is using nouns, one is manipulating the symbols of a self-subsistent reality.' . . . Nouns give one the impression of something stable, even permanent and immutable, or at least beyond the immediate limits of subjectivity." See Edward Schiappa, *The Beginnings of Rhetorical Theory in Classical Greece* (New Haven: Yale University Press, 1999), 24.

29. An incidental thought: "ineffable": not + *effabilis*: capable of being expressed, from *effari*: to speak out—a nonspeakable reality may be the fetish of those who want something more than signs and signifieds, and so we invent through rhetorical means the nonrhetorical.

30. Cintron, "Bus Trip Named Desire."

31. Max Tegmark, *Our Mathematical Universe: My Quest for the Ultimate Nature of Reality* (New York: Alfred A. Knopf, 2014).

32. In light of what has been just said, consider again the what-is-question and logical connectors. Both presume the idea of presence. Both are energy forms, forms of desire. In this sense, they are visceral needs. That is, we pursue ontological inquiry (what is the nature of such and such?) in order to encounter the thing itself, the thing as such in its completed presence, a presence not projected from us but from outside of us. Further, we polish and refine our logic in order to establish the powerful presence of certainty.

33. Mark Bevir, "Meaning, Truth, and Phenomenology," in *Presence: Philosophy, History, and Cultural Theory for the Twenty-First Century*, ed. Ranjan Ghosh and Ethan Kleinberg (Ithaca: Cornell University Press, 2013), 60.

34. Ibid., 58–59.

35. An example of institutional studies that I have relied on is Larry Diamond and Marc F. Planner, eds., *Democracy After Communism* (Baltimore: Johns Hopkins University Press, 2002). At the darker end of the spectrum, in my view, are Freedom House (http://www.freedomhouse.org) and other Washington, D.C.–based think tanks that have instrumentalized these modes of analysis. A much deeper analysis of democracy's institutions is Timothy Mitchell's brilliant *Carbon Democracy: Political Power in the Age of Oil* (London: Verso, 2013).

36. James Woodburn, "'Sharing Is Not a Form of Exchange': An Analysis of Property-Sharing in Immediate-Return Hunter-Gatherer Societies," in *Property Relations: Renewing the Anthropological Tradition*, ed. C. M. Hann (New York: Cambridge University Press, 1998), 48–63; Stephen Gudeman, *The Anthropology of Economy: Community, Market, and Culture* (Malden, Mass.: Blackwell, 2001).

37. The book starts and ends as parody. Many anthropologists of the first half of the last century began their books with an arrival scene, a kind of grand entry to or overview of their field sites, pen and notebook in hand, their observant eye shaped by scientism and colonialism—yes, everything at the ready. They wrote sincerely about the romanticized Other because this figure liberated them from the doldrums of Euro-American secularization (ah, the escape into animacy), even as they reduced these exotic ways of life to rational structures. The arrival scene was a kind of high-pitched beginning. My arrival scene is more

low-pitched with a few comic characters thrown in: smiling faces, motorboats, the pleasantries of skyscrapers and wherewithal. I end with a slapstick homage to the French Revolution, both a promise and a disaster that still broods inside of me. But if readers want to know who I "really" am below these "masks" of parody, read closely all references to Gracchus Babeuf and his commitments to absolute egalitarianism.

Chapter 2

1. "Two years ago, the world values survey was clear as a bell. While older respondents (over the age of 60) were resolute that democracy was 'essential' to their lives, this was true of less than half of those under 30. Almost a quarter of American 'millennials' now think democracy 'a bad way' to run a country. A sixth—17%—of young Europeans think likewise, double the figure for 1995. In Germany, Spain, Japan and America, a full 40% of people overall would prefer 'a strong leader who does not have to bother with parliaments or elections.'" Simon Jenkins, "Blame Liberal Democracy's Flaws for Erdoğan's Win, Not the Voters," *Guardian*, June 25, 2018, https://www.theguardian.com/commentisfree/2018/jun/25/blame-liberal-democracy-flaws-erdogan-win-turkish.

2. *Illegal*, *undocumented*, and *unauthorized* are three terms that describe the same population but with different political overtones. *Illegal* is used most commonly by immigration restrictionists. The opposite position typically defends the rights of the *undocumented*. Over the past decade or so, some on both the right and left have used *unauthorized*, intending it to be a more neutral term. I'm not yet convinced that it is.

3. https://www.congress.gov/bill/109th-congress/house-bill/4437.

4. For a brief overview of Athenian democracy, see Christopher W. Blackwell, "Athenian Democracy: A Brief Overview," in "Athenian Law in Its Democratic Context," ed. Adriaan Lanni, Center for Hellenic Studies Online Discussion Series, republished in C. W. Blackwell, ed., *Dēmos: Classical Athenian Democracy*, ed. A. Mahoney and R. Scaife, *The Stoa: A Consortium for Electronic Publication in the Humanities*, http://www.stoa.org/projects/demos/article_democracy_overviewpage=1.

5. The "principle of perfection" is an important rhetorical device for Kenneth Burke. One of his claims is that the premises of an argument demand elaboration if the argument is to become convincing. So, if the premise "all men are created equal" is fundamental to democracy, then considerable rational effort will be applied to establishing the "truth" of that premise, eventually for all humans. Burke, "Epilogue: Prologue in Heaven," 273–316.

6. Fukuyama, "End of History?"

7. An interesting fact about these marches is that there is good data indicating that many of the marchers were citizens; this fact adjusts but does not alter the question: Can noncitizens legitimately protest? See Pallares and Flores-Gonzalez, *!Marcha!*.

8. William Walters, "Deportation, Expulsion, and the International Police of Aliens," in *The Deportation Regime: Sovereignty, Space, and the Freedom of Movement*, ed. Nicholas De Genova and Nathalie Peutz (Durham: Duke University Press, 2010), 72–83.

9. David Miller, *Strangers in Our Midst: The Political Philosophy of Immigration* (Cambridge, Mass.: Harvard University Press, 2016), 13.

10. Luciano Canfora, *Democracy in Europe: A History of an Ideology*, trans. Simon Jones (Oxford: Blackwell, 2006), 22, 8. I cannot offer enough of Canfora's analysis, but here is a little more:

> Perhaps we will never fully unravel the web that linked the leaders with the mass of the people—a "circular" set of interactions which constitutes the essence of politics. What is

> important to note here is that in Athens democracy did not give rise to a "people's government" but rather to control of the "people's regime" by that substantial section of the "rich" and the "gentry" who accepted the system.
>
> Now, the arrival of democracy—in the form of the extension of citizenship to non-property owners—triggered a powerful phenomenon that led to upheaval. Faced with this new power of the non-property owners, the ruling groups, who thanks to their high social position also benefited from a political education and thus had mastered the art of speaking (and therefore were natural candidates for governing the city) *became divided.* Some—we might say the greater part, but we have no means of measuring this—agreed to run the system in which non-property owners were now the prevailing force. From this substantial section of the upper classes (powerful families, rich *hippies*, and so forth) the political class who ran the city . . . emerged. (28; emphasis original)

11. From Napoleon III: "Among different peoples and in revolutions the aristocracy always survives; if you destroy it in the nobility, it immediately finds a home in the rich, powerful houses of the third estate; destroy it there, and it resurfaces and takes refuge among factory foremen and the leaders of the common people." Napoleon III, *Précis des guerres de César*, chap. 16, trans. in Canfora, *Democracy in Europe*, 214. From Tocqueville: "I have an intellectual taste for democracy, but I am an aristocrat by instinct—that is, I despise and fear the mob. I passionately love liberty, the rule of law, and respect for rights, but not democracy. . . . I hate demagogy . . . I belong neither to the revolutionary party nor to the conservative party. However, when all is said and done I care more for the latter than for the former. . . . Liberty is the greatest of my passions. This is the truth." Tocqueville, *Scritti, note e discorsi politici, 1839–1852*, ed. Umberto Coldagelli (Turin: Bollati Boringhieri, 1994), 13, translated in Canfora, *Democracy in Europe*, 19. Tocqueville : "American society has . . . a surface covering of democracy, beneath which the old aristocratic colors sometimes peep out." Tocqueville, *Democracy in America*, ed. Phillips Bradley, trans. Henry Reeve (New York: Everyman's Library, 1994), 45. From Robert Michels: "Reduced to its most concise expression, the fundamental sociological law of political parties (the term 'political' being here used in its most comprehensive significance) may be formulated in the following terms: 'It is organization which gives birth to the dominion of the elected over the electors, of the mandatories over the mandators, of the delegates over the delegators. Who says organization, says oligarchy.'" Robert Michels, *Political Parties: A Sociological Study of the Oligarchical Tendencies of Modern Democracy*, trans. Eden and Cedar Paul (New Brunswick, N.J.: Transaction Publishers, 2004), 365.

12. The NATO protests in Chicago in late May 2012 offer a glimpse of how vertical accumulation of power controls space. During these marches, security snipers were stationed across many key buildings. "For four days, and nearly around the clock, Chicago police guided, cajoled, and blockaded roaming groups of NATO protesters, following a set of strategic goals: . . . Keep protesters from damaging property or hurting anyone, keep any trouble south of the city's famous Michigan Avenue retail district, where many international dignitaries were staying, and do it all with a 'soft look' that belied the overwhelming police presence and kept violent confrontation to a minimum." Tribune staff, "Police Tactics Kept Crowds Off Balance," *Chicago Tribune*, May 22, 2012, 1.

13. Walter Benjamin, "Critique of Violence," in Jephcott, *Reflections*, 283.

14. Political philosopher Susan Buck-Morss repeats Weber's and Benjamin's analyses with her own twist:

> As Walter Benjamin argued in the early 1920s, when the police are brought in to put down popular demonstrations such as workers' strikes or antiwar mobilizations, their purpose is to protect, not law, but the monopoly of the right to establish law. . . . If one

> . . . attempts to redeem the violent state through liberal-democratic theory, appealing to the legality of popular sovereignty, one faces the problem that, in the case of the use of violence by popular sovereignty against a mass demonstration of popular will, it becomes questionable whether the law that the sovereign is upholding is itself legitimate. When democratic sovereignty *confronts* the people with all the violence that it monopolizes as the legitimate embodiment *of* the people, it is in fact attesting to its *non*identity with the people.

Susan Buck-Morss, *Dreamworld and Catastrophe: The Passing of Mass Utopia in East and West* (Cambridge, Mass.: MIT Press, 2002), 6–7 (emphasis original).

15. Snippets from ethnographic fieldwork: first, in the early 2000s, Kosova was moving from Serbian rule into a kind of receivership under the authority of the United Nations Mission in Kosova (UNMIK). UNMIK needed to dampen both the nationalist and socialist impulses of the Kosovars. Vetëvendosje (Self-Determination) became the largest opposition party to UNMIK's efforts. On those occasions when violent riots broke out that targeted both UNMIK policies and the continuing presence of Serbian meddling, leaders of Vetëvendosje were labeled instigators and quickly put under house arrest. Second, in another part of the world, PRA has cultivated a particular topos over decades concerning the transcendent nature of Chicago's Puerto Rican riots of the late 1960s. The topos is often articulated this way: "No matter what you think about violence, the riots of the 60s is where it all starts. Puerto Ricans rose up against oppression and against colonialism to claim the value of their own lives and spaces. They established initiatives for housing, education, economic development, the preservation of culture—we started to determine our lives for ourselves. Today is the legacy of that historic moment." If my analysis via Benjamin regarding the law-making character of violence is correct, we might understand the use of violence by horizontal forces as the attempt to transcend existing law, which represents the reigning vertical authority, with a new, world-forming or order-instituting law, no matter how inchoate the process may seem.

16. Two examples of the full force of mathematical reasoning arriving at uncertainty in economic theory: (1) In an IMF paper, three economists question the thesis that there is a "threshold effect whereby debt above 90 percent of GDP is associated with dramatically worse growth outcomes." They conclude that debt matters, but when it comes to the relationship between debt and growth, they cannot "establish what the underlying structural relationship is." Andrea Pescatori, Damiano Sandri, and John Simon, "Debt and Growth: Is There a Magic Threshold?" IMF Working Paper (WP/14/34), International Monetary Fund, February 2014, 4, 14–15. (2) Economists have long known that GDP calculations are artful constructs, more specifically an artificial aggregate of selective measures that could be calculated with a different set. Consequently, the GDP has not captured the well-being of society and has reified the pursuit of economic growth as the most important global political objective: "GDP omits many dimensions for the quality of life that matter to people. This occurs by design rather than being a flaw in the concept of GDP, because GDP is a measure of goods and services exchanged in markets and is not intended to include the value of nonmarket activities that matter to people. Second, the growth of GDP, even on its own terms as a measure of market activity, is systematically understated, for price indexes used to convert current-dollar spending into constant inflation-adjusted 'real' dollars overstate price increases." Robert J. Gordon, *The Rise and Fall of American Growth: The U.S. Standard of Living Since the Civil War* (Princeton: Princeton University Press, 2016), 9. See also Robert A. Dahl, *On Political Equality* (New Haven: Yale University Press, 2006), 107–14.

17. The economic anthropologist Keith Hart suggests, rightly, that in abstract mass societies the resort to number is a way of "demarcating phenomena" in order to make it "perceptible

to the senses." Keith Hart, "The Persuasive Power of Money," in *Economic Persuasions*, ed. Stephen Gudeman (New York: Berghahn Books, 2009), 142.

18. I have had a long-standing interest in statistical data, which, in my view,

> negotiate the rhetorical relationship between the visible and invisible. That is, they produce knowledge that is not visible through any other means, for it is not as if a total population or the totality of the poor versus the wealthy can be witnessed. These are foundationally invisible to any naked eye, but through the statistical arts they become formidably visible to that same eye. Consider how statistics in particular function as a type of synecdoche (part to whole). In order to make the necessary representative sample (the part), it needs to strip away contextual "noise." In this sense the visibility of the part is produced by producing invisibility. It is a kind of rounding off. Through such means the part acquires the power to point to an abstracted whole—voila, the "nation" becomes visible.

From Cintron, "Bus Trip Named Desire."

19. Douglas Walton compares enthymemes to abductive logic. "They are eikotic, in the sense that they are based on presumptions shared by speaker and hearer concerning the way things can normally be expected to go in a kind of situation that is familiar to them both." Walton's central conclusion is that the enthymeme allows us to understand the democratic political system as "reason-based, under the right conditions." Douglas Walton, "Criteria of Rationality for Evaluating Democratic Public Rhetoric," in *Talking Democracy: Historical Perspectives on Rhetoric and Democracy*, ed. Benedetto Fontana, Cary J. Nederman, and Gary Remer (University Park: Pennsylvania University Press, 2004), 329–30.

20. What is the distinction between ratio and dialectics? This paragraph and the two prior ones outline some of the distinctions. Points of agreement: (1) both are polar habits of thought; (2) polar habits of thought tend to perfect themselves as advocates clarify their premises during agonistic exchanges. Points of disagreement: (1) dialectics presumes an identifiable thesis and antithesis; (2) ratio does not presume that polar habits of thought have a "thingness" that can be identified; (3) ratio instead presumes entailment (i.e., one thought constitutes the other, or helps to invent the other, and thus cannot exist as a stand-alone); (4) traditional dialectics presumes a telos; (5) ratio instead presumes that polar habits of thought, because they exist variably in the minds of a people, can change quickly according to the context. They are dynamic memories, which, if institutionalized, endure over time.

21. Deirdre Nansen McCloskey, "How To Be a Humane Libertarian: Essays in a New American Liberalism," unpublished manuscript, 9.

22. James Madison, "No. 10," in *The Federalist Papers* (New York: Mentor Books, New American Library, 1961), 80.

23. Michels, *Political Parties*.

24. Aristotle, *The Politics*, trans. Carnes Lord (Chicago: University of Chicago Press, 1984).

25. Hegel translated some of these ideas into his notion of the individuation of both person and nation: "Knowledge is knowledge of oneself as an object purely self-identical. Individuals and nations have no personality until they have achieved this pure thought and knowledge of themselves. . . . Hence the imperative of right is: 'Be a person and respect others as persons.'" Georg Wilhelm Friedrich Hegel, *Hegel's Philosophy of Right*, trans. T. M. Knox (London: Oxford University Press, 1967), 37.

26. Samuel Fleischacker, *A Short History of Distributive Justice* (Cambridge, Mass.: Harvard University Press, 2004).

27. David Graeber, *Toward an Anthropological Theory of Value: The False Coin of Our Own Dreams* (New York: Palgrave, 2001), 115.

28. Bill Maurer, *Mutual Life, Limited: Islamic Banking, Alternative Currencies, Lateral Reason* (Princeton: Princeton University Press, 2005), 112.

29. I am thinking here of Gerard Hauser's description of a Greek concept that Quintilian rendered as *fantasia*. Hauser describes this "uniquely rhetorical mechanism" as a vivid, verbal display that emotionally evokes "its audience's expectations and beliefs" and thus impels "a person toward a certain outcome." Gerard A. Hauser, *Prisoners of Conscience: Moral Vernaculars of Political Agency* (Columbia: University of South Carolina Press, 2014), 162.

30. Ole Bjerg, *Making Money: The Philosophy of Crisis Capitalism* (London: Verso, 2014).

31. Tegmark, *Our Mathematical Universe*, 260. See also Richard D. Mckirahan, *Philosophy Before Socrates* (Indianapolis, Ind.: Hackett, 1994).

32. Maurer, *Mutual Life, Limited*, 112–13.

33. Burke, *Rhetoric of Religion*, 25–26. As a useful analytic device, *god terms* in rhetorical analysis are often thought of as generalizations whose truths seem undisputable so that in the midst of public argument they immediately coalesce a range of sympathies that automatically win: among libertarians, the "free market"; among the Taliban, the holiness of the Koran; among the progressive left, the evils of neoliberalism.

34. Gracchus Babeuf, *The Defense of Gracchus Babeuf Before the High Court of Vendome*, ed. and trans. John Anthony Scott (Boston: University of Massachusetts Press, 1967).

35. https://www.ssa.gov/history/paine4.html.

36. Naomi Klein, *This Changes Everything: Capitalism vs. the Climate* (New York: Simon and Schuster, 2014), 10.

37. https://www.ssa.gov/history/paine4.html.

38. Jeffrey D. Sachs, *The Age of Sustainable Development* (New York: Columbia University Press, 2015), 441–43.

39. Babeuf, *Defense of Gracchus Babeuf.*

40. Immanuel Kant, *Critique of Judgment*, trans. Werner S. Pluhar (Indianapolis, Ind.: Hackett, 1987). See particularly book 2, "Analytic of the Sublime."

41. I borrow the term *nomosphere* from David Delaney in order to describe the rule of law spreading not just across a nation but the globe itself. This expansion of law enables managerial modernity to extend its influence across the animate and inanimate. The legal is always happening at every moment, everywhere on the globe. "It is performed not only by those we identify as 'legal actors' (police, guards, lawyers, judges, notaries, ICE agents, mayors, and diplomats) but by everyone who acts in accordance with (or with transgressive reference to) understandings of rules, authority, rights, permissions, prohibitions, duties, and so on (employees, teachers, tenants, consumers, neighbors, doctors, thieves, coyotes, protestors, inmates, students, social workers, citizens)." David Delaney, *The Spatial, the Legal and the Pragmatics of World-Making: Nomospheric Investigations* (New York: Routledge, 2010), 19.

42. Klein, *This Changes Everything*, 172–73.

43. Gordon, *Rise and Fall of American Growth*, 4.

44. John Maynard Keynes, "Economic Possibilities for Our Grandchildren," *Essays in Persuasion* (New York: W. W. Norton, 1963), 358–73, http://www.econ.yale.edu/smith/econ116a/keynes1.pdf.

45. For two classic essays in rhetorical studies on the idea of the "people," see Michael C. McGee, "In Search of the People: A Rhetorical Alternative," *Quarterly Journal of Speech* 61, no. 3 (October 1975): 235–49, and Maurice Charland, "Constitutive Rhetoric: The Case of the Peuple Québécois," *Quarterly Journal of Speech* 73, no. 2 (May 1987): 133–50.

Chapter 3

1. Monarch butterflies migrate between the United States and Mexico. Because their numbers have been fluctuating in recent years, their image has also been appropriated by the environmental movement. To see politicized images of the monarch butterfly, search for "mariposa" and "immigration rights" together on Google Images.

2. The PRA's Statement on Sanctuary, March 2017.

The PRA supports the growing sanctuary movement in the city of Chicago and the nation. As such, the PRA, its members and institutional conveners, encourages Paseo Boricua and greater Humboldt Park neighborhoods to become a sanctuary district, where individuals or groups can seek protection through a safe-haven from the recent immigration and deportation policies of the federal government.

On February 20, 2017 the United States Department of Homeland Security issued two memoranda ("Implementing the President's Border Security and Immigration Enforcement Improvement Policies" and "Enforcement of the Immigration Laws to Serve the National Interest") that greatly expand who might qualify as a deportable criminal. For instance, provision #2 of "Enforcement . . ." permits the deportation of undocumented persons who "have been charged with any criminal offense that has not been resolved," meaning that the charge of an offense, and not the conviction, is sufficient for deportation.

The PRA opposes these expansions, and affirms instead the 2011 Cook County sanctuary ordinance as well as Chicago's 2012 sanctuary city law, the "Welcoming City Ordinance." These sanctuary ordinances allow the county and city to not use their resources (e.g., police, fire, administrative services) to enforce national immigration policy.

The PRA also supports the municipal ID ordinance, which, we understand, will provide the undocumented with official IDs that can be used at banks and other places of business. At the same time the PRA encourages the city to maximize the protection of the undocumented if their names are to be entered into municipal data bases. Finally, we urge the city to use the revenues from the IDs to support issues important to the undocumented.

The right to take sanctuary is an ancient practice that lies in customary law. Historically, it has asserted that there are moments when spiritual convictions can take precedence over the laws of the state, and we are in just such a period in our country where we stand with our immigrant friends, families and neighbors in spiritual and moral solidarity.

It is estimated that the city has 183,000 undocumented residents. We encourage all businesses, agencies, and churches along Paseo Boricua and elsewhere to welcome refugees and asylum seekers, and to not ask patients, clients, and workers about their immigration status. There is precedence for these actions in the restaurant industry. Restaurants that do not wish to allow police or ICE to enter their establishments without a valid search warrant can search the restaurant sanctuary website, https://sanctuaryrestaurants.org, for more information.

Information on the national sanctuary movement can be found here: https://www.nytimes.com/video/us/politics/100000004969152/safe-haven-the-sanctuary-movement.html.

3. Nicholas De Genova, "Theoretical Review," in *The Deportation Regime: Sovereignty, Space, and the Freedom of Movement*, ed. Nicholas De Genova and Nathalie Peutz (Durham:

Duke University Press, 2010), 59. De Genova seems to be arguing that the freedom of movement is a right that supersedes all "political regimes." Is there such a right? In 1948, the Organization of American States adopted the "American Declaration of the Rights and Duties of Man." Article VIII states that "every person has the right to fix his residence within the territory of the state of which he is a national, to move about freely within such a territory, and not to leave it except by his own will." The right to a freedom of movement in this document is state-centric. There is no abstract, deterritorialized movement outside the control of the state. Again, I am not so much critiquing De Genova as pointing to unresolvable tensions between deterritorialized and territorialized notions of democracy. See https://www.cidh.oas.org/Basicos/English/Basic2.american%20Declaration.htm.

4. Jean-Luc Nancy, *The Truth of Democracy*, trans. Pascale-Anne Brault and Michael Naas (New York: Fordham University Press, 2010), 17–18:

> It is precisely the expectation of a political sharing (out) of the incalculable that leads to disappointment with democracy. We have remained prisoners of a vision of politics as the putting to work and activation of an absolute sharing (out): the destiny of a nation or republic, the destiny of humanity, the truth of relation, the identity of the common. In short, everything that might have seemed to be subsumed by the glories of monarchy and that various "totalitarianisms" wanted to replace with a literally demo-cratic glory: the absolute power of a people identified in its essence and in its living body, an indigenous people or a people of workers, the self-production and autochthony of a principle substituted for the princes of yesteryear.

5. Milton Friedman with Rose D. Friedman, *Capitalism and Freedom* (1962; Chicago: University of Chicago Press, 2002).

6. Michel Foucault, *The Birth of Biopolitics: Lectures at the College de France*, ed. Michael Senellart, trans. Graham Burchell (New York: Palgrave, 2008), 63.

7. Ibid., 65.

8. An interpretation of Foucault's other work on care of the self suggests, ironically, that the tropes of nature and the natural undergird his conceptions of freedom. In sum, this interpretation suggests that Foucault may have had a double mind about these matters. At one point, he may have thought that freedom was produced by liberalism, but then at another produced by nature. My thanks to David Bleeden for this insight.

9. We might think of the United States Constitution (and all nation-state constitutions) as potentialities that move toward actualization when laws are passed. These actualizations are often contradictory. Consider the First Amendment's right to free speech. It establishes the potentiality of government neutrality, but neutrality is a contentious commitment regarding how governance should proceed. Moreover, as the legal theorist Louis Seidman argues, governance and free speech cannot be neutral because they are wedded to property interests. Consequently, there is no abstract neutrality that can ground the contrary claims and needs that write our laws. Louis Michael Seidman, "Can Free Speech Be Progressive?," Georgetown University Law Center, https://scholarship.law.georgetown.edu/facpub.

10. For a more complete discussion of Arellano's case, see Maura Toro-Morn, "Elvira Arellano and the Struggles of Low-Wage Undocumented Latina Immigrant Women," in *Immigrant Women Workers in the Neoliberal Age*, ed. Nilda Flores-Gonzalez, Anna Romina Guevarra, Maura Toro-Morn, and Grace Chang (Urbana: University of Illinois Press, 2013), 38–55.

11. See Bleeden, Gottschalk-Druschke, and Cintrón, "Minutemen and the Subject of Democracy."

12. Interview with Elvira Arellano and others at a sanctuary church, Chicago, May 26, 2006.

13. In 2008, Dallacroce shut down her organization because the donations she depended on dried up. Nevertheless, she has maintained a presence both in Arizona and with occasional interviews on Fox News. She and her adventures are easily accessible on YouTube and the internet. For a left-leaning analysis of Dallacroce, see Mary Romero, "'Go After the Women': Mothers Against Illegal Aliens' Campaign against Mexican Immigrant Women and Their Children," *Indiana Law Journal* 83, no. 4 (2008): 1355–89.

14. See Bleeden, Gottschalk-Druschke, and Cintrón, "Minutemen and the Subject of Democracy."

15. From a talk given at the conference "Globalization and Mobilities: The Theory and Methods of Human Movement," University of Chicago, May 3–4, 2013.

16. Robert Jackson, *Sovereignty: Evolution of an Idea* (Cambridge: Polity Press, 2011), 50–51.

17. Gilberto Rosas, *Barrio Libre: Criminalizing States and Delinquent Refusals of the New Frontier* (Durham: Duke University Press, 2012).

18. For a personal as opposed to a legal-theory account, see Luke Mogelson, "The Deported," *New York Times Magazine*, December 9, 2015.

19. Michelle Innis, "Australia Allows Abuse of Refugees to Deter Others, Rights Groups Say," *New York Times*, August 3, 2016, https://www.nytimes.com/2016/08/04/world/australia/nauru-refugees-abuse-conditions.html.

20. Maurizio Albahari, *Crimes of Peace: Mediterranean Migrations at the World's Deadliest Border* (Philadelphia: University of Pennsylvania Press, 2015).

21. The best examples of abuse legalized are the increasing deaths over the past decade or so of border crossers at the southern United States and in the Mediterranean. These deaths typically are not attributed to policies, such as the long-standing U.S. policies to steer undocumented migrants toward the dangerous deserts of the southwest. Rather, guilt is placed on the migrants themselves because of the rights of self-determination attached to the ethos of the nation-state. These deaths that do not create outrage, then, speak to the disposability of migrants themselves. Those who succeed, arrive at their destination, and find work are just as disposable, and, indeed, their disposability makes them cheap labor vulnerable to wage theft and dismissal by employers interested in driving down costs.

22. Nicholas P. De Genova, "Migrant 'Illegality' and Deportability in Everyday Life," *Annual Review of Anthropology* 31 (2002): 424. See also Mae M. Ngai, *Impossible Subjects: Illegal Aliens and the Making of Modern America* (Princeton: Princeton University Press, 2004), 6; Alicia Schmidt Camacho, *Migrant Imaginaries: Latino Cultural Politics in the U.S.-Mexico Borderlands* (New York: New York University Press, 2008).

23. 1790: http://legisworks.org/sal/1/stats/STATUTE-1-Pg103.pdf; 1795: http://legisworks.org/sal/1/stats/STATUTE-1-Pg414a.pdf; 1798: http://web.csulb.edu/~jlawler/Course%20DW/NaturalizationAct_1798.htm; 1802: http://legisworks.org/sal/2/stats/STATUTE-2-Pg153a.pdf.

24. Walters, "Deportation, Expulsion, and the International Police."

25. This right is foundational in the immigration literature. Linda Bosniak's body of work dissects all the dimensions behind such claims. See Linda Bosniak, "Being Here: Ethical Territoriality and the Rights of Immigrants," *Theoretical Inquiries in Law* 8, no. 2 (July 2007): 389–410.

26. "And it shall be the duty of the clerk, or other officer, or person authorized, who shall receive such report [sex, place of birth, age, nation, place of allegiance or citizenship, condition or occupation, and place of actual or intended residence within the United States] to

record the same in a book to be kept for that purpose." "An Act to Establish an Uniform Rule of Naturalization" (Naturalization Act 1798).

27. https://www.ourdocuments.gov/doc.php?flash=true&doc=47&page=transcript.

28. David Bacon, *Illegal People: How Globalization Creates Migration and Criminalizes Immigrants* (Boston: Beacon Press, 2008), 6.

29. Nicholas De Genova, "Conflicts of Mobility, and the Mobility of Conflict: Rightlessness, Presence, Subjectivity, Freedom," *Subjectivity* 29 (2009): 447.

30. Erik Camayd-Freixas, "Interpreting After the Largest ICE Raid in US History: A Personal Account," June 13, 2008, https://cdn1.nyt.com/images/2008/07/14/opinion/14ed-camayd.pdf.

31. Macias's work points to proceedings so bizarre and deceptive that they are worth quoting. In the following court scene, "voluntary departure," on the one hand, looks like an easy out, but the prosecutor's refusal sets up a protocol of background checks that will necessitate extra detention time. This action suddenly makes "deportation" look like the better choice, but the migrants do not know the consequences of that choice. They are in a liminal moment. Their choice of words—*prior to whatever actions they might take*—is a kind of switch plate that establishes either their continuing potential to remain what they are, economic migrants, or establishes a new potential in which they may become criminals. Again, I am emphasizing here that criminality, as such, is not an ontological condition of the migrant in the normal understandings of the term *criminality* but rather, it is a potential produced within the spectacle of the court system. Within such settings the migrant in choosing one word over another funnels himself or herself toward potential criminality:

> "Do you know what a voluntary departure is?" asks the judge. "*Si.*" "Would you like to apply?" "*Si.*" "Does the government oppose?" the judge asks the federal prosecutor, an attorney for DHS. "Yes," the government attorney replies. The judge reschedules another hearing in a week in order to determine eligibility for voluntary departure. Confused that his response prompted another hearing that would prolong his time in detention, the detainee became visibly nervous and requested—through the translator—formal deportation instead. "I didn't understand," he said. "I accept deportation." Within seconds, the judge issues an order of deportation and barred him from future entry for ten years. Violating that deportation order, he warns, will result in criminal prosecution and imprisonment.
>
> The entire hearing lasts minutes. The judge calls the next detainee and then another. One by one, each detainee anxiously follows the lead of the one before and asks for deportation. . . . Like falling dominos, every detainee asks to be deported.

Patrisia Macias, "Victims and Culprits," unpublished manuscript.

32. Linda Bosniak, *The Citizen and the Alien: Dilemmas of Contemporary Membership* (Princeton: Princeton University Press, 2006), 74.

33. A remarkable case of a group "feeling rightless" concerns Puerto Ricans as citizens, which is an offshoot, of course, of the colonial status of the island itself. If the case of slaves and later African Americans is the quintessential paradigm of rightlessness despite having some rights, the case of Puerto Ricans is not far behind. Bosniak, *Citizen and the Alien*, 88–89. See also José A. Cabranes, "Citizenship and the American Empire: Notes on the Legislative History of the United States Citizenship of Puerto Ricans," *University of Pennsylvania Law Review* 127, no. 2 (December 1978): 391–492.

34. Plyler v. Doe, 457 U.S. 202 (1982).

35. Constructed from interviews with immigration restrictionists during 2006 and 2007. See Bleeden, Gottschalk-Druschke, and Cintrón, "Minutemen and the Subject of Democracy."

36. Constructed from three interviews with Elvira Arellano in 2006.

37. Étienne Balibar, *We, the People of Europe? Reflections on Transnational Citizenship*, trans. James Swenson (Princeton: Princeton University Press, 2004).

38. It is commonly understood that both these actions are acts of hubris. Both civil war and revolution declare, on the one hand, to be acting in the name of the people. And yet these actions or wars typically precede the action of "constituting" the people. Even the action of constituting a people is problematic, for no constitution can absorb the utter singularities of all its members. What we face in these examples are the rhetorical urgencies that belong to democratic ideology—namely, the urgency to create legitimacy as a consequence of "the people" and, consequently, the social ironies and impossibilities that emerge. These are not just academic matters. The recent actions of Ukraine, the Russian response, including the Crimean response and the responses of other Russian sympathizers in the Ukraine, seem to be deeply entangled in these rhetorical and social problems. All actors are compelled to claim legitimacy as manifestations of the "will of the people." Even though "the will of the people" is an impossible concept and project, our standards of legitimacy demand the use of this rhetorical trope. How would these actions manifest and frame themselves if these rhetorics were not so firmly in place? For a political analysis of the "constitutive," see chapter 3 in particular, "Potentiality and Law," in Giorgio Agamben, *Homo Sacer: Sovereign Power and Bare Life*, trans. Daniel Heller-Roazen (Stanford: Stanford University Press, 1998), 39–48. For a more rhetorical analysis of the "constitutive," see Charland, "Constitutive Rhetoric," 133–50.

39. Some caveats: The condition of the noncitizen is not a fixed condition. In the United States, the distinction between secure communities and sanctuary cities allows noncitizens different degrees of freedom. In sanctuary cities, for instance, it is common for the police to not ask about the status of those they are questioning. Not so in secure communities. Similarly, some states have passed provisions making it easier for undocumented youth to attend higher education while other states have not. At the level of nation-states, citizenship does not function monolithically. Some states allow the undocumented to qualify for citizenship status with relative ease, while others, such as the United States, do not. Generally speaking, a broad distinction might be drawn between nation-states with highly developed economies and surveillance capacity that draw peoples from around the world and less developed economies with less surveillance capacity. The undocumented in the former face many more restrictions than the undocumented in the latter. In other words, in some locations distinguishing between the citizen and noncitizen is a major concern, but not so in other locations.

40. Coutin, Stevens, and De Genova all have separate commentaries on the natality-naturalization distinction. It is interesting to read the conclusion of *Arizona v. U.S.* where Justice Kennedy writes of a swearing-in ceremony that had been held in the Smithsonian Institution: "These naturalization ceremonies bring together men and women of different origins who now share a common destiny. They swear a common oath to renounce fidelity to foreign princes, to defend the Constitution, and to bear arms on behalf of the country when required by law," Arizona v. U.S., 567 U.S. 387 (2012). See Susan Bibler Coutin, *Nations of Emigrants: Shifting Boundaries of Citizenship in El Salvador and the United States* (Ithaca: Cornell University Press, 2007); Jacqueline Stevens, *States Without Nations: Citizenship for Mortals* (New York: Columbia University Press, 2010); Nicholas De Genova, "The 'Native's Point of View': Immigration and the Immigrant as Objects of U.S. Nationalism," in *Working the Boundaries: Race, Space, and "Illegality" in Mexican Chicago* (Durham: Duke University Press, 2005), 56–94.

41. Michel Foucault, *Fearless Speech*, ed. Joseph Pearson (Los Angeles: Semiotext[e], 2001).

42. Aristotle, *Politics* 1.9–15 (trans. Lord, *Politics*, 37).

43. Johann Fichte, *Fichte: Addresses to the German Nation*, ed. Gregory Moore (New York: Cambridge University Press, 2008), 104. The prior chapter talked of the modernist political orders as embodying different sorts of potentiality, and that nationalism's version placed potentiality in the "spirit of the people," or, in more deadly versions, the "spirit of the race."

44. Stevens, *States Without Nations*, 5.

45. Anthropologist Ivo Strecker has recovered the ancient term *genius loci* (spirit or general atmosphere of a place) from reading the work of the architectural critic Christian Norberg-Schulz. (Related ideas are embedded in essays by Heidegger and in *The Poetics of Space* by the French philosopher Gaston Bachelard.) What is salient in all this work is the human need to find significance in the spaces/places that one inhabits. Genius loci points to the human translation of the material landscape into deeper structures of meaning and significance. As Strecker suggests, indigenous communities that have inhabited specific natural geographies for a long time understand their environments via the spirits and demons that are said to live there, or the specific topographical features that are said to resemble specific animals or human body parts. Strecker's observations suggest that in these contexts, genius loci is seen as naturalized rather than invented. In my view, traditional communities may tend to see their symbolic material as having emerged from the womb of the immediate environment, whereas moderns may tend to see a community's symbolic material as emerging from and hence satisfying some psychological, social, and/or economic motive. Ivo Strecker, "The *genius loci* of Hamar," in "Cultural Variation in Southern Ethiopia Regional Comparative Studies," ed. Jon Abbink, special issue, *Northeast African Studies* 7 (2002): 2–3.

46. "It is not that one is born here or there that makes a place or land sacred but the sacral myths that render one's birthplace a community totem. New stories of belonging imbuing one's place of birth with the insignificance actually due this random mundane event and discrediting the fantastic and fanatic myths about birth might help liberate us from the craziness of repressing the open secret that differences attributed to birth are impossible and ludicrous, especially as legitimation of the state." Stevens, *States Without Nations*, 78.

47. Under international law, the refugee seeking asylum has to be able to prove state persecution. Other forms of persecution do not necessarily count because, historically, refugee law has resisted further liberalization. Hence, I claim that "more democracy" has yet to eliminate the real abuses suffered by many migrants. For a stunning analysis of refugee law, see Alexander Betts, *Survival Migration: Failed Governance and the Crisis of Displacement* (Ithaca: Cornell University Press, 2013). For a real-world example where other forms of persecution do not count, see Miriam Jordan, "Her Husband's Killers Told Her That She Was Next. These Days, That's Not Enough for Asylum," *New York Times*, August 7, 2018, https://www.nytimes.com/2018/08/07/us/asylum-aclu-migrants-border.html.

48. This idea of an archaic metaphysics, which is deeply problematic, underwriting birthright citizenship is my tentative answer to Bosniak's remarkably salient questions: "Why should the fortuities of birthplace and parentage—which today establish the background rules for distribution of territoriality through domicile or residence—be permitted to dictate people's life chances so unalterably? Why should national states be able to stand in the way of those individuals lacking in privileged pre-given birthplace or parentage ties who wish to improve their life chances through cross-border movement to other territories?" Bosniak, "Being Here," 399.

49. Today, we are able to correlate the "human turmoil" of moving populations by overlaying "United Nations data on nearly 64 million 'persons of concern,' whose numbers have

tripled since 2005," against "data from NASA's Common Sense Climate Index." Jessica Benko, "Hot Zones," *New York Times Magazine*, April 23, 2017, 56–57.

50. Arizona v. United States, 567 U.S. 387 (2012).

51. Support Our Law Enforcement and Safe Neighborhoods Act (S.B. 1070), 49th Legislature, Second Regular Session, 2010.

52. Support Our Law Enforcement and Safe Neighborhoods Act (S.B. 1070), 1.

53. Self-deportation has been a cornerstone of immigration policy for the Republican Party. It was mostly authored by Kris Kobach, a lawyer who, in 2018, lost the governor's race in Kansas. Self-deportation was adopted by Mitt Romney during his presidential campaign in 2012, and Kobach headed up the voter fraud inquiry at the beginning of President Trump's administration. Self-deportation represented at its moment a remarkable rhetorical innovation. It suggested that Arizona or any other state that adopted a similar policy was not in the business of deporting. Thus deportation would not be a state action but a choice that an individual could make or not make. Hence the finality of deportation would remain in the hands of individuals or the federal government. In so doing, Arizona in *Arizona v. United States* claimed that S.B. 1070 remained within the constitutional boundaries of the federal government's plenary powers and the Supremacy Clause regarding immigration policy.

54. Again, Bosniak, in her inimitable way, articulates one version of this argument. In effect, it repeats Justice Brennan's argument that we saw earlier: "If we do not extend rights and recognition to co-inhabitants, if we allow for the maintenance of what Walzer calls 'a class of live-in servants' who are perpetually disadvantaged under law, we will, to that extent, poison the democratic community at its heart" Bosniak, "Being Here," 407.

55. The political standing of the undocumented through Fourteenth Amendment protections has been well established since at least the late nineteenth century. Yick Wo v. Hopkins, 118 U.S. 356 (1886); Wong Wing v. United States, 163 U.S. 228 (1896).

56. To be sure, history suggests that there are no pure prepolitical conditions, not even slavery. Not everyone "hears the call of democracy" in the same way. Consider that each slave state in the United States prior to 1860 had its own "slave code," some more moderate than others. See https://archive.org/details/americanslavecodoolcgood/page/n15. Also consider that slavery, which most approximates the quintessential prepolitical condition, persists as debt slavery in many parts of the world.

57. "Submission to the United Nations Human Rights Committee: Review of the Dominican Republic," Open Society Justice Initiative and the Center for Justice and International Law, March 12, 2012, 4. See also "Country Reports on Human Rights Practices for 2011: Dominican Republic," U.S. Department of State, https://www.state.gov/j/drl/rls/hrrpt/2011humanrightsreport/#wrapper; "A Crisis of Nationality: Dominicans of Haitian Descent," Fact Sheet, Open Society Justice Initiative, October 2013, http://www.justiceinitiative.org; "Racial Discrimination against Dominicans of Haitian Descent in Access to Nationality," Open Society Justice Initiative, February 28–29, 2008; Randal Archibold, "Dominicans of Haitian Descent Cast into Legal Limbo by Court," *New York Times*, October 24, 2013, https://www.nytimes.com/2013/10/24/world/americas/dominicans-of-haitian-descent-cast-into-legal-limbo-by-court.html; "Dominican Republic Must Retract Ruling That Could Leave Thousands Stateless," Amnesty International, October 18, 2013, https://www.amnesty.org/en/latest/news/2013/10/dominican-republic-must-retract-ruling-could-leave-thousands-stateless; "UNHCR Concerned by Potential Impact of Dominican Court Decision on Persons of Haitian Descent," UNHCR (The UN Refugee Agency), October 1, 2013, https://www.unhcr.org/news/press/2013/10/524c0c929/unhcr-concerned-potential-impact-dominican-court-decision-persons-haitian.html; Sentencia TC/0168/13, República Dominicana, Tribunal Constitucional, September 23, 2013, http://www.refworld.org/docid

/526900c14.html; "'Without Papers, I Am No One': Stateless People in the Dominican Republic," Amnesty International, London, November 2015, https://www.amnestyusa.org/sites/default/files/without-papers_stateless-people-dominican-republic.pdf.

58. The following quotation from the Open Society Justice Initiative, one of the driving forces behind the "rights of nationality" on behalf of Dominicans of Haitian descent, reveals both the looking back and looking forward points of views:

> The Dominican delegation refused all nationality-related recommendations, arguing that the country's constitution was not open to interpretation by external norms. . . . Contrary to what the Dominican government maintains before human rights monitoring bodies and its own citizens, it does not enjoy unfettered authority to regulate matters bearing on nationality. Its powers to set citizenship policies are circumscribed by legal obligations to ensure the full protection of human rights to those on its territory. . . . One of the most important international legal restrictions on state discretion in matters of nationality is the prohibition of arbitrary deprivation of nationality.

"Submission to the United Nations Human Rights Committee," 11.

59. The condition of the Haitians in the DR will change multiple times in the foreseeable future. In May 2014, DR legislators, responding to local and international pressures, passed a law declaring "foreigners living in the Dominican Republic between 1929 and 2007 and who are registered with the government" eligible for citizenship. This law responded to the Constitutional Court's decision from September 2013 that had "directed the government to purge [all] birth registries of non-citizens." Thus the law improved matters by giving immediate relief to twenty thousand Haitians, but this was only 10 percent of the total Haitian population. The law continued to split the registered from the nonregistered, a split that, as explained earlier, was arbitrarily determined. However, the law also stated that "those who are not registered can apply to become residents and then apply to become naturalized citizens two years later." Advocates for the Haitian cause claimed that the two hundred thousand nonregistered continue to remain vulnerable. Ezequiel Lopez and Danica Coto, "New Dominican Law Aids Some 'Stateless' Migrants," Associated Press, May 22, 2014, https://www.washingtonexaminer.com/new-dominican-law-aids-some-stateless-migrants.

60. De Genova, "'Native's Point of View.'"

61. "'Without Papers, I Am No One.'"

62. Ralph Cintron, "What Next? Modernity, Revolution, and the 'Turn' to Catastrophe," in *The Texture of Political Action: Studies in Rhetoric and Political Culture*, ed. Robert Hariman and Ralph Cintron (Oxford: Berghahn Press, 2015), and Enrique Dussel, *Twenty Theses on Politics* (Durham: Duke University Press, 2007).

63. The text here comes from fieldnotes written during the event and is not a transcript.

64. After the conversation, I looked into this claim. The number and purpose of these bases are disputed. Those who defend the bases claim that their real purpose is drug interdiction, not surveillance of Venezuelan military operations or the destabilization of the socialist-leaning Venezuelan government. More broadly, however, these bases represent a confluence of security issues, which, all totaled, can be described as a security regime, a manifestation of the "anxious nation" as coined by anthropologist Gilberto Rosas (personal conversation). Here are some of the activities of the security regime: espionage, interdiction of illegal trafficking (drugs, immigrants, weapons, etc.), terrorist surveillance and interdiction, securing political stability and the flows of minerals and oil, and the training of foreign militaries. The eleven bases (at least in 2010) are located in Aruba, Curaçao, Ecuador, El Salvador, and seven bases under a United States–Colombia joint agreement. Some commentators claim thirteen

bases by including Panama. See Ignacio Ramonet, "Bases militares estadounidenses cercando a Venezuela," *La Republica*, January 12, 2010, http://www.larepublica.com.uy/editorial/396416-bases-militares-estadounidenses-cercando-a-venezuela. Interestingly, the United States–Colombia joint agreement was declared invalid by the Colombian Constitutional Court in August 2010, and even though this affected the stationing of U.S. soldiers on Colombian soil, it did not seem to affect joint operations between the U.S. and Colombian militaries. See John Lindsay-Poland and Susana Pimiento, "U.S. Base Deal for Colombia: Back to the Status Quo," *Foreign Policy in Focus*, October 8, 2010, http://www.fpif.org/articles/us_base_deal_for_colombia_back_to_the_status_quo.

65. Some selected passages from Michael Hardt and Antonio Negri, *Commonwealth* (Cambridge, Mass.: Belknap Press of Harvard University Press, 2009): "A first freedom necessary is the freedom of movement, by which we mean the freedom to migrate within and across national borders, and also the freedom to stay in one place. . . . Freedom of movement would thus configure a freedom of space, allowing the multitude to flow to where it can be the most creative, organize the most joyful encounters, and establish the most productive relationships. Establishing some form of open citizenship is the only means we see to support this freedom" (309). "Every singularity is a social becoming. What the multitude presents, then, is . . . a society constantly in the process of metamorphosis. . . . Rather than a static mosaic of many-colored parts, this society is more like a kaleidoscope in which the colors are constantly shifting to form new and more beautiful patterns, even melding together to make new colors" (112). See also Michael Hardt and Antonio Negri, *Empire* (Cambridge, Mass.: Harvard University Press, 2000); Michael Hardt and Antonio Negri, *Multitude: War and Democracy in the Age of Empire* (New York: Penguin Press, 2004).

66. The following texts would agree with Hardt and Negri: De Genova and Peutz, *Deportation Regime*; Coutin, *Nations of Emigrants*; and Rosas, *Barrio Libre*.

67. Andrew Higgins, "Right Wing's Surge in Europe Has the Establishment Rattled," *New York Times*, November 9, 2013, https://www.nytimes.com/2013/11/09/world/europe/right-wings-surge-in-europe-has-the-establishment-rattled.html; Christina Pazzanese, "In Europe, Nationalism Rising," *Harvard Gazette*, February 27, 2017, https://news.harvard.edu/gazette/story/2017?/02/in-europe-nationalisms-rising.

68. The concept of the "natural" needs further elaboration. Is there a "natural" that implies some sort of separation between itself and a "nonnatural"? Ultimately, I think not, and hence we ought to question why we privilege the "natural" and why we grant special status to such legal concepts as birthright citizenship. Is nature divided from some nonnature? It is hard to understand how one would argue such a division, particularly if one believes, as I do, that nature is totality that ceaselessly projects totality. From such a perspective, there is no division between the natural and the unnatural. There is only the human propensity to divide the two. Moreover, division occurs at the moment when humans begin to observe nature. That is, when nature becomes "objectively" observed, it becomes an "it" with an "itness" all its own, and outside that "it" is the human observing and differentiating, and, as a result, profoundly differentiated from totality. This is the sort of work that division performs.

69. All of these projects are part of the policies emerging via Mercusor, the common market of the southern cone, Mercado Común del Sur.

70. Since at least 2013, Governor Jerry Brown of California and a willing legislature have been advancing the mobility and freedom of the undocumented. (1) Laws have been passed to prohibit local law enforcement agents from cooperating with holds requested by ICE except in matters of serious crimes; (2) undocumented immigrants can obtain California driver's licenses and (3) can become licensed lawyers; (4) employers cannot coerce the undocumented with the fear of deportation; (5) those who help the undocumented gain legal

status must observe fee restrictions; (6) the undocumented can apply for state-financed scholarships and aid at state universities; and (7) legal residents who have yet to acquire citizenship are eligible to be poll workers. See Assembly Bill No. 4, California Legislature—2013–14 Regular Session; Jennifer Medina, "Veto Halts Bill for Jury Duty by Noncitizens in California," *New York Times*, October 7, 2013, http://www.nytimes.com/2013/10/08/us/veto-halts-bill-for-jury-duty-by-noncitizens-in-california.html.

71. Here is Nigel Farage, who engineered the British exit from the EU:

> What happened last Thursday was a remarkable result, it was indeed a seismic result, not just for British politics, for European politics, but perhaps even for global politics too. Because what the little people did, all the ordinary people did, what the people who have been oppressed over the last few years and seen their living standards go down, they rejected the multinationals. They rejected the merchant banks, they rejected big politics, and they said, "Actually, we want our country back. We want our fishing waters back, we want our borders back. We want to be an independent, self governing, normal nation." That is what we have done, and that is what must happen.

John Ashmore, "Full Text of Nigel Farage's Speech in the European Parliament," June 28, 2016, https://www.politicshome.com/news/europe/eu-policy-agenda/brexit/news/76683/full-text-nigel-farages-speech-european-parliament.

72. Again, I return to Bosniak: "The idea that we could be compelled to extend solidarities of justice to the world at large is politically utopian and sociologically naïve. There is, however, an important case to be made—and it is one that some scholars and activists have been making—first, that responsibilities of justice extend beyond the bounds of the territorial nation-state and, second, that as a matter of fact, people are increasingly experiencing themselves as ethically and politically connected to others across national borders." Bosniak, "Being Here," 407.

73. The "forgotten man" is a trope that dates to the dawn of the Progressive Era.

> That this "forgotten" American could be used both to uphold and to dismantle liberalism suggests that this American political identity has never been especially fixed: Democrat or Republican, liberal or conservative, but populist above all. Since the 1960s, the phrase has also implied that the country was paying too much attention to the wrong sorts of people—most notably, to African-Americans—at the expense of the white working class. It is no coincidence that the "forgotten men and women of our country" began their migration into the Republican Party at the very moment that African-Americans were asserting their right to vote, and voting Democratic, in large numbers for the first time. Mr. Trump's victory will go down as one of the great upsets in United States history, but it is also the product of a long and bitter struggle over race and class in this country.

Beverly Gage, "Who Is the 'Forgotten Man'?" *New York Times*, November 9, 2016, https://www.nytimes.com/interactive/projects/cp/opinion/election-night-2016/who-is-the-forgotten-man.

74. Michels, *Political Parties*. See also Juan J. Linz, *Robert Michels, Political Sociology, and the Future of Democracy*, ed. H. E. Chehabi (New Brunswick, N.J.: Transaction Publishers, 2006).

Chapter 4

1. The distinction between the active and passive citizen has direct roots in Kant's political writings: All citizens, including passive ones, reap the benefits of freedom and equality, but "it does not follow that they [passive citizens] also have a right to influence or organize the state itself as *active* members, or to co-operate in introducing particular laws" (emphasis original). But, arguably, the distinction also appears in Aristotle's *Politics* in his concern with the establishment of merit and virtue in the polis, along with the confluence of citizenship, rights, the vote, and property ownership in ancient Athens. Also the distinction famously appears during the French Revolution in the Constitution of 1791. Here the distinction upheld a number of principles, including that the right to vote became limited to those who annually paid taxes equaling, at least, three days of wages paid to the unskilled laborer. In the American context, the now illegal practice of passing a literacy test or owning property in order to vote also seems to reflect the distinction between the active and passive citizen. Immanuel Kant, *Political Writings*, ed. Hans Reiss, trans. H. B. Nisbet, 2nd ed. (Cambridge: Cambridge University Press, 2003), 140.

2. Interestingly, the "ritualized into" may also subscribe to the rhetorics of merit and meritocracy. Here is Mr. Ma, a citizen immigrant who, according to the *New York Times*, opposes sanctuary for the undocumented:

> As an immigrant I really feel it [being in America is a high privilege]. . . . You cannot easily give that privilege to somebody without going through some kind of process. It's like giving lots of gold for one dollar. . . .
>
> Growing up in China, J. D. Ma shared a small room with his parents and sister in a communal apartment in a working-class district of Shanghai. They had to take turns with two other families—14 people in all—to use a single bathroom. . . . Today, Mr. Ma, 45, is a patent attorney, living in a stately home in Clarksville, Md., after years of study at universities in New York, Utah and Virginia and a first career as a software engineer. . . . Mr. Ma voted for Hillary Clinton. But hearing liberals talk about undocumented immigrants confuses him: The fact that their entering the country broke the law is somehow sidestepped, like a crude remark at a polite dinner party. Democrats oppose deportation on the grounds that it breaks up families, Mr. Ma said. But so do other aspects of the justice system—without setting off the same outcry.

Sabrina Tavernise, "Sanctuary Bills in Maryland Faced a Surprise Foe: Legal Immigrants, *New York Times*, May 8, 2017, https://www.nytimes.com/2017?/05/08/us/legal-immigrants-who-oppose-illegal-immigration.html.

3. I am following Lanham's entry for enthymeme. Enthymemes are more than abridged syllogisms. They are "abridged" because they rely on tacit knowledge, perhaps the ideological presumptions of a community of speakers. In this sense, they enable us to act and argue quickly and unconsciously. Consider how a group of people who believe in human rights can quickly arrive at the concept of fetal rights. Enthymematic logic and metaphorical expansionism seem to be some of the devices enabling this movement of thought. A theory of rhetorical resonance would be able to discuss such moves in some detail. Richard A. Lanham, *A Handlist of Rhetorical Terms*, 2nd ed. (Berkeley: University of California Press, 1991), 65–66.

4. The idea of autonomy is a cornerstone of the modernist imaginary, and, as in so many matters, Kant is a resource for understanding the pervasiveness of modernist terms.

> [Kant] introduces the term "autonomy" to indicate what is distinctive about his own view. The word had long been current in political discussions. An autonomous state was one that ruled itself. It could make its own laws without asking permission from rulers of other states. Kant took the term from political discourse and changed its meaning. He applied it to individuals and to the morality that ought to govern the relations of persons to themselves and to one another, regardless of the political laws under which they lived. He said that morality is a human creation. It is the legislation that comes from our own rational will.

J. B. Schneewind, "Why Study Kant's Ethics?," in Immanuel Kant, *Groundwork for the Metaphysics of Morals*, ed. and trans. Allen W. Wood (New Haven: Yale University Press, 2002), 84–85.

5. The well-respected Keynesian economist Joan Robinson made this point crystal clear in her analysis of Adam Smith and other classical economists:

> There is one solid unchanging lump of ideology that we take so much for granted that it is rarely noticed—that is nationalism. . . . Policy means nothing unless there is an authority to carry it out, and authorities are national. The subject by its very nature operates in national terms. Marxism also, though theoretically universalist, had to be poured into national moulds when revolutionary administrations were set up. The aspirations of the developing countries are more for national independence and national self-respect than just for bread to eat.
>
> The hard-headed Classicals made no bones about it. They were arguing against the narrow nationalism of Mercantilists in favour of a more far-sighted policy, but they were in favour of Free Trade because it was good for Great Britain, not because it was good for the world.

Joan Robinson, *Economic Philosophy* (1962; London: Aldine Transaction, 2006), 124.

6. See Schneewind, "Why Study Kant's Ethics?," 4.

7. The legal scholar Carol Rose reads the utilitarianism of Jeremy Bentham as saying, in effect, that "property is designed to do something, and what it is supposed to do is to tap individual energies in order to make us all more prosperous." For Rose, contemporary neo-utilitarians continue the same argument: "Property rights are a good thing because they encourage people to invest their efforts in things they claim (since each owner reaps the rewards of investment decisions as well as bearing the costs) and because they encourage trade (since clear entitlements are a precondition to trade). All this activity and trade, of course, makes us collectively wealthier." Carol M. Rose, *Property and Persuasion: Essays on the History, Theory, and Rhetoric of Ownership* (Boulder, Colo.: Westview Press, 1994), 3.

8. Nicholas Blomley makes the point that "the boundary has long been used within English legal culture as a symbolic and practical marker of the bounds of property. We take as a given the idea that a property claim can be spatially delimited, and that the boundary itself has a determinative meaning (marking mine and thine)." Nicholas Blomley, *Unsettling the City: Urban Land and the Politics of Property* (New York: Routledge, 2004), 7.

9. C. M. Hann, "Introduction: The Embeddedness of Property," in Hann, *Property Relations*, 12; emphasis original.

10. Alan Macfarlane, "The Mystery of Property: Inheritance and Industrialization in England and Japan," in Hann, *Property Relations*, 109.

11. Ibid., 112.

12. Ibid., 113.

13. Ibid., 112.

14. Ibid., 113.

15. Manning Nash, *Primitive and Peasant Economic Systems* (San Francisco: Chandler, 1966).

16. Macfarlane, "Mystery of Property," 114.

17. See Bleeden, Gottschalk-Druschke, and Cintrón, "Minutemen and the Subject of Democracy."

18. "No system of government control will ever be able to unleash or spur the creative or entrepreneurial elements of the human spirit. It is therefore incumbent that any government should seek to facilitate but not direct these efforts. The best and the brightest will be able to succeed only if they receive breathing room for their own activities. They can receive that space only if our collective power and intelligence support and nourish systems of private property, on which the advancement of public welfare so heavily depends." Richard A. Epstein, *Skepticism and Freedom: A Modern Case for Classical Liberalism* (Chicago: University of Chicago Press, 2003), 260.

19. I am following the lead of legal theorist Mark Tushnet and his reading of constitutional law:

> The distinction between negative and positive rights reflects and perhaps is based on a fundamental aspect of our social life. We fear that others with whom we live will act so as to crush our individuality, and thus we demand negative rights. But we also know that we need other people to create the conditions under which we can flourish as social beings, and thus we need positive rights. In our culture, the fear of being crushed by others so dominates the desire for sociality that our body of rights consists largely of negative ones. . . . The contemporary rhetoric of rights speaks primarily to negative ones. By abstracting from real experiences and reifying the idea of rights, it creates a sphere of autonomy stripped of any social context and counterposes to it a sphere of social life stripped of any content. . . . I find it striking that the rights actually recognized in contemporary constitutional law are almost all negative ones.

Mark Tushnet, "Symposium: A Critique of Rights; An Essay on Rights," *Texas Law Review* 62 (May 1984): 1363.

20. *Unlikely Heroes of the Arab Spring* with Hernando de Soto, dir. Jim Taylor, Free to Choose Media for WTTW National Productions, December 30, 2015.

21. Hernando de Soto, *The Mystery of Capital: Why Capitalism Triumphs in the West and Fails Everywhere Else* (New York: Basic Books, 2000).

22. The Ronald Coase Institute (https://www.coase.org/coasepublications.htm), which honors the life of this Nobel Prize–winning economist, contains a list of his publications as well as a working paper series by other economists writing on property rights. I quote the last sentence from one of these papers. The paper observes a living experiment in Buenos Aires, Argentina, between squatters that were able to get titles for their land versus their neighbors who were unable to do so: "In sum, entitling the poor increases their investment both in the house and in the human capital of their children, which should contribute to reduce the poverty of the future generations." Sebastian Galiani and Ernesto Schargrodsky, "Property Rights for the Poor: Effects of Land Titling," Ronald Coase Institute, Working Paper Number 7, January 19, 2009, 32.

23. Alain Badiou, *The Rebirth of History: Times of Riots and Uprisings* (London: Verso, 2012), 111, 113–14.

24. Ibid., 51–52.

25. Ibid., 48–49.

26. Ibid., 18.

27. Joseph Persky, "Retrospectives: The Ethology of *Homo Economicus*," *Journal of Economic Perspectives* 9, no. 2 (Spring 1995): 225.

28. Foucault, *Birth of Biopolitics*, 270, 114.

29. Ibid., 278. "The will of each, the interest of each, and the way in which this interest is or is not realized are bound up with a mass of elements which elude individuals. At the same time, this individual's interest, without him knowing it, wishing it, or being able to control it, is linked to a series of positive effects which mean that everything which is to his advantage will turn out to be to the advantage of others" (277). In passages such as this, Foucault is digesting Adam Smith's "invisible hand" and Hayek's "spontaneous order." Adam Smith, *The Wealth of Nations* (New York: Bantam Classic, 2003), 572; Friedrich A. Hayek, *Law, Legislation, and Liberty*, vol. 2, *The Mirage of Social Justice* (Chicago: University of Chicago Press, 1976). Another version of the same idea appears in the work of the recent Nobel Prize winner Eugene Fama, who in interviews has declared himself an "extreme libertarian." Jeff Sommer, "Eugene Fama, King of Predictable Markets," *New York Times*, October 26, 2013, https://www.nytimes.com/2013/10/27/business/eugene-fama-king-of-predictable-markets.html. Hence Foucault emphasizes in these passages how self-interested economic choices are bound up in a totality of actions that pay an even larger benefit to the commons of humankind. The totality itself, the sum of all self-interested actions in the market, is outside understanding and control. Here is one reason why classical and neoclassical economists have a difficult time understanding capitalism or the free market as exploitative—they have an ethical theory directed toward the commons, as do socialists, but directed differently. For instance, the classical and neoclassical thinkers suspect that government interventions, via, say, subsidies or excessive regulation of markets, tend to create unnatural distortions that eventually favor special interests. These thinkers do not want rigged systems disrupting the spontaneous order of markets, which if left alone would right themselves naturally. Hence neoclassicals believe that ethicality appears when markets are left to rise and fall on their own until they naturally balance themselves. But socialists also do not want rigged systems. For socialists, the festering divisions between concentrations of wealth versus poverty mean that capitalism's nature favors profit and wealth-making and that only government interventions through, for instance, poverty programs can rebalance the playing field. For socialists, then, ethicality appears when governments intervene to address "injustices" due to the inability of the markets to "fairly" distribute resources. Conceptually, homo economicus belongs to neoclassical thought—everyone's self-interestedness, if left alone, will naturally, and in ways that we cannot fully predict or comprehend, enhance everyone else. (Further comment: special interests seem to take advantage of both regulated and deregulated markets, suggesting that economies are always rigged and that the idea of an unrigged system is a fetishization.)

30. Meeting of aldermen and activists in the offices of DSBDA, July 29, 2014.

31. Ralph Cintrón, Maura Toro-Morn, Ivis Garcia Zambrana, and Elizabeth Scott, *60 Years of Migration: Puerto Ricans in Chicagoland* (Chicago: Puerto Rican Agenda, 2012), https://voorheescenter.uic.edu/wp-content/uploads/sites/122/2018/03/puertorican-agenda.compressed.pdf.

32. Volumes have been written explaining the complexities of Puerto Rican status. I choose here two leaders of the independence movement who have been incarcerated for their views. Both voices, particularly the last one since he is a Chicagoan, represent well the views of the Puerto Rican activists in Humboldt Park. "We have to show workers why independence is in their interests as workers: so they can be the owners of their country and their factories, so they can be the owners of what they produce. So that everything doesn't end up

in the coffers of Wall Street. So that it stays here for their development. We have to explain what annexation would mean. If Puerto Rico were to be made a state, they would treat us exactly like they treat our communities in New York, Connecticut, Chicago, and Los Angeles." Rafael Cancel Miranda, *Puerto Rico Independence Is a Necessity* (New York: Pathfinder, 1998), 13. See also Oscar López Rivera, *Between Torture and Resistance*, ed. Luis Nieves Falcón (Oakland, Calif.: PM Press, 2013).

33. The Blue Line train has a Division Street stop at Ashland and Milwaukee. Division Street is 1200 north and very attractive to homebuyers who want easy access to Chicago's downtown Loop. There are two other reasons to buy in the area. Humboldt Park itself is one of the roomiest and most significant parks in the city, and the new Bloomingdale Trail and Park is an elevated, long-abandoned track that is being transformed into a 2.7-mile multiuse recreational trail. These amenities are driving property values, http://www.cityofchicago.org/city/en/depts/cdot/supp_info/bloomingdale_trail.html.

34. Ralph Cintron, *Angels' Town: Chero Ways, Gang Life, and Rhetorics of the Everyday* (Boston: Beacon Press, 1997).

35. Darryl Holliday, "Humboldt Park's Reclaimed 'WOW District' Thrives West of Western," *DNAinfo Radio*, June 16, 2014, https://www.dnainfo.com/chicago/20140616/humboldt-park/humboldt-parks-reclaimed-wow-district-thrives-west-of-western.

36. We interviewed the "goddess of WOW" in July 2014. She is neither white nor Puerto Rican, had lived in Humboldt Park for decades, and was as offended as the Puerto Ricans by a group of white gentrifiers intent on driving the Puerto Ricans out. She was emphatic about her entrepreneurial values. Her position was largely class driven and individualist insofar as she had a professional education and aspired to ever-greater economic success. She was confident of her special business acumen and thought that the Puerto Rican community had isolated themselves and were afraid of change.

37. Potentiality was a major preoccupation for the pre-Socratics. Aristotle's work picks up those interests across multiple texts. In the *Physics*, for instance, the concept of potentiality (*dunamis*: also power, force, change, ability, energy) is fundamental: "Things exist either only actually or both potentially and actually." Aristotle, *Physics* 3.1, 200b (trans. Robin Waterfield [New York: Oxford University Press, 1999], 56). Further, the explanatory notes claim that "only God contains no potentiality" (trans. Waterfield, 245). Giorgio Agamben takes up contemporary inquiries into language and potentiality in *Potentialities: Collected Essays in Philosophy*, ed. and trans. Daniel Heller-Roazen (Stanford: Stanford University Press, 1999).

38. "Part of the problem is that it's a tale of two cities—downtown Chicago and neighborhood Chicago. There's no correlation between them. If you go to [the wealthy] Michigan Avenue, you'll see a cop on every corner. If you go to [the poorer] Madison and Pulaski, you see nothing but potholes. That's unacceptable. What the Progressive Caucus wants to do is make those two Chicagos one." Ethan Corey, "Chicago Aldermen Want a $15 Minimum Wage in Their City, Too," *In These Times*, June 17, 2014, http://inthesetimes.com/working/entry/16849/chicago_15_dollar_minimum_wage.

39. Division/California and Division/Campbell are sites for very significant affordable living spaces built because of the efforts of the Puerto Rican activists. Roberto Clemente High School and the Humboldt Park Vocational Educational Center, a branch of the City Colleges of Chicago, are institutions also deeply supported by the Puerto Rican activists. Bloomingdale Trail is an abandoned, elevated train track that has been converted into a walking and biking trail, and cuts through the city for several miles. One segment runs just north of North Avenue and has been attracting the interests of developers. The discussions among affordable housing advocates from approximately 2013 to the time of this writing is that the trail is now the driver of the newest wave of gentrification in northwest Chicago.

40. Consider Milton Friedman's and other libertarians' preference for "freedom" as choices in the marketplace above and beyond the more abstract "freedoms" of democratic politics (Friedman, *Capitalism and Freedom*). There are even those who claim that the United States Constitution itself is the document that makes this translation and thus is rightly described as an economic document. See M. Lane Bruner, *Democracy's Debt: The Historical Tensions between Political and Economic Liberty* (Amherst, N.Y.: Humanity Books, 2009).

41. Henri Lefebvre, *The Production of Space*, trans. D. Nicholson Smith (Malden, Mass.: Blackwell, 2011).

42. Don Mitchell, *The Right-to-the-City: Social Justice and the Fight for Public Space* (New York: Guilford Press, 2003), 17. See also Blomley, *Unsettling the City*, and virtually the entire corpus of David Harvey.

43. Rose, *Property and Persuasion*, 11.

44. John Locke, *Two Treatises of Government and a Letter Concerning Toleration*, ed. Ian Shapiro (New Haven: Yale University Press, 2003), 111–12.

45. Rose, *Property and Persuasion*, 11.

46. Ibid.

47. Ibid., 12.

48. Ibid., 11–23.

49. How can any rhetorical theorist worth his salt resist commenting as long as possible on the idea of a "clear act," particularly when it plays an important role in judicial rhetoric, one of the central sites where rhetoric makes its appearance? The idea of a clear act should be particularly appealing for rhetorical scholars because of its proximity to rhetoric's interests in presence and presencing. That is, presence is related to the supposed clarity of sensory verification, as when one says "such and such is present before me because I see it or feel it." The empirical sciences seem to be burdened by the need for a kind of clear "sight-line" running from object to subject that reduces ontological matters and even subjecthood to the clear realities (presence) of the object. But these sensory matters regarding clarity (the presence of things) are also translated from empirical matters to conceptual ones. This is the sort of translation work that Descartes accomplishes in the *Meditations* when he establishes "clear and distinct" ideas as a basis for distinguishing true ideas from false ones. If "presence" (hence clarity) seems to be part and parcel of truth claims derived both empirically and conceptually, "presencing" seems to belong to the rhetorical art of making matters so apparent, so palpable, that they drive us toward conviction. Thus the term *the arts of presencing* seems to capture the intrusion of rhetoric so as to manufacture a powerful sense of truth, conviction, and verifiability. Stating it rather crudely, presence, particularly in the sciences, relies on clarity—and, ultimately, the power of self-evidence as a kind of gold standard—to help establish proof, whereas the arts of presencing relies on the force of rhetoric to create the appearance of proof. Finally, there is another account of presence and presencing that belongs to the phenomenological tradition. I am thinking, for instance, of the work of Heidegger and Merleau-Ponty, who do not accept the "sight-line running from object to subject" that has shaped methods of proof-making in the sciences and the courts. The upshot of this discussion is to unpack the premises underpinning the "clear act" as a basis for proof and, in the process, to suggest how the ontological and rhetorical cross into each other during the making of both clarity and proof. See Ralph Cintron and Jason Schneider, "The Things of the World: Migration, Presence, and the Arts of Presencing," *Philosophy and Rhetoric* 2019, 115–41.

50. In the Supreme Court decision *Johnson and Graham's Lessee v. M'Intosh, 21 U.S. 543 (1823)*, Chief Justice Marshall declares "the rights of discovery" and the "rights of the conqueror," but he also notes that indigenous peoples did not make productive use of the land. "The tribes of Indians inhabiting this country were fierce savages, whose occupation was war,

and whose subsistence was drawn chiefly from the forest. To leave them in possession of their country was to leave the country a wilderness." Long before 1823, early colonial theorists John Winthrop, John Cotton, and Roger Williams debated indigenous conceptions of property. Williams's defense of indigenous rights lost to the likes of Winthrop and many others. Here is how the historian William Cronon works through Winthrop's arguments: "'As for the Natives in New England,' [Winthrop] wrote, 'they inclose noe Land, neither have any setled habytation, nor any tame Cattle to improve the Land by, and soe have noe other but a Naturall Right to these Countries.' By this argument, only the fields planted by Indian Women could be claimed as property, with the happy result, as Winthrop said, that 'the rest of the country lay open to any that could and would improve it.' The land was a *vacuum Domicilium* waiting to be inhabited by a more productive people." William Cronon, *Changes in the Land: Indians, Colonists, and the Ecology of New England* (New York: Hill and Wang), 56.

51. Personal conversation with fieldworker and cultural geographer Ian Baird.

52. Anna Lowenhaupt Tsing, *Friction: An Ethnography of Global Connection* (Princeton: Princeton University Press), 181.

53. Cary Wolfe, *What Is Posthumanism?* (Minneapolis: University of Minnesota Press, 2010).

54. Blomley, *Unsettling the City*, 7.

55. Ibid., 32.

56. Ibid., 56; emphasis original.

57. Ibid., 57.

58. "Racist Newcomers Unite to Deny Puerto Rican Parade Beer Garden," *La Voz del Paseo Boricua*, The Puerto Rican Cultural Center, Chicago, May 2013.

59. The emergence of a "new lifestyle" in the Humboldt Park area is, for newcomers, a sign of safety as poor Latin@s and street gangs disappear. But at a more innocuous level, improving property values also bring new consumption patterns. What I find interesting in the following quotation from a newcomer is the combination of mundaneness, innocence (as opposed to transparent racism), and crude classism as an old Humboldt Park is displaced by a new Humboldt Park:

> Here is one small indication of positive change in the area (at least to me): The Foremost Liquors at Spaulding and North [about two blocks west of Humboldt Park] only carried Corona/Tecate and Budweiser/Bud Light type stuff when I moved there 6 years ago. The closest they had to a micro-brew was dusty 6-packs of Sam Adams well past their sell by date, and some Heineken. Now today, they have a huge selection of craft/micro brews (well over a hundred varieties) and I can assure you, it's not the longtime residents buying those products. Again, it's just a small indicator of change and of the type of people moving into that specific area, but it's a positive one, I think.

Quigboto, City-Data Forum, March 10, 2011, http://www.city-data.com/forum/chicago/1219043-how-safe-humboldt-park-specifically-kedzie-2.html.

60. Darryl Holliday, "'California Nights' Returns to Humboldt Park This Weekend," DNAinfo Chicago, July 18, 2014, http://www.dnainfo.com/chicago/20140718/humboldt-park/california-nights-returns-humboldt-park-this-weekend.

61. See quigboto, City-Data Forum, March 7, 2011, http://www.city-data.com/forum/chicago/1219043-how-safe-humboldt-park-specifically-kedzie.html.

62. The Puerto Rican Cultural Center in Chicago has established a number of initiatives and institutions. The terms *critical space*, *community as ecosystem*, *inclusivity*, and *democracy* circulate widely through these sites, helping to establish coherence and virtue.

These terms are also popular among those activists who are, at most, indirectly related to the center.

63. These discussions were occurring in July 2014 and were voiced again in June 2018 during a housing summit staged by the Puerto Rican activists and the Latino aldermen responsible for the Humboldt Park area. In addition to these maneuvers, the activists and aldermen tried to push banks to become more transparent regarding the foreclosed properties that they held. Before these homes could hit the open market, they were being sold to bulk investors or to preferred customers and agents who had no commitment to the community. In these instances, social ownership claims were opposed to more abstract, free market practices.

64. Such a claim emerges from focus group interviews as well as formal and informal individual interviews. A common theme among young Puerto Rican entrepreneurs is that Puerto Ricans, generally, are not entrepreneurial. In other words, they do not subscribe to the values of homo economicus—a good thing, maybe. Our research team gathered both comparative occupational data and employment-by-industry data. We found that in the Humboldt Park area, "whites were almost twice as frequently represented in . . . leadership-oriented business occupations." We also found that Puerto Ricans are well represented "in clerical or skilled professions," but they have the lowest rates of self-employment compared to whites, African Americans, and Mexicans. They also have high rates of government employment. See Cintrón, Toro-Morn, Garcia Zambrana, and Scott, *60 Years of Migration*, 33, 34.

65. "Consider the effect [of] introducing into the law terms like 'motive,' 'intent,' and 'due process.' These terms work a subtle shift into the rhetoric of explanation available to judges; with them, new ways of thinking and new insights come to be explored and developed. In such fashion, judges who could unabashedly refer to the 'legal rights of the environment' would be encouraged to develop a viable body of law—in part simply through the availability and force of the expression." From legal theorist Christopher D. Stone, *Should Trees Have Standing? Law, Morality, and the Environment* (New York: Oxford University Press, 2010), 22–23.

66. The term itself was coined, to the best of my knowledge, by Garrett Hardin in "The Tragedy of the Commons," *Science* 162 (1968): 1243–48.

67. Rose, *Property and Persuasion*, 106.

68. Harold Demsetz, "Toward a Theory of Property Rights," *American Economic Review* 57, no. 2 (1967): 347–59.

69. See Lawrence Lessig, *The Future of Ideas: The Fate of the Commons in a Connected World* (New York: Random House, 2001). The classic analysis of the tensions between the commons and enclosures is Karl Polanyi, *The Great Transformation: The Political and Economic Origins of Our Time* (Boston: Beacon Press, 2001).

70. For instance, the volatility surrounding the creation of new markets becomes visible in the many layers of bad-debt markets. These markets are where uncollectable debts go that even institutional lenders such as banks and credit card companies have given up on. That is, even uncollectable debts can be priced, and different profit-making markets can emerge depending on the age of the bad debt. Small, shadowy collection agencies earn enormous profits in these markets, and poor communities such as Humboldt Park tend to hold a lot of bad debt. Jake Halpern, "Paper Boys: Inside the Dark, Labyrinthine, and Extremely Lucrative World of Consumer Debt Collection," *New York Times Magazine*, August 14, 2014, https://www.nytimes.com/interactive/2014/08/15/magazine/bad-paper-debt-collector.html?searchResultPosition=1.

71. Elinor Ostrom, *Governing the Commons: The Evolution of Institutions for Collective Action* (New York: Cambridge University Press, 1990), 2–3.

72. Hardin, "Tragedy of the Commons," 1248.

73. I am reflecting here on a number of community meetings where LUCHA, a nonprofit affordable housing agency whose executive board I lead, has had to defend its projects against the complaints of homeowning neighbors who would prefer not to have affordable housing close to them.

74. Essentially, today's homeowners are a consequence of the bourgeois state whose characteristics were articulated by Hobbes, Locke, and many others. These theorists also had a hand in shaping today's democratic rhetorics. They hoped that these apparatuses might solve the problems of their own era—namely, its religious and civil wars and its domination by hierarchical authorities. Thus theirs was an important step in the making of a new social order and, eventually, our own era of managerial modernity. Here are some of the interlocking premises of this emerging new order: (1) all humans by "nature" are free according to the "state of nature"; therefore, the freedoms of civil society may be limited but are still linked to that absolute freedom; (2) civil societies are contractually obligated to align their laws, within reason, to freedom as such—that is, to the ontological condition of freedom; (3) each human has a right to freedom and, therefore, a right to self-realization, meaning, in effect, the right to release their potentiality; (4) the release of human potentiality is enabled, in part, through the release of the potentiality stored within nature; hence the emphasis on private property; (5) in this sense, private property represents the individuation of the world under the ownership of individuated selves, but it also offers a management system that observes pricing and costs versus benefits; thus owners may have the right to exploit the abundance of what they own, but they are simultaneously discouraged from "over-grazing." Perhaps this sampling of interlocking premises becomes clearer as modernity unevenly unfolds because the premises need time to be fully elaborated. Nevertheless, there seems to be an emerging paradigm here of rights, freedoms, contract, and the superiority of private property over and against the commons, a paradigm that will constitute a revolution against the king's rights of ownership. Ultimately, a politics based on the rights of horizontality to release its own potentiality will upend vertical concentrations of power and wealth, but the deep irony, as I have been arguing, is that this revolution is accomplished by giving horizontality the right to become vertical. That is, each individual as a member of the horizontal masses has the freedom and right to extend herself vertically, dependent on her abilities, but if a cap is placed on the amount of power and wealth that she gathers, then the society has contradicted the principles of freedom upon which the society rests. Hence the eventual emergence of modern meritocracy, which has become nothing less than stealth aristocracy with its accumulations of wealth and power, is already taking shape within the premises of early liberalism. Here are the origins of the oligarchic condition and the centrality of ownership in the making of such a condition.

75. Rose, *Property and Persuasion*, 127.

76. In economic theory, the long-standing discussion regarding the relationship between value and price echoes Aristotle's distinction in the *Rhetoric*, which understands persuasion as moving from contingency toward certainty. Most economists have understood that the "value" of something is subject to all sorts of opinions. Value is indeterminable or contingent. However, when something is given a price, its value appears less contingent and more certain. That is, price fixes value, even if only temporarily. Similarly, rhetoric concerns itself with contingent matters, meaning that the goal of persuasion is to move matters from indeterminacy or contingency toward the clarity of a winning argument. The movement from value to price, then, mimics how persuasion is a movement from contingency toward the appearance of certainty.

77. Bjerg, *Making Money*, 238.

78. Board of Governors of the Federal Reserve System, Division of Reserve Bank Operations and Payment System, 2017 Currency Budget, https://www.federalreserve.gov/foia/files/2017currency.pdf.

79. Board of Governors of the Federal Reserve System, December 27, 2018 (last update), http://www.federalreserve.gov/faqs/currency_12771.htm.

80. Paolo Virno, "General Intellect," in *Lessico Postfordista*, ed. Adelino Zanini and Ubaldo Fadini, trans. Arianna Bove (Milan: Feltrinelli, 2001), http://www.generation-online.org/p/fpvirno10.htm.

81. Anna Lowenhaupt Tsing, *The Mushroom at the End of the World: On the Possibility of Life in Capitalist Ruins* (Princeton: Princeton University Press, 2015).

82. "Universal basic income is a catchall phrase that describes a range of proposals, but they generally share one feature: All people in society get a regular check from the government—regardless of their income or whether they work. These funds are supposed to guarantee food and shelter, enabling people to pursue their own betterment while contributing to society." Peter S. Goodman, "Free Cash in Finland. Must Be Jobless," *New York Times*, December 17, 2016, https://www.nytimes.com/2016/12/17/business/economy/universal-basic-income-finland.html.

83. Rose, *Property and Persuasion*, 105–6:

> The right to exclude others has often been cited as the most important characteristic of private property. . . . Because they can exclude outsiders, owners alone may capture the value of their individual investments in the things they own, and as a consequence property rights encourage them to put time, labor, and care into the development of resources. . . . Moreover, exclusive control makes it possible for owners to identify other owners and for all to exchange the things upon which they have labored until these things arrive in the hands of those who value them most highly. . . . Thus it is peculiar to find a long-standing notion of public property [in the sense of the customs of an unorganized public] in the law of the Western world. . . . And despite the power of the classical economic argument for private property, a curious countercurrent has continually washed through our own American law.

Chapter 5

1. Buck-Morss, *Dreamworld and Catastrophe*, xiii–xiv.

2. Ibid., 15; emphasis original.

3. It is important to recall Hobbes here. Hobbes's version of the social contract states that our natural right to kill to get what we need should be sacrificed to the Leviathan, who, in exchange, will grant everyone protections and restricted rights. I have argued that the corporeal conflict in "the war of all against all" was eventually transposed into a legal conflict over rights. The war thus never quite disappeared but became attenuated and transmuted upon entering the social contract and particularly the courts. The courtroom has now become the arena of battle. Hobbes, *Leviathan*.

4. "Rights are often spoken of in the language of possessions. . . . The idea of rights as moral property, as belonging to individuals the way property does, is an important aspect of the concept of rights. It focuses attention on the person to whom something is due, just as property law focuses attention on the possessor of property. The individual person with his needs and desires is the central motif." Elizabeth Wolgast, *The Grammar of Justice* (Ithaca:

Cornell University Press, 1987), 29. Saying much the same thing from a legal theory perspective is Tushnet, "Symposium."

5. Stanley N. Katz, "Thomas Jefferson and the Right to Property in Revolutionary America," *Journal of Law and Economics* 19, no. 3 (1976): 475.

6. Ibid., 473; see also Joseph R. Blasi, Richard B. Freeman, and Douglas L. Kruse, "Capitalism for the Rest of Us," *New York Times*, July 17, 2015, https://www.nytimes.com/2015/07/18/opinion/capitalism-for-the-rest-of-us.html. These ideas continue to inform the American imaginary. Consider the contemporary conservative journalist David Brooks: "The coming debate about capitalism will be between those who want to restructure the underlying system and those who want to help people take advantage of its rough intensity. It will be between people who think you need strong government to defeat oligarchy and those who think you need open competition." The point is that both the horizontalists and verticalists are seen as defeating oligarchy. Brooks, "Two Cheers for Capitalism," *New York Times*, July 31, 2015, A23.

7. Georg Wilhelm Friedrich Hegel, *Phenomenology of Spirit*, trans. A. V. Miller (Oxford: Oxford University Press, 1977).

8. Hegel, *Hegel's Philosophy of Right*, 41–42.

Index

Note: page numbers in italics refer to figures. Those followed by n refer to notes, with note number.